From
The Connoisseur
UP NORTH

DINING IN
DINING OUT
In Northern Michigan

————

The food lover's guide to the region's
restaurants, cafes, taverns and
resources for the home chef

Traverse City, Petoskey, Charlevoix, Harbor Springs, Leelanau, Benzie, Elk Rapids, Torch, Boyne, Mackinac

————

Sherri and Graydon DeCamp

————

bayShore Books
Elk Rapids, Michigan
publishers

The Connoisseur
UP NORTH

DINING IN
DINING OUT

In Northern Michigan

_____

Sherri & Graydon DeCamp

Illustrations & cover : Graydon DeCamp
Cover concept : Sherri DeCamp
Design concept : Thomas Kachadurian
Copy editing & assistance:Kris Elbert, Louis Sanford

Inquiries & orders:

Bayshore Books
PO Box 549, Elk Rapids, MI, 49629

WWW.BAYSHOREBOOKS.COM

E-mail: Dining@bayshorebooks.com

ISBN 0-9651442-3-2

PRINTED IN THE UNITED STATES OF AMERICA

COVER: Photographed at
the Grey Hare Inn Vineyard B&B,
Old Mission Peninsula.

To all the friends and family with whom we have shared love, laughs, tears, ideas, and prayers over good food and wine.

Table of Contents

Dining In

Dining Out

Chefs' Cookbook

Index to Restaurants

Complete index — P.236   **"New as we go to press" — P. 233**
On-line guide to good food Up North — BAYSHOREBOOKS.COM

Forewords

The entire Black Star Farms team joins me in welcoming Graydon and Sherri DeCamp's homage to the people who make Northern Michigan such a grand place for the food lover. This book is a tribute not only to chefs and restaurants, but also to all the winemakers and cheese-makers, vineyard, orchard and farm managers, innkeepers, and distillers who celebrate the region's agricultural abundance.

What we as "artisans" produce only begins to maintain a vibrant family-farm economy. It's one thing to grow good grapes and make good wine, but quite another to establish Northern Michigan as a premier wine region. This book helps us do that. The DeCamps are the bards of our craft, capturing the essence of the farm-to-table movement and portraying the unique and varied personalities involved. They are dedicated to the environment and quality of life of our region, whose unique foods and wines can be fully described only by writers who live, travel, and eat here on a daily basis.

Our challenge is to preserve and build our agricultural heritage in the face of urban sprawl, a historically depressed farm economy, and the homogenization of society. The residents and visitors who make the region's food and wine part of their daily lives validate our efforts and investments. We welcome this book, and urge you to use it to discover the essence of our lands and lakes. Join Graydon and Sherri in their travels and their discovered pleasures, and help ensure the wonders of the "Up North" experience for generations to come.

–Don Coe, Black Star Farms

My, we've come a long way! When I opened the Rowe in 1972, the North was a place where broiled whitefish and prime rib passed for fine cooking. By 1996 there were enough good restaurants to warrant a fine book, *The Connoisseur Up North.* Since then Northern Michigan has drawn the attention of connoisseurs the world over, including major coverage in *Food Arts* and the *New York Times,* and even in England's *Sunday Guardian.* What a marvelous evolution! I am proud the Rowe had a part in it.

This success would never have come without the thousands of knowledgeable people who appreciate good food and wine and patronize our restaurants. Two of the most passionate among them are Graydon and Sherri DeCamp. These two love great food and wine, and have a keen eye for both. The Rowe has been written up hundreds of times over the years, but no one has ever captured the essence of what we do better than they. You can trust what they tell you. If you love food and wine and Northern Michigan as much as I do, you need this book.

–Wes Westhoven, The Rowe Inn
Foreword to the Connoisseur Up North

Introduction

Adventure is one of the things that attracts people to Northern Michigan, whether it's the adventure of sailing a new course, hiking a new trail, or seeking out a new artist. This region also delights the culinary adventurer who comes in search of new and interesting restaurants and dishes and the fresh, seasonal products of farms, wineries, cheese makers, and specialty food shops. These are the food adventurers we write for.

Once upon a time here in resort country, "gourmet" dining meant a clean tablecloth and planked whitefish. "Fancy" restaurants operated only in summer for the benefit of resorters. Over the last 30 years, however, tens of thousands of long-time visitors have become year-round residents, and Northern Michigan has become a new culinary marketplace, complete with its own highly regarded wine appellations.

The region's restaurants range from knotty-pine casual to white-tablecloth elegant. The choice is broad, and people often ask our advice about where to go or take houseguests. We try in our books to answer that question. While our newspaper columns are reviews and must sometimes be critical, this book embraces places we'd go and take friends when we're not working. We know most of the proprietors and chefs; we have enjoyed their food and their cellars. We believe them to be assiduous and inventive in the selection, preparation, and presentation of food, and to have gracious, welcoming, knowledgeable staffs. In most cases, in fact, the owner is present every day, either at the door or in the kitchen. There certainly are some fine exceptions, but we've found that very few good restaurants are operated effectively *in absentia* or by some formula written in a distant home office.

Cuisine need not be haute to be fine, of course, and many simple cafés and taverns offer outstanding fare even if they don't have two escargots to rub together. This book includes many such places. If you don't expect them to be something they're not, we think none will disappoint you.

Remember, too, that our economy is highly seasonal, and many restaurants streamline service and simplify menus in the off-season. Some just close. We try to judge them by high-season performance, and you may have a different experience in April than in July. At the lowest ebbs, such as spring break, we personally stick to places that are still busy; nothing keeps a restaurant on its game better than a lot of customers.

At any season, however, we encourage you to seek new experiences in places you've never been. That's what adventure is about.

Y ou'll find high food adventure in Northern Michigan today without setting foot in a restaurant. Vineyards and wineries have proliferated Up North in the last 15 years. So have bread makers and cheese makers, patisseries and delis, wine stores and specialty food shops. Some roadside fruit stands have become full-scale farm markets, offering a wide range of fine, home-grown produce. Much of it is produced on community-based farms for a pre-paid clientele; much is produced by dedicated organic growers. Many towns now also have weekly market days, when farmers and orchardists bring their produce to town to sell from stalls and truck beds.

Seeking and sampling this bounty is a pleasure as unique and rewarding as the lakes and the dunes themselves.

A few words about editorial independence: We treasure ours and guard it jealously. Some so-called guides are little more than advertising, and some expect restaurants to pay to be included. Some "critics" even take free meals. We value our reputation far too much for any such nonsense.

Let us be very clear about this:

No restaurant pays to be in our book.

No chef tells us what to say.

We buy every bite we eat with our own money.

Only in this way can we be free to report and write objectively about the restaurants where we eat.

W hile we do know our way around the kitchen, we certainly don't pretend to know how to run a restaurant, and we hardly have the skills of experienced professionals. We are only dimly aware of the rigors of preparing fine cuisine for hundreds of fussy patrons day in and day out. What little we *do* know makes us respect and admire the many chefs and owners we write about. We regard them with awe.

But we never forget that the audience we write for consists of paying restaurant patrons just like ourselves.

– Sherri and Graydon DeCamp
Elk Rapids, Michigan, May 2004

We solicit notice of errors and welcome readers' comments, applause, and criticism. Write to PO Box 549, Elk Rapids, MI 49629 or E-mail dining@bayshorebooks.com

To Market, to Market

One June day, on our way home from the Straits, we detoured to Bluff Gardens in Harbor Springs to get some baby asparagus for dinner and a bunch of spring radishes for the salad. Back on the road, we sampled a radish to see if they were as good as they looked. The first was so good, we had another, then another, and . . . by the time we got home, they were gone.

Nothing counts like freshness when it comes to food. One of the delights of traveling about Northern Michigan in summer and autumn is the farm stand. At these roadside markets you can buy fruits and vegetables that were alive and growing only hours before.

Some stands are full-fledged stores, with refrigerated display cases and merchandise that transcends produce. Some are tiny affairs where you may or may not find someone tending the till. Often as not, especially in midweek, you'll just find an old box and a hand-lettered sign saying to help yourself and put what you owe in the box, and make change if you can. As far as we know, no one ever cheats.

Each spring we eagerly await the opening of the farm stands and stores. The one we watch most closely is the **Wells Family Farm** in Williamsburg. Their year starts with asparagus, maple syrup, and the earliest spring greens. The seasonal delights then parade through summer and into autumn—strawberries, leaf lettuces, broccoli, cucumbers, beans, beets, raspberries, squash, and pumpkins. One of our peak moments each summer is when Wells' green zebra-stripe tomatoes appear on the counter.

Wells is one of a handful of Northern Michigan farms offering "community-supported agriculture" to folks who want produce at its peak. Customers pay in advance for a share of the grower's output, and then each week pick up their portion of whatever's ripe and ready. Wells is part of a national network of such "CSA" farms *(www. localharvest.org)*. The Michigan Department of Agriculture maintains a registry of farm markets at *www.michigan.gov/ mda*. Wells Family Farm is about five miles south of Elk Rapids at *9490 Elk Lake Rd., Williamsburg (231-264-9522)*.

We don't pretend to list all the region's farm markets, and we knowingly omit roadside "cherry stands" and places that sell their own tree fruit but someone else's garden produce, pies, and whatnot. The farm markets we talk about here, however, are all places we know and enjoy, either for consistently good quality or some specialty or other.

For instance, **Altonen Orchards** on US-31 a mile or so south of Elk Rapids would be one of our favorite market stands even if we didn't live nearby. We don't even *think* about going anywhere else for sweet corn or seasonal fruit pies. Their strawberries are awesome in spring, too. They have seasonal fruits and vegetables up to and including pumpkins, from mid-May into November *(231-264-8052)*.

Now, let's go back up north and more or less work our way down the coast, farm by farm, and see what's what. **Bill's Farm Market** is a beloved, perennial fix-

ture in and around Petoskey. Bill McMaster grows and hand-picks almost all his own produce on the 150-acre farm, including sweet corn, lettuces, beans, peas, and asparagus, plus such happy eccentricities as purple cauliflower, blue potatoes, and sweet mini-corn you can eat raw. The farm dates to McMaster's

great-grandparents, who were 19th century immigrants from Germany. Bill opened the farm market in 1976 as a table by the road. Now it's a store that spills over into outdoor displays. Bill opens in June, hits full stride in August, and in autumn winds down to squash and pumpkins. His year ends Dec. 24 when the last Christmas trees and homemade wreaths sell out. At Christmastime you can pick and cut your own tree. The farm is nine miles east of town at *9950 E. Mitchell Rd. (231-347-6735)*.

Bluff Gardens is a real old-timer. On the hill above Harbor Springs, it's now in its eighth decade. Hand-painted Faience pottery is a specialty here, but they offer knowing cooks some of the most unimaginably fresh miniature vegetables in sight, plus a wide array of preserves. In addition to those luscious baby veggies, they sell preserves, dips, dressings, relishes, and sauces at retail or mail-order. Their extensive line of Faience is custom-made for them in France, and includes pots, lamps, and porcelain-handled cutlery in a dozen styles and colors. You stay-at-homes can buy their preserves and dips by catalog if you wish, but you'll never get any of those baby radishes if you do. The store is at *721 W. Lake Rd. (231-526-5571).*

Pond Hill Farm, north of Harbor Springs, is a visitor-friendly place, selling its own free-range eggs, fruits and veggies (some of them hydroponic), and home-canned preserves, salsas, and maple syrup. The farmers, Jim and Sharon Spencer, are people of many interests and a firm belief that in an era of specialization, farms can still survive by producing a little of everything. They run an international internship program, sell produce and products at the store in

Cheese It!

John and Anne Hoyt's Leelanau Cheese Co. is not exactly a farm market, but attached to the wine-tasting room at Black Star Farms. The Hoyts turn cheese making into a sort of spectator sport for visitors: The operation is behind a wall of windows, and you can see cheese in the making while you decide whether to take home some cherry port with your case of Black Star Arcturos Riesling. John Hoyt learned his craft in Switzerland, where he and Anne met. They founded Leelanau Cheese in 1995 in a bayside shed in Omena, then moved to Black Star a few years ago. Using fresh, local milk from a farm near Cedar, they make a mellow, nutty raclette (their signature product) and a Boursin-like herbed spread.

Raclette is the traditional base for Swiss fondue. It is also a dish unto itself: Oven-melt the cheese on a plate and serve it surrounded by slices of potato, some cornichons, red onion, capers and grainy mustard. You'll find this on the menu at Grand Traverse Resort's Trillium. The name "raclette" comes from *racler,* the French word for "scrape," because the Swiss heat the whole cheese and scrape it off as it softens. The dish is easy to do at home, too. All you need is the raclette — and this is the place to get it.

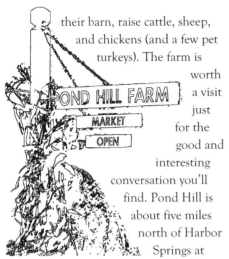

their barn, raise cattle, sheep, and chickens (and a few pet turkeys). The farm is worth a visit just for the good and interesting conversation you'll find. Pond Hill is about five miles north of Harbor Springs at *5581 S. Lake Shore Dr. (231-526-3276).*

Kiteley Farm outside of Charlevoix is a bit hard to find, but worth the effort. It's famous locally for U-pick berries and fruit, as well as for herbs and seasonal produce. From the light by the airport in Charlevoix, go south for 3.3 miles on M-66, turn right on Shaw, and quickly left on Brock. The farm will be on your right at *3805 Brock Rd. (231-547-2318).*

It's no surprise that many of the area's farm markets are along US-31, because it's Northern Michigan's main drag. We have several regular stops in the stretches south of Charlevoix.

Most visible among them is **Friske's Farm Market** in Atwood. Olga Friske herself will probably greet you in the store, and if she does, you'd be wise to accept her suggestions. It's worth hunting about among the gifts and knickknacks to find the seasonally fresh fruit and produce. They also bake pies and pastries on the premises and serve café lunches. You can't miss this establishment on *US-31 in Atwood (231-599-2604).*

Just south of Atwood, **Heritage Farms** is often our choice when it isn't quite the season for tomatoes, lettuce, cucumbers, peppers and herbs. They grow it all hydroponically from May through November. So, when most markets have nothing but pithy southern imports, we get freshly picked tomatoes so ripe and juicy and sweet we sometimes eat them like apples. Heritage is at *7435 US-31.*

When it comes to apples, there are few bigger players than **King Orchards** (*www.kingorchards.com*). The brothers John and Jim King started farming there almost a quarter-century ago, and now John and Betsy and Jim and Rose have neighboring spreads with more than 90 acres of apples, 70 of cherries, plus peaches, sweet corn, and various other garden veggies as well. They also partner with their neighbor, Mark Doherty in **Russell Ridge Farms**, with the goal, Doherty says, of "the best apples Northern Michigan has ever seen." King Orchards has two markets, one on US-31 at Creswell Rd., and the other on M-88, three miles east of Eastport, atop the highest hill around. It's worth going just for the wide-angle view *(231-544-6479).*

A bit further on you'll find the small **Cherry View Orchards** stand, with the usual seasonal berries and fruit. What we like to stop there for are the excellent sugarless fruit butters, jams, and jellies that we can send in good conscience to a diabetic relative. Cherry View is at *1644 US-31 N, Kewadin (231-264-9807)*.

Guntzviller's, on US-31 at the south edge of Elk Rapids, is our favorite berry patch. We watch the sign out front like hawks for the arrival of strawberries, raspberries, and blackberries. And when they cover their sign with a blue tarp, we drive on by; that's their way of saying, "Sold out." (*231-264-5597*).

Over near Torch River, the ladies at **Sage Meadow Farm** sell herbs and vegetables they grow from organic seeds, using no pesticides or synthetic fertilizers. The farmers are Mary Nemeth and Carolyn Royal, who moved to the area in 1999 to establish an organic farm and "live from it in a sustainable way both for ourselves and for the earth." Their specialty is herbs—whole plants and cut fresh culinary herbs in summer, and dried herbs and herbal products in winter. We've found that the best way to do business with them is to visit Elk Rapids' Saturday-morning outdoor market. They do business from the farm itself, but call ahead to be sure they're open; we've

A Brief History of Cherries

We Michiganders are so saturated with cherry stuff that it sort of drifts through our lives unnoticed . Cherries have been growing in North America since French colonists introduced them. Peter Dougherty, the Presbyterian missionary who built Old Mission, was first to plant them here. To everyone's surprise they did quite well, and so many people took to growing cherries (mostly tart Montmorencies for pie) that surpluses became a chronic issue. Dried cherries took up slack for a long time. Then just when we were running out of things to say about cherries, along came tart cherry concentrate. It's for sale everywhere Up North these days and Cherry marketers cheerfully quote (and fund) research into how cherry juice relieves pain, fights arthritis, prevents colon cancer, and helps you sleep. We haven't a clue about any of that, but it sure tastes good. Mixed with water it's a great cool drink. Tossed in a blender with banana, yogurt, OJ and ice, it makes a killer smoothie. First-timers may gasp at the price until they realize that a quart of concentrate is a two-month supply. Shop around! Some health food retailers ask three times what we pay our neighboring orchardists, whose concentrate fights insomnia and cancer just as well. Use what you save to attend the National Cherry Festival in Traverse City in July. Begun in the 1920s as a "blessing of the blossoms," it has now evolved into a week-long orgy of parades, sports events, beauty and talent contests, rock concerts, pit-spitting and binge-eating competitions, and low-flying combat aircraft.

KING ORCHARDS

"TART IS SMART"

TART CHERRY JUICE CONCENTRATE

King Orchards—Central Lake MI 49622
Ingredients: 100% tart cherry juice

Market Days

As anyone who has traveled in Europe knows, every town of any size has its weekly market day, when farmers and crafters set up stalls in the town square or sell from the backs of trucks and wagons. The custom arrived in Traverse City some years ago and has since spread to several other communities Up North where the region's farmers take their wares to sell at a weekly market. Traverse City's weekly market days are the ones most closely resembling a French *marché* in size, scope and character. The TC market operates 8 a.m. to noon each Saturday, May through October, plus Wednesday mornings in July and August. The market, along the Boardman River, draws growers come from all corners of the state with their fresh, seasonal fruits, vegetables, herbs and flowers. Stall space is first-come, first-served so you never know who'll be where, and food-lovers know to arrive early to get the ripest, freshest and plumpest. Similar, if smaller, civic markets have sprung up in recent years in other Northern Michigan towns. Here's a roster of regular market days where you can find asparagus and strawberries in spring, berries and cherries in summer, plump broccoli in summer, and the ripest apples, squash and pumpkins in fall. Keep in mind that hours and seasons vary.

Boyne City, Saturdays, June to October

Cadillac, Tuesdays and Fridays, mid-July through October

Cheboygan, Saturdays, July through October

East Jordan, Thursdays, May through October

Elk Rapids, Fridays, June through October

Empire, Saturdays, mid-June through September

Leland, Tuesdays, mid-June through August

Petoskey, Saturdays, July through September

Suttons Bay, Saturdays, June through October

Traverse City, Saturdays, May through October (plus Wednesdays in July and August). Closed during Cherry Festival

found that their days and hours of operation are not exactly etched in stone. One regular customer we know says she prefers going to the farm anyway, however, because "the lettuce is all washed and ready to go on my salad plates, and they present it to me in a bag as if it were pure gold." They do free-range chickens and eggs, too, but for those you'll have to get on their waiting list. Sage meadow is at *12486 Hickin Rd. (231-322-4720).*

Across the bay in Leelanau, John and Phyllis Kilcherman's **Christmas Cove Farm** is the go-to place for apples. It's a veritable apple museum, with 200 varieties, antique and modern, including (they say) the very variety Eve gave Adam. It's north of town at *11573 Kilcherman Rd. (231-386-5637).*

Leelanau's **Bellwether Herbs** is a perennial nursery and flower farm with display gardens and a shop for garden lovers. Open daily except Monday, May though August, it's about seven miles south of Suttons Bay at *10203 E. Shady Lane (231-271-3004).*

TLC Tomatoes, also south of Suttons Bay, is one of a growing number of hydroponic farms that extend the season for the stuff of fresh salads. They produce red and gold cherry tomatoes, beefsteak tomatoes, Bibb, red and green leaf lettuce, peppers, cucumbers and herbs. Jim and Toni's retail store is open daily in season, dawn to dusk. Ask nicely and they'll give you a tour of the operation, which is at *4030 Setterbo Rd. (231-271-4754).*

We've just scratched the surface of the region's farm bounty. If you want to spare yourself a lot of driving, let the markets come to you. The list of towns with regular market days *(see preceding page)* grows each year.

Well-known chef and instructor Nancy Allen once wrote that "the Traverse City farmer's market on a September morning is my idea of heaven." Here's someone who knows her way. From her travels around the globe, she remembers the mile-long Beijing market as a maze of vegetables she couldn't even identify. Yet she once wrote that Northern Michigan's markets "offer some of the best food anywhere . . . sweet summer squashes and shiny eggplant from Cherry Center Farm Market; Flossie Armstrong's piles of red peppers; Millie Hathaway's rich red baby plum tomatoes; Garthe's organic apples and pears . . . . Who could resist Ocanas Farm Mar-

The Sweet Life

We Northerners often refer to summer visitors as "fudgies," because of a sweet tooth many of us locals share. Nowhere does fudge count as much toward the gross national product as on Mackinac Island, where its aroma almost makes us forget how many horses are on the island. Fudge, however, is relatively new to the region. Maple sugar predates history. The Ojibwa celebrated spring by moving from their winter camp to their "sugar bush" maple grove and made sugar to preserve food with. Europeans were hooked the day they tasted it, and on 19th-century Mackinac, the first sign of rising sap sent everyone off to the maple groves on nearby Bois Blanc Island where for three weeks they boiled sap by day and partied by night. For all we know, this was the origin of our famous Michigan spring break. Those islanders weren't just feeding a sweet tooth. They sold their sugar as far away as Chicago and New York. One way we know spring is near where we live is when the sap barrels appear by roadside maple trees. The stenciled name "Maple Acres" tells us they belong to the Luchenbill farm at US-31 and Campbell Road in Kewadin (231-264-9265). Two other big producers are Robert Weisbrodt's Johnny Appleseed Farm on Pioneer Road in Beulah (231-882-4041) and Kerry Gedge's Kodiak Farms near Alanson (231-548-3146). The Michigan Maple Syrup Association, online at *www.mi-maplesyrup.com*, can tell you maple syrup is good for more than waffles and pancakes. Try it on mixed fruit, or with butter and dry mustard to glaze the carrots you get at the farm market. Next time you grill a nice salmon, spread on a glaze of equal parts syrup, brown sugar, and thyme.

kets' tart tomatillos or the perfume and blush of Popp's peaches?"

We like browsing farm markets without a shopping list. The joy lies in discovering what's available today and then building a meal around it. We once came home with two mammoth hunks of celery root and no idea how we'd use it. We're lucky it has shelf life, because it was days before it had all found its way into our diet, some mashed in with potatoes and horseradish, some in a soup, and some thinly sliced and sautéed. It was terrific.

A few weeks later we found chilled celeriac soup in a restaurant that knocked our socks off, and we appreciated it all the more for having been down the same road in our own kitchen with good stuff from our own neighborhood.

Real Bottles, Real Milk (and Cream on Top)

Are you old enough to long for real milk that came in glass bottles and had cream floating on top? Long no more. The real thing, just the way you remember it, is available all over Northern Michigan thanks to George and Sally Shetler and their clan, who own and operate the Shetler Family Farm in Kalkaska.

They produce and sell whole milk, skim milk, chocolate milk, heavy cream, half-and-half, and two-percent milk. They also produce eggnog at Christmas. Their milk comes in pints, quarts, and half gallons.

For 15 years or so, the Shetlers sold their milk to a commercial processor. But shortly before the turn of the new century they set themselves the goal of doing all their own bottling. They built a new processing plant on the farm and acquired and installed vintage milk-processing equipment.

Doing things the old fashioned way, they've been able to involve the entire family in the business at all levels, from production to marketing. They want their customers to think of buying their milk as an investment in the future of small, family farms.

The Shetlers don't homogenize their milk because they believe cream is more digestible when left to rise to the top intact. And, they say, milk tastes better when it comes from glass bottles than from plastic or cartons. (Glass bottles are obviously more expensive, so the Shetlers also ask customers to return them for re-use.)

The Shetlers feed their 40-cow herd no antibiotics or hormones, and they keep the herd in pasture six to eight months a year. Even in winter the herd is let out when weather permits. The cows are milked twice daily.

All of Shetler Dairy's milk is pasteurized, of course, and enriched by the addition of vitamins A and D.

The Shetlers produce most of their own feed, which they grow without man-made chemicals or herbicides, and fertilize with composted manure.

You'll find their milk at groceries and delis in Kalkaska, Mancelona, Elk Rapids, Traverse City, Charlevoix, Petoskey, Harbor Springs, and Gaylord. It is easy to recognize. Just look for those glass bottles with all that rich cream on top.

You can buy right from the farm, too. The Shetlers will be happy to see you.

Shetler Family Dairy
5436 Tyler Rd. SE, Kalkaska
231-258-8216

Great Northern Resources

Sometimes a terrific recipe calls for an ingredient you just know your neighborhood store won't have. A daikon radish, maybe, or white truffle oil, or four Anaheim peppers. It might not even be something you consider exotic. Northern Michigan's stores stock far more variety than they used to, but you can never be sure. What you can buy one week may vanish the next. We once spent an hour scouring a local supermarket for ginger paste only to learn the store had stopped carrying it.

Later, however, we found it at any number of stores and specialty shops. Happy is the cook who has good resources.

There are a lot of happy cooks Up North these days. We enjoy good resources in new profusion.

Even smaller towns have their fine delis, and the larger centers enjoy a truly sophisticated variety. The wealth of good foods available Up North today means we needn't fret if we come across a recipe for rabbit fricassee or pan-seared duck breast and want to serve it to company next week.

Let's start with Traverse City's **Meijer** store, because that's where we often begin our own culinary scavenger hunts.

Aside from being one of the area's largest supermarkets, it has produce no other can match. If you suddenly find yourself in need of fresh celeriac or a pair of pomegranates, here's where the odds favor you the most. It's the go-to place for the likes of quince or cactus pear, Maradol papayas, Fuyo persimmons or chayote squash. The cheese counter there is our most reliable source of smooth, flavorful French feta. Meijer's produce is so diverse that we often just browse the exotica in search of something new to try, and *then* seek recipes calling for it. This is where we discovered the pul qua squash and the plum-size South American tamarillo with its bitter skin and deliciously sweet-tart flesh.

Meijer, however, is a huge place, and getting in and out can take a long time when all you need is a can of coconut milk or a little flax seed. What has truly transformed Northern Michigan into a happy hunting ground for the cook-at-home food lover are all the smaller delis and specialty food stores..

Some, of course, have been around for years. One of the oldest of these marvels is **Symons General Store** in downtown Petoskey. One of the newest is Pram and Sue Acharya's **Esperance**, on US-31 in north-side Charlevoix. What they have in common is that both specialize more in wine than food, but still manage to make available to us mortals some delicacies seldom seen this side of Elysium. Symons is your source for, oh, a few peppered walnuts, or some soft, rich, Taleggio cheese from Lombardy, either of which might make your next salad unusually interesting. They carry hundreds of cheeses. Chandler Symons, grandson of the founder, is the third generation involved in the operation and also runs the little restaurant next door. His folks, Tom and Lynne, started running the store almost half a century ago. The wine shop downstairs from the general store has a wide and very interesting range.

While Esperance probably stocks wine from every region on earth where good grapes grow, it is also where we'd be likely to go for duck breast or pheasant, should we take a sudden notion to roast some. We know, too, that here we'll find unusual cheeses we've probably never even heard of so we can dazzle the next food-snob we invite for dinner. Esperance also has a coffee-sandwich bar where you can get something to nibble and sip while you browse, and it's also a source for out-of-the-ordinary carryout. One such to-go item is what Pram calls a "noshing platter" of pâtés, cheeses, artichoke hearts, olives, and roasted peppers.

When we asked him once to suggest a Valentine's Day treat, he put us on to "Pappadews," which turned out to be a sweet-hot, pickled, South African fruit he had just discovered at a trade show. He also offered us a "Red Fire Bar" of dark chocolate with ancho and chipotle chili. You won't find *that* at your local Shell Mini-Mart. We haven't a clue what wine we'd pair with it, although we're sure Pram would have a few good suggestions.

Every food lover Up North knows, of course, that the mother lode of specialty foods is on a two-block stretch of West Front Street in Traverse City. We call it "Gourmet Row" because of all the culinary bounty there.

Mary's Kitchen Port, at the west end of "Gourmet Row," is another of those institutions that every food lover treasures. A sort of combination deli, sweet-shop, and kitchen store, it's where local foodies buy their mortars and mandolines, spatulas and graters, coffee-mills and tart pans. It's also where they go to buy carry-out lunches built around the salads, soups and pastries turned out by founder Mary Boudjalis's son, Mike, who now runs the store.

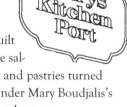

Mike knows that nothing puts foodies into a buying frenzy faster than the prospect of good food, so when they come in to browse the woks and whisks, he sneaks up on them with the sight and scent of his deli salads and exquisite cookies, cakes and desserts. That's why you find mid-day customers queued not just for flan pans but for precious pints of pasta, chicken, and seafood salads, and little sacks of chocolate opulence. Mary's is the place to find something extraordinary for the cook in your life as well as something for your own work-day lunch by the bay.

Folgarelli's, at the east end of Gourmet Row, is a Traverse City institution. This classic deli specializes in sensuous Italian foods, from *prosciutto di Parma* and papardelle to pesto and Parmesan. It also has extensive shelves of delicacies from Asia, Europe, and the Middle East. It is such a regular stop for local food lovers that a trip there often has the feel of a social event. Make a quick stop for a baguette and some basmati and you might find yourself spending half an hour exchanging recipe ideas with a neighbor who came in for a little fresh mozzarella or some kalamatas. This store has such a following that when the cops once busted Proprietor Donna Folgarelli for the "crime" of bringing her dog to work, customers defended her with a blizzard of letters to the editor. Like any deli worth its salami, they'll make you lunch on the spot from a menu of 45 sandwiches, some of them downright heroic. Pick from sub buns, rye, baguette, or focaccia, and then think turkey, prosciutto, mortadella, salmon, corned beef, pastrami, salami, provolone, Cambozola, Jarlsberg, lettuce, tomato, peppers, onion, pesto, cucumber, sprouts . . . . Well, you get the picture. The guys behind the deli counter will also put up a platter for your party, and send you next door to the wine shop for the perfect pairing.

In the little strip mall between these two anchors is **Burritt's,** which incorporates **Carlson's** Fish Market next door and makes a nifty one-stop solution for both the sea bass you want to grill for guests and the *mousse de foie de canard* you'll surely want to serve with their champagne cocktails. The staff is eager to answer questions and give guidance. A treat we once found there, when we'd gone to get some veal scalloppine, was butternut squash agnolotti. It meant great dinners back to back: savory veal piccata one night, then those agnolotti the next, cooked al dente in a savory to-mato-fennel broth.

("Do you really eat like this all the time?" people sometimes ask us. "You bet," we reply. And it is places like these that let us do it. It's no harder to grill some salmon steaks and whisk up a little honeyed ginger-lime sauce than to assemble a casserole with mushroom soup and Hamburger Helper.)

Almost next door to Burritt's, at Denise and Mike Busley's **Grand Traverse Pie Co.,** we love the glorious, flaky crusts and fruit fillings that are neither glutinous nor overly sweet (as is too often the case in fruit pies). We're particularly fond of their cherry pie, because their tart cherries taste, well . . . *tart.* They make some awfully good cream pies, too, as well as lunch-time pot pies, soups, salads and sandwiches. Don't be deceived by the modest appearance of this little outlet. Since opening the TC store in 1996, the Busleys have built quite a chain (stores in Brighton, Okemos, and Indianapolis), and their products appear in groceries and supermarkets practically everywhere in Michigan. They also sell fruit preserves, salsas and BBQ sauce by catalog and Internet.

If you're after cheesecake rather than pie, we'd steer you uptown to the cheerful little **Underground Cheesecake Co.** They make cheesecakes in a wide variety of flavors and sizes, but we love the little five-inchers, which we somehow manage to stretch into two yummy nights' worth of dessert.

Fans of genuine, south-of-the-border Mexican food know they can find the real thing at the Traverse City grocery, **Osorio El Mexicano.** What some might not know is that owner Miguel Osorio, who also owns Taqueria Margarita next door, is an unofficial Godfather to the region's Hispanics. He received Michigan's" Civic Duty Award" in 2002 for "serving as translator, provider to the hungry, and bus driver when his neighbors need transportation."

For folks up the coast from Traverse City, **Folgarelli's Wine Shop at Summer's Place** in Elk Rapids has a fine inventory of wine and expert help in choosing it. They also sell invariably interesting carry-out soups, salads, and pizzettas, made on site. Our advice: If they have a plum tart to sell, snap it up!

As we said up front, the good delis and resources aren't all in the big city, either. One of the best new resources Up North is the **Galley Gourmet** in the Marina District at Bay Harbor. It's stocked to the gunwales with exotic goodies — tinned, packaged and fresh — from ports on all oceans. Down in the galley itself, the chefs prepare an ever-changing menu of pastas, pizzas and casseroles, sandwiches and soups, salads and desserts. With enough notice they'll even whip up a custom meal from your own recipes. You can just take it home, warm it up, and plate it for your guests; that way you get to enjoy the food, avoid the work, and still get the applause. Aboard the yachts in the harbor, this place makes galley slaves look downright brilliant when folks from the next slip unexpectedly come aboard for supper. It is every bit as fine a resource, however, for the poor landlubber who hasn t a yacht to his name and must arrive by SUV.

Once upon a time, commercial Great Lakes fishing was a noble enterprise employing whole families who sold their catch right off the dock in every harbor town. Alas, times change, and species come and go. Only the Carlsons remain from the fleet that once worked out of Leland harbor.

One hardy perennial that still serves a huge region, however, is **John Cross Fish Market** in Charlevoix. The store lies on the south side of Round Lake, right down by the water with the dock at the back door, and big bins of the fresh, iced catch

Why, Naturally!

We're never sure whether "natural food stores" are a business or a belief system, but it's just the ticket for anyone seeking foods untainted by man-made chemicals and such. Traverse City's Oryana and Petoskey's Grain Train, for instance, promise foods produced in "ecologically sound" ways. They also espouse "cooperative economics" as an effective way of meeting consumers' needs (and possibly even as the one true path to the well-being of the planet). Speaking personally, we find our fresh produce needs very effectively met in a somewhat less political atmosphere like Meijer, where it  tends to look as good and cost less. But, then, we don't mind if someone used a little fertilizer to grow our food. If you do mind, then these stores are for you. And they're the only source for some things you just won't see at a supermarket, such as kelp. We needed some miso a while ago and could find it only at Oryana. Traverse City's Edson Farms is another "natural" food outlet, rich with vitamins and supplements and such essentials as broccoli extract and spirulina, which are algae said to keep your brain from going south when you get old. Our personal cuisine seldom calls for it, but if yours does, Edson's is your source. They also have black elderberry syrup that they say was developed by the renowned virologist, Madeleine Mumcuoglu.

inside. One of our most memorable visits there was in our little runabout, at the end of a long day's cruising around Lake Charlevoix. Before heading home, we put in at their dock and strolled ashore to buy some perch to take home. It somehow made dinner that night both more satisfying and more authentic.

Sonny's Market in Torch Lake Village has a huge following around Torch Lake and from as far away as Elk Rapids and Charlevoix. Sonny Szejbach and his dad used to run a market in Elk Rapids. When Sonny and his wife, Chris, opened a new store on US-31 in Torch Lake Village, it seemed like sheer folly at first because it was practically out in middle of nowhere. But it filled a huge neighborhood food vacuum, and the Szejbachs parlayed their good reputation into a brilliant success, with the help of a lot of top-quality meat, seafood and service and a well-chosen array of deli and specialty foods. Chris took to serving breakfasts and deli lunches in a little seating area up front, too, and next thing she knew the restaurant had a following all its own. After only a couple of years, they built an addition so they could expand both the restaurant and the store. This is a fine source for good black angus beef cut to your specs, and Sonny is very accommo-

dating when it comes to special orders for a cut or critter you can't find elsewhere. Two of the Szejbachs' daughters work the store with them, and their son-in-law, Matt, makes some of the best pizza we've ever found west of the Hudson River. It's the same sort that turned the USA into a nation of pizza-eaters half a century ago — with good, fresh toppings, savory tomato sauce, a modest coat of good cheese, and a crust thin enough to bubble up in the oven.

American Spoon Foods is not just a Northern Michigan resource, but a treasure. It's where we turn when we want to give distant friends a gift with something of

Northern Michigan in it. We always include some of their unsweet-ened "Spoon Fruits." Our friends invariably write back to ask where to get more, so we send along a cata-log or suggest they check their local deli or gourmet store. Ameri-can Spoon's good stuff seems to be sold anywhere food-lovers shop. They have five stores Up North — in Petoskey, Harbor Springs, Charlevoix, Acme and Traverse City. The latter two are operated inde-pendently by Peter and Kim Schmitz. American Spoon was built to promi-nence by a Detroit grocer's son named Justin Rashid, who once sold foraged berries and morels at a market near his family's Indian River cottage. With New York restaurateur Larry Forgione, to whom he had been selling morels, he went big-time in 1981. American Spoon Foods now sells its Spoon Fruits, fruit butters, salsas, relishes , dressings, mari-nades, dips, and grilling sauces world-wide, at retail and by mail-order and Internet. One of the company's newest ventures is a line of low-fat fruit gelatos and sorbets, sold in the Traverse City stores and at the Gelato Cafe, next door to the American Spoon Foods store in Petoskey.

Another local entrepreneur has built an empire out of just one fruit: cherries.

Bob Sutherland's **Cherry Republic** peddles its cherry-themed products by mail-order and on-line catalog all over the world.

The empire's capital is a funky deli and store in Glen Arbor where you can get a cherry sandwich, cherry salad with cherry dressing and maybe some cherry pie with cherry-butter-pecan ice cream, and a Cherry Re-public T-shirt and passport. It began about 15 years ago, when Sutherland tried selling cute "Cherry Republic" T-shirts from the trunk of his car, and 3,500 shirts later he decided cherries might be able to support his entire per-sonal lifestyle (motto: "life, liberty, beaches and pie"). Since then he has probably done as much to erase the re-gion's cherry surplus as all the subsidies in Washington.

When we're out cycling, we often like to picnic by the water, and **Cornichons** in Harbor Springs is a favorite

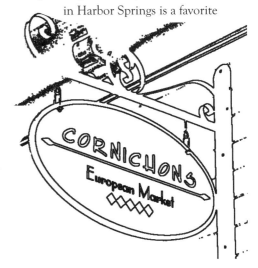

stop for our lunches — something like a fresh tuna *salade Niçoise,* maybe or a turkey-and-tomato wrap overflowing with greens, red onion, cucumber, roasted red pepper, and feta. The deli case is well stocked, too, with cheeses, meats, and bread from the fabled Zingerman's in Ann Arbor. You can even stay right there and enjoy your picnic at small tables indoors or in the secluded courtyard.

Never know what you'll find in a strip mall, either. At **Nutmeg,** in a strip mall along the Harbor-Petoskey Road, we once found some of the best tomato-basil cream soup in memory. **Cormack's Deli** outside Petoskey is also in a place where you might look for an optometrist, maybe, or an insurance agency, but not a pastrami on rye. Good, home-made deli food keeps it packed at lunchtime.

Great Northern Resources — the Data

American Spoon Foods, PO Box 566, Petoskey; 800-222-5886 www.Spoon.com
> Stores:
>> 411 E. Lake St., Petoskey; 231-347-1739
>> 315 Bridge St., Charlevoix; 231-547-5222
>> 230 E. Front St., Traverse City; 231-935-4480
>> Grand Traverse Resort, Acme; 231-938-5358
>> 245 E. Main, Harbor Springs; 231-526-8628

Burritt's and Carlson's, 509 W. Front St., Traverse City; 946-3300

Cherry Republic, 6026 S. Lake St., Glen Arbor; 800-206-6949; www.cherryrepublic.com

Cormack's Deli, 2569 Charlevoix Ave. (US-31S), Petoskey; 231-347-7570

Cornichons, 248 State St., Harbor Springs; 231-242-0020; www.cornichonsmarket.com

John Cross Fisheries, 209 Belvedere Ave., Charlevoix, 231-547-2532

Esperance, 12853 US-31N, Charlevoix; 231-237-9300

Folgarelli's, 424 W. Front St., Traverse City; 231-941-7651; www.folgarellis.com

Folgarelli's Wine Shop at Summer's Place, 100 River St., Elk Rapids; 231-264-9000

Galley Gourmet, 4181 Main Street, Bay Harbor; 231-439-2665

Grand Traverse Pie Co., 525 W. Front, Traverse City; 231-922-7437; www.gtpie.com

L'Chayim, 274 S. Benzie, Beulah; 231-882-5221

Mary's Kitchen Port, 539 W. Front St., Traverse City; 231-941-0525

Meijer, 3955 S. Division (US-31 S), Traverse City; 231-933-1800; www.meijer.com

Nutmeg, Harbor Plaza on M-119; 231-347-0712

Osorio el Mexicano, 1319 W. South Airport Rd., Traverse City; 231-935-1890

Silvertree Deli, 119 St. Joseph St., Suttons Bay; 231-271-2271; www.thesilvertreedeli.com

Sonny's Market, 2786 US-31N, Torch Lake; 231-599-9477

Symons General Store, 401 E Lake St., Petoskey; 231-347-2438

Underground Cheesecake Co., 406 S. Union St., Traverse City; 231-929-4418;
> www.undergroundcheesecake.com

Dining In, Dining Out

For the Culinary Gear-head

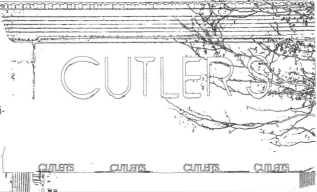

Quick: Where would you go if you needed a new Mouli grater right away, or a mandoline? Sometimes the thing you're looking for isn't an ingredient at all, but a device. Maybe an asparagus steamer that will get the most from the spring's tender spears, or a raclette cooker to let you enjoy some good Leelanau raclette properly.

Ordinary tongs and whisks are one thing, but when we need something out of the ordinary, our treasure hunts tend to be more productive when we start at places like Mary's Kitchen Port in Traverse City, and Cutler's in Petoskey. They have long been favored by home chefs seeking kitchen gear, both essential and exotic. Gas-powered wine-opener? Ravioli mold? Zojirishi bread maker? Where but here?

After all, when the in-laws are coming tonight and you desperately need a decent tomato mill or a hot-milk frother, you don't want to be floundering around in search mode all day. At Traverse City's Peppercorn, you can even do a little wine tasting while you seek the perfect gadget. Mary's, while part deli-patisserie, specializes in kitchen gear. While Cutler's also handles gifts, china and linens, books and gear for food lovers are key parts of the game plan.

Suttons Bay's Front Porch and Beulah's Crystal Crate and Cargo are two more fine resources for the food-lover, with kitchen hardware to keep any culinary gear-head happy.

Crystal Crate & Cargo, 262 S. Benzie, Beulah; 231-882-5294; www.crystalcrate.com
Cutler's, 216 Howard St., Petoskey; 231-347-0341
Front Porch, 207 St. Joseph St., Suttons Bay; 231-271-6895
Mary's Kitchen Port, 539 W. Front St., Traverse City; 231-941-0525
Peppercorn, 226 E. Front St., Traverse City; 231-941-4146

Celebrate Bread!

No escaping the aggressive marketing of low-carb diets these days. From the hysteria on TV about the "obesity epidemic," you'd think a baguette deadlier than cigarettes and SUVs combined.

Well, we are *not* about to give up the very staff of life, especially now that a wave of artisans has come along with such glorious breads. Every neighborhood grocer Up North, it seems, has crusty baguettes, neatly chained epis, rustic boules, and good sourdoughs that curl the tongue.

Personally speaking, we are grateful for physicians who merely advise us to eat less, exercise more, and live moderately—preferably on a diet that includes bread. It has been our most basic food since Jacob gave some to Esau to go with his lentil soup. Who ever beseeches God to give us this day our daily nutritional supplement?

Good bread, like good wine, is an art. Each loaf reflects the bread maker's creative interpretation of a few, simple ingredients. Good bread has more than flavor. It has soul and integrity. It is pleasing to hold and to look at, and has the scent of sweet, toasted grains and dark, robust crust. Northern Michigan's Stone House extols the purity of bread it makes with just wheat, water, yeast and salt. Anyone who can make bread that good must be using a secret fifth ingredient. Call it love. Call it soul. Call it art. Stone House's Bob Pisor calls it "passion."

Like him, we can't imagine a full and happy life without good bread. Bay Bread Company gives us multi-grain boules with plenty of fiber, perfect for a hearty breakfast of toast with cheese or jam. Crooked Tree Breadworks in Petoskey provides baguettes crusted with toasted sesame, flax and fennel seeds, an ideal tear-apart complement to a hearty winter soup. On Thursdays, Stone House's Asiago appears — terrific by itself but also ideal for grilled-cheese lunches or toasted croutons that enliven our salads and soups. Traverse City's Great Harvest Bread Co. may be part of a chain, but we'd never hold that against someone who provides such good dill-onion rye for a sandwich of Atkins-approved liverwurst and Swiss.

Bay Bread Co., 601 Randolph Street, Traverse City; 231-922-8022
Great Harvest, 895 S.Garfield, Traverse City; 231-947-9670; greatharvestbreadtc.com
G.T. Bagel & Bakery, 1327 S. Airport Rd.&1650 Barlow,Traverse City; 231-946-3941
Stone House Bread, 407 S. Main, Leland; 800-252-3218; stonehousebread.com
Crooked Tree Breadworks, 2286 M-119, Petoskey, 888-591-8688; breadworks.com

Welcome to Wine Country

After a century as the world's cherryland, Northern Michigan is drawing serious attention to itself these days as wine country. This all came about because of a farmer's hunch 30-odd years ago that the lakeshore microclimate could work its magic on vineyards as well as orchards. What happens along the shoreline is that in spring the icy lake tends to delay buds until frost danger is past, and the lake's stored-up warmth keeps frost at bay in early autumn. It's why autumn color comes earlier inland than along the coast.

It was Bernie Rink, a former Ohio farm boy, who put two and two together and came up with wine. Librarian at Northwestern Michigan College at the time, he set out in 1970 to see if he might grow wine grapes on his farm near Lake Leelanau. (He says he did it to keep his kids out of trouble, but we

suspect otherwise). His first crop a few years later demonstrated that it was, indeed, possible to produce wine Up North.

This seems obvious now, to anyone who has toured the wineries of the Leelanau or Old Mission peninsulas, or read of the prestigious awards they've brought home. But back then, it was quite a leap of intellect, faith, and thirst.

The loquacious Rink, now retired from the college, regales visitors to his Boskydel Vineyard with nonstop yarns and he is a master at pairing wines and aphorisms. If you can get a word in edgewise when you visit his winery, be sure to say thanks, because it was he who led the way. (You'll find a delightful personal reminiscence about the founding of Boskydel and the origins of the region's wine industry at *www.michiweb.com/wine/rink.html.*)

In recent years grapes have been blossoming all over cherryland. Every year, it seems, more orchards yield to vineyards as old-time orchardists realize they can get more revenue per acre from grapes than from trees. One of those old-time fruit-farming clans, the Kroupas of Old Mission, brought new fame to the region in 2003 when one of their wines was named *the* best white wine at a prestigious international competition. (More about that in a minute.)

By 1990 the region had six wineries, and by century's turn there were 16. Grapes had become so significant a crop that the state established a wine council in 1985 to help market the output (*www. michiganwines.com*).

Most of the region's wineries are on the Leelanau Peninsula. The rest lie across the bay on Old Mission, where the O'Keefe family built upon Rink's happy discovery by producing good varietal wines from vinifera grapes, the classic fruit of most European wines. The

O'Keefes' Chateau Grand Traverse, senior among Old Mission wineries, markets its Rieslings throughout the Midwest.

Other growers, having concentrated at first on hardy hybrids to build a reliable crop, soon followed with vinifera of their own. Nowadays, Northern Michigan wineries produce a wide variety of classic varietals and are best known for their whites — notably Riesling, Chardonnay, Gewurztraminer, and Pinot Gris.

The Raftshol brothers, Warren and Curtis, early pioneers when it came to producing reds up north, were first to grow commercial quantities of red vinifera grapes (on what once was the family dairy farm). Today they produce wines from Merlot, Cabernet Franc, and Cabernet Sauvignon, as well as Rieslings.

Silvio (Tony) Ciccone is known to local red-wine fans for his persistence at making reds work in Michigan. He produces whites as well, but somehow he always brings the conversation around to the hearty reds of his ancestral Italy, particularly Dolcetto and Nebbiolo. Tony, a physicist and engineer, is the son of a vegetable farmer, and grew vegetables in his backyard while working for General Dynamics in De-

troit. He always yearned to grow grapes, however, and one day he ripped out his garden and planted vines. When his wife, Joan, bought him an antique press, he was a winemaker for good.

As retirement loomed, Tony and Joan began seeking property Up North where they

might get serious about wine. Eventually they found their dramatic hilltop acreage in Leelanau where they now produce Cabernet Franc and Pinot Noir, as well as that Dolcetto he loves to talk about.

Other local wineries, notably Lee-

lanau's Black Star Farms, have also had pleasing success with red wines, despite the relatively short growing season Up North.

(Weather can be cruel: Many vines were damaged in 2003 by an unusual sub-zero spell in March after an equally unusual thaw melted the protective snow. Wineries seem to have recovered, however.)

Northern Michigan drew international attention to its prowess when the Kroupas' tiny Peninsula Cellars turned the wine world on its ear in 2003. The Kroupas entered winemaker Bryan Ulbrich's 2002 Semi-dry Riesling in the San Francisco International Wine Competition. This prestigious event, organized by *Bon Appetit* Magazine, had nearly 4,000 entries, and when the judges finished their blind tasting and the bottles were unmasked, their choice as "best white wine" was Ulbrich's. The shock among the *cognoscenti* is said to have been palpable.

Where on earth, they wondered, is Old Mission?

One San Francisco dealer was able to place it "well west of the Moselle and well east of California." (But who, he wondered aloud, would ever

expect "the state with the Detroit Tigers to be making such stellar Riesling?")

Peninsula Cellars' accomplishment in San Francisco has brought Northern Michigan wine an altogether new level of prestige.

Whether it was cause or effect, we can't say, but soon afterwards the *New York Times* devoted the front of its Sunday Travel section to the food and wine of Northern Michigan. The prestigious, pacesetting culinary-trade monthly, *Food Arts*, beat the *Times* by four years; it featured our region's chefs, restaurants and wine in 1999.

Kroupa and Ulbrich's local wine-making competitors were almost as proud of the accomplishment as they themselves were. That says a lot about the esprit de corps among Northern Michigan wineries. It's not easy to grow anything Up North. That we can make good wine here both amazes and delights us!

A poignant post-script to this yarn is that Peninsula Cellars is so small, the prizewinning vintage was gone within days. "I wish I had more to sell," said Ulbrich, offering solace by saying he expected his 2002 Select Riesling would turn out to be even better.

The 2002 Semi-Dry Riesling was also named "best white wine" and "world Riesling champion" at that year's International Eastern Wine Competition in upstate New York.

Chateau Grand Traverse's 2002 late-harvest Riesling won double gold and seven Silver Medals in the same competition. The winery's Sean O'Keefe said it just confirmed his confidence in Riesling as Northern Michigan's "signature grape."

These are hardly the first awards the region's vintners have brought home to Northern Michigan, and they surely won't be the last.

Many wine lovers Up North think the region's best wines are the sparklers that Larry Mawby produces at his Suttons Bay winery. Mawby once told us he doesn't want to have to grow more grapes, so his only way to increase profit is to make better wine. Each year he seems to do just that.

Mawby is known not only for his fine wines and the passion he brings to making them, but for a keen and wry sense of humor. He once labeled a wine "P.G.W. Pun," explaining to anyone who asked that "P.G.W." stood for "pretty good wine."

This brings us to the subject of Sex.

Among our favorite events each year are the vineyard dinners Mawby puts on with Jim Milliman of Hattie's restaurant for 80 or 90 food-lovers, under a tent by the Leelanau tasting room. It's a favorite partly because of the lovely setting, partly because of the small-plate delicacies Milliman sets out, and partly because of the entertaining way Mawby has of introducing the sparkling wine that accompanies each course.

Sex first reared its pretty head at one of the vineyard dinners in 2003. Sex, in this case, was one of Mawby's new offerings, a soft, pink, sparkling wine. He was surprised to discover that no one had a wine labeled "Sex," so on a whim he proposed such a label to the federal authorities who oversee such matters. He was almost certain they'd reject his application. But they must have been distracted that week by searching little, old ladies at airports, because next thing he knew, the Feds had approved "Sex" as a label.

It was a marketing coup whose effects are limited only by the acreage of Mawby's vineyards. Within hours the puns were flying from Mawby's lips and

landing on fertile soil. At the first vineyard dinner after the wine appeared, everyone had great fun turning to total strangers and saying, "Let's have Sex."

Many regard Mawby as the region's premier winemaker. He planted his first vines in 1973 and produced his first wine in 1978. His vines cover 12 acres, and no matter what he once said about not wanting to work harder, he proposes to add another half dozen someday. Most of his efforts go into producing sparkling wines, and his products are widely regarded as among the nation's best *mèthode Champenoise* wines.

Most Northern Michigan wineries are small. Mawby, for instance, produces but 2,500 cases a year. The region's largest, Chateau Grand Traverse, produces 15 times that — still small by California standards.

There's virtue in this, however. "Modest volume," Mawby says, "allows us the pleasure of winemaking in the style we enjoy — barrel fermented, small lots, minimal handling."

The Grand Traverse region has so many wineries now that an entire week's holiday can be built around wine touring. "Agritourism" has almost become an industry in and of itself.

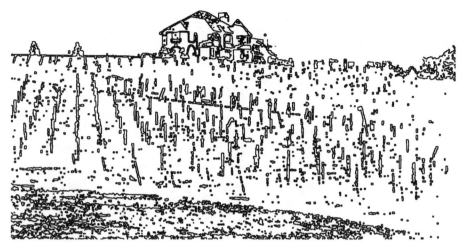

Maybe "agritourism" is just a fancy word for farmers' squeezing extra revenue from the north 40 by charging folks to watch, but it seems quite sensible in a region where tourism and agriculture have always been the economic mainstays. The U-pick fruit farm and farmhouse tearoom are old examples. With the rise of winemaking, it's no surprise that some wineries now offer bed-and-breakfast lodging as well.

The idea was launched here a few years ago at Chateau Chantal on Old Mission Peninsula. This did not happen easily; many newly arrived suburbanites still seem horrified by the notion of actual commercial activity on any of those "scenic" farms. But farms are *not* mere scenery, and the winery B&B is a perfectly logical extension of the tasting room (which is really no more than the winery version of the roadside cherry stand).

Chantal and Leelanau's Black Star Farms have taken agritourism to new levels. Black Star's managing partner, Don Coe, converted a palatial farmhouse south of Suttons Bay into a luxurious, 8-room inn among his vineyards, winery, distillery and tasting room. His winemaker is Lee Lutes, a Traverse Citian who trained in Italy and was quick to challenge the notion that northern summers are too brief for good reds. His first Pinot Noir vintage was immensely promising, and with several years under his belt, he seems to be proving his point. (At the risk of being snubbed by wine snobs, we'll add that we consider his dry cherry "port" one of the best new uses anyone has found for the cherry in decades.)

Chateau
Grand
Traverse
Winery & Vineyards

The Limits of Chauvinism

We readily acknowledge that ours is not the only good wine region, and that we sometimes crave a Malbec or a nice Côtes du Rhône. On such occasions, we're grateful for good retailers whose opinion we can seek and whose judgement we can trust, such as:

Blue Goat, 875 E. Front St., Traverse City; 231-941-9463

Esperance, 12853 US-31N, Charlevoix; 231-237-9300

Folgarelli Wine Store, 426 E. Front St., Traverse City; 231-947-8466

Folgarelli's at Summer's Place, 100 River St., Elk Rapids; 231-264-9000

Gurney's, 215 E. Main St., Harbor Springs; 231-526-5472

Hansen's Foods, 91 W. Fourth St., Suttons Bay; 231-271-4280

Silvertree Deli, 119 St. Joseph Ave., Suttons Bay; 231-271-2271

Sonny's Torch lake Mkt., 2786 N US-31, Torch Lake; 231-599-2357

Symons General Store, 401 E. Lake St., Petoskey; 231-347-2438

Wine Country Market, 541 W. Front St., Traverse City; 231-935-1776

We have also had fine advice from a few restaurants that retail wine, such as the Rowe Inn, Tapawingo, Lulu's, Hattie's and The New York.

Coe has also been distilling other Northern Michigan fruit into America's first *eaux de vie,* fruit brandy. (The local zoning board, leery at first of the revolutionary idea of letting winery visitors stay overnight, warmed to the idea when they learned that *eau de vie* would require a *lot* of good local fruit.)

Agritourism takes new turns every year, and the region's wineries work together to promote it. Coe, retired president of Hiram Walker distillery and a long-time Leelanau cottager, is a tireless advocate, constantly working with colleagues in the culinary arts to enhance Northern Michigan's reputation.

Some visitors are still amazed when they discover what a lively wine trade we enjoy up here in a land that's halfway to the North Pole, where it sometimes seems to be winter half the year. They shouldn't be surprised at all! They need only look at a map to see that that Leelanau and Old Mission lie at precisely the same latitude as Bordeaux.

Or is it the other way around?

Est. 1980

GOOD HARBOR VINEYARDS

Sales & Tasting Room

A Northern Michigan Wine Tour

Wine touring has become a popular way to spend a weekend in Northern Michigan, especially in autumn after the grapes are in. Vineyards, in fact, almost rival beaches and golf courses as tourist destinations. Some wineries have luxurious bed-and-breakfast operations, and some B&Bs have their own vineyards. (Our cover photograph was made at Grey Hare Inn Vineyard B&B on Old Mission.) All the wineries have tasting rooms, and some offer tours. Always call ahead, because hours and days vary, especially in the off-season. Winery websites are listed at *OldMission.com* and *LPWines.com*. If you plan an extended tour, please designate a driver, or hire one. GT Limo will even help you plan your tour (231-946-5466, *GTLimo.com*). Other limos: Majestic (231-938-1746) and Lodi (231-369-3333).

Leelanau Peninsula

Bel Lago Vineyards, 6530 S. Lake Shore Dr. (C-643), Cedar; 231-228-4800

Black Star Farms, 10844 E. Revold Rd., Suttons Bay; 231-271-4882

Boskydel Vineyards, 7501 E. Otto Rd., Lake Leelanau; 231-256-7272

Chateau Fontaine, 2270 S. French Road, Lake Leelanau; 231-256-0000

Chateau de Leelanau, Hilltop Road at M-22, Suttons Bay; 231-271-8888

Ciccone Vineyard, 10343 E. Hilltop Rd., Suttons Bay; 231-271-5551

Good Harbor Vineyards, M-22, four miles south of Leland; 231-256-7165

Gills Pier Vineyard & Winery, 5620 N. Manitou Tr., Northport; 231-256-7003

L. Mawby Vineyards, 4519 S. Elm Valley Rd., Suttons Bay; 231-271-3522

Leelanau Cellars, 12683 Tatch Rd., Omena; 231-386-5201

Raftshol Vineyards, 1865 N. West Bay Shore Dr., Suttons Bay; 231-271-5650

Shady Lane Cellars, 9580 Shady Lane, Suttons Bay; 231-947-8865

Willow Vineyards, 10702 E. Hilltop Rd., Suttons Bay; 231-271-4810

Old Mission Peninsula

Bowers Harbor Vineyards, 2896 Bowers Harbor Rd.;
  231-223-7615

Chateau Chantal, 15900 Center Rd.;
  231-223-4110

Chateau Grand Traverse, 12239 Center Rd;
  231-223-7355

Peninsula Cellars, 11480 Center Rd.;
  231-933-9787

What is "Regional Food," Anyway?

Talk with enough chefs in Northern Michigan and sooner or later you'll hear the term "regional cuisine." Restaurants Up North have used it to describe their style since Wes Westhoven introduced the notion 30-odd years ago at The Rowe Inn.

It is not nearly as fancy as it sometimes sounds. The practice is old-hat in Europe, which has not traditionally had the pervasive food-distribution industry that so homogenizes American restaurant fare. European chefs rely more on local farms and markets, and their menus reflect distinctive local variations. Where olives grow, they use olive oil in their cuisine; In mushroom season, they use mushrooms.

In Northern Michigan, then, "regional" means maple syrup tapped from the trees in March, ramps, or "wild leeks" we dig from the forest floor in April, tender baby asparagus in May, strawberries in June, blueberries in July, and raspberries and blackberries in August. We have perch, walleye, trout, and salmon. Above all, we have whitefish and cherries. Apples and other fruits grown hereabouts also figure heavily in "regional" Northern Michigan cooking. Squashes have been staples

since Indian days, as have duck, and venison.

One historical account of an early Mackinac Island feast speaks of "partridge and goose kept frozen from the fall hunt, and bear paws and beaver tails and stuffed rabbit roasted whole at the end of long sticks."

Much "regional" food is now regional only in the historical sense. Restaurant walleye, perch and trout are likely to be farm-raised, for they are no longer plentiful enough in the wild to fill all the menus. Perch often come from commercial farms in Europe. Lake Michigan salmon are there only because they were planted.

The best chefs, however, buy locally produced fruits, vegetables, meat and fish whenever possible, and spend time with neighbors who have herbs, morels, asparagus, morels, sprouts, watercress, and fruit to sell.

In like fashion, when we at home prepare delicious meals using produce we find at farm stands and farmers' markets, we, too, are putting good "regional" food on our own tables.

Dining Out

Gold Coast Dining

In our first food-lovers' guide, *The Connoisseur Up North*, we took the easy way out and presented our restaurant profiles geographically. Ho hum. This time around, since one of our themes is that good food is an adventure, we've taken a different tack. We've profiled restaurants by category and are leaving the navigation to you.

We'll be first to admit that our categories and assignments might, in some cases, be a bit arbitrary. What, for instance, is the difference between "Gold Coast" and "On the Waterfront" or "By the Lake?" Frankly, not much. Let's just say the difference is that this was how we looked at things the day we did it. What does matter is that these are all lovely places, deserving of acknowledgement. And if you've not been, we think they deserve discovery.

We deal first, in this chapter, with what we're calling the "Gold Coast," by which we more or less mean restaurants that take themselves very seriously. We take them seriously, too, but we certainly do not believe that the meal you'll get tonight on the Gold Coast will be any better than the one you have next week in in your neighborhood tavern. We hope that nothing in any of our arbitrary categories even vaguely suggests superiority or rank. Do we have our own favorites? Sure we do. But food isn't a contest or sport, even if TV's "Iron Chef" tries to make it one. Where restaurants Up North are concerned, we're like those parents who keep saying they love all their children equally, but in different ways and for different reasons. No two restaurants are any more alike than any two diners' tastes.

Now, go have an adventure!

Here are some good places to start.

Andante

A few years ago, in the course of researching a story about a day in the life of a chef, we spent 16 hours here in the kitchen with owner-chef Bob Stark. We had planned to do this in several restaurants, but one day with Stark persuaded us we had no need to go anywhere else. Stark is a complete chef, and when it comes to designing, preparing, and serving exquisite meals, he has few peers. His charming restaurant in Petoskey's Gaslight District is one of the region's stars.

Our day with Stark began at 8 a.m., making bread for the evening to come. It ended at midnight after the last order of barbecued duck breast and Acadian peppered shrimp had been dispatched and the last dessert dish washed. We attended the preparation of sauces, marinating of meats, seasoning of soups. We survived some mid-day crises shopping for missing ingredients. And we had an evening full of grilling, sautéing, simmering, ladling, and plating. It left us in awe of what a good chef can do in a small kitchen.

All may seem to teeter at times on the brink of chaos, but once an evening is under way, the focus is intense and Stark is utterly absorbed and in total charge. He assembles every plate, knows what table it was going to (and often knows the patron by name and preference). He checks every returning plate to assess reactions, and never loses track of the details of each table's meal or of the status of various meals-in-progress scattered among sauté pans, grill, and ovens.

In the dining room, by contrast, an elegant calm prevails. Muted conversations curl and murmur against a foil of classical music and impressionist paintings, and dinner is punctuated by the gentle clink of silver and the twinkle of lights from the far shore of Little Traverse Bay. Andante, in an unpretentious house on the edge of Petoskey's downtown Gaslight District, is a sanctuary where the food-lover can find respite from the ordinary.

It is also a family operation. Stark's

wife, Lori Steighner, handles the front of the house, while he runs the kitchen with help from Bob Black, whom he refers to as his "co-chef."

Stark is fond of definite flavors, and over the years he has used barbecue rub on tender veal (then served it with chili, grits, and grated Asiago). Chilean sea bass might be marinated in miso and citrus juices and served with a spicy mango salsa. How about gravlax cured in green tea or Cognac, and served on pineapple with a honey-mustard vinaigrette? Even a comfy butternut-squash bisque may show up laced with Marsala and chipotle, and garnished with gorgonzola.

As you can tell, Andante is attuned to the world and strives to stay on the cutting edge. Stark is what marketers would call an "early-adopter." He was quick to use flavors from the bayous and the Southwest when they were in vogue—spicy rubs and chiles, andouille and chorizo. Now he and co-chef Bob Black often steer a more easterly, Asian-fusion course.

Still, Stark lays claim to no set game plan. "I'm through with that. We do what we do, and that's gonna be what we do. I just can't take all the brainstorming any more." Traditionalists will be pleased to know that this means that several long-time regional favorites remain on the menu (including a potato-crusted whitefish that many regulars have loved for a decade).

Andante's wine list is extensive, solid, and gratifyingly far-ranging, and the service is the equal of the food and wine. That is to say, it is refined and worldly, hospitable and attentive, knowledgeable and helpful. You can trust recommendations, and the servers see to it that there is always close communication between his kitchen and the tables out front. If you vacillate in ordering between two equal delights, Stark might just send out a sample of whatever you don't choose, just to see if you like it. Leave something uneaten, and there will be questions asked in the kitchen. Rave, and the chef will know — and be pleased.

So if you enjoy something you have at Andante, let your server know, because in the interests of good food Up North, we want to keep these people happy in their work.

Andante

321 Bay Street, Petoskey
231-348-3321

Hattie's

First-timers at Hattie's are somewhat surprised to find it more urban, spare, and contemporary than knotty-pine rustic, but the quiet elegance, muted conversation and delicious aromas soon make it very clear that Hattie's is about food more than place.

The fellow behind this gem of a restaurant, Jim Milliman, was in the van of a culinary revolution that swept the region in the 1980s. He opened Hattie's in 1987 (and named it for the grandmother who was an early culinary tutor). He'd honed his skills as chef at Ellsworth's Rowe Inn, but once on his own Milliman extended his reach beyond the Rowe's "regional" French style by adopting global influences, inscrutable flavor combinations, and exquisitely artistic presentation.

Almost everything about Hattie's is understatement—soft lighting, restful grey tones—that helps concentrate the senses. Behind the unadorned facade on Suttons Bay's main street you'll find some of Northern Michigan's most inventive and interesting food.

Hattie's has a devoted following of regulars who tend to care about food, so Milliman enjoys revealing something of ingredient and method on his menus. It gives appreciative diners a glimpse of the complexities behind "Grilled Rack of Venison," or "pan-seared scallops." Even so, not all is revealed up front, and part of the fun here for the food lover is deciphering the code for each course.

Milliman understands, of course, that Northern Michigan diners treasure certain things, so you'll routinely find things like whitefish, pork and beef — although a bit more exquisitely prepared than elsewhere.

A comprehensive wine cellar offers a balanced list of vintages from New World and Old, as well as a loyal representation of local wines. The restaurant works closely with neighboring wineries and, in the off-season, keeps the juices flowing with an extensive calendar of special events ranging from cigar dinners to Valentine's celebrations and *prix-fixe* meals before the flicks across the street at the Bay Theater.

Milliman does considerable catering, too, and one of our favorite Hattie's meals isn't at Hattie's at all, but under a tent at L. Mawby Vineyards outside of town. There, two or three times a summer, appreciative food lovers enjoy exquisite dinners that appear as if by magic from what amounts to a field kitchen—each course paired with a different sparkling wine from Mawby. The indoor formality of crisp white tablecloths, white tri-corn napkins, simple silverware and sparkling goblets and flutes somehow seems in perfect harmony with the earthy vineyard. Your tablemates are likely to be from all over the map, many of them drawn to Leelanau just for the evening, and all of them serious about food. One recent vineyard menu described a dish simply as "grilled sea scallops with mango salad." This typifies the understatement that permeates everything about Hattie's. The scallops were browned and slightly crisp outside, sweet and succulent — almost molten — within. They were twinned over fresh mango slivers that had been tossed with orange zest, lime juice, and fresh ginger. Murmurs of appreciation rippled up and down the table as 80 diners parsed the subtleties.

That same meal also featured a wonton cup of stir-fried shiitake mushrooms tossed with ginger and chopped tomato, a plate of grilled duck breast fanned out in pink slices garnished with zucchini julienne vinaigrette, and a dessert of strawberries atop lemon-thyme mascarpone on an almond *tuile*. In the restaurant, such food is merely outrageously good. At a picnic, prepared from scratch in what amounts to a field kitchen, it is miraculous.

One of the amenities at Hattie's is that the restaurant also serves as a gallery, displaying the works of an ever-changing roster of local artists. It's a natural fit in Leelanau, a peninsula where artists seem to outnumber seagulls. But make no mistake: The art at Hattie's isn't all on the walls. Some of the best art comes from the kitchen.

Hattie's
111 St. Joseph St., Suttons Bay
231-271-6222   www.hatties.com

The Rowe Inn

Among food lovers in Northern Michigan The Rowe is a sort of living shrine as the place where most people Up North first encountered "regional cuisine" in the manner of the French provinces.

The style arrived with a one-time history teacher named Wes Westhoven in 1972, when he bought a little knotty-pine, plate-lunch roadhouse near Ellsworth called The Rowe Inn and transformed it. In an era when planked whitefish and sirloin surf-and-turf was about as haute as the cuisine got Up North, Westhoven introduced new ideas — fresh, local asparagus in June; local strawberries in July and raspberries in August; perch and whitefish without the benefit of deep-frying, and dishes that were inventively sauced and garnished with locally grown herbs.

Some of the neighbors were a bit puzzled at first. Westhoven recalls that they couldn't understand why he went into the woods to pick morels when perfectly good mushrooms were available in the grocery. "Maybe," he says, "they thought we were too poor to buy food from the grocery like everyone else." Before long, however, some of those same people took to

showing up at the Rowe each spring to sell morels they had picked.

Inspired, perhaps, by Westhoven's frequent visits to France, today's fare at The Rowe has a decidedly Provençal accent, but it is still Northern Michigan food. A year or so ago, as if to demonstrate that he and the Rowe are as enthusiastic as ever about good food, and always ready to adapt, Westhoven unveiled a new, off-season menu he calls "Bistrot Bridgette." It bowed to the burst-bubble era of fading demand for high-end destination dining by making outstanding cuisine eminently affordable without losing a petit four's worth of quality. (Now you have no excuse; anyone who thinks dining at the Rowe need cost an arm and a leg has some adjustments to make.)

Our first such meal there started with baked onion soup, rich with flavor, and an *omelette aux cèpes* that conveyed all the

earthiness of a sun-drenched Provençal hillside. The entrees were *crêpes aux fruit de mer* that enfolded generous chunks of richly sauced seafoods, and roast chicken in a hunter's sauce that seemed to have been simmering for days in the pot of a *ferme auberge* near Avignon. And that's just the Rowe's midwinter economy version. Imagine what delights summer brings!

High season, of course, starts around the time morels appear, so the Rowe always has a couple of morel weekends. Westhoven considers pecan-stuffed morels to be a house specialty. ("I've never seen it done as well as we do it," he says, with the undeniable credibility of an old champ.)

Rowe regulars appreciate that a good restaurant need not be fancy, formal, or even elegant. They know, too, that good meals require good wine and conversation. Much of the charm of The Rowe is in the utterly relaxed nature of a meal there. However good its food and wine, the Rowe is still essentially a simple, unpretentious roadhouse where, on a slow night, the proprietor may well pull up a chair for a little conversation.

The topics likely will include good wine. The Rowe also has an extraordinary cellar. "Wine," Westhoven says, "is as important as the food, and together they make something far more than the two separate entities."

Part of the charm of the Rowe is the attentive and knowledgeable service. Courses are invariably delivered with impeccable timing by unobtrusive servers who hover unnoticed in the background and make sure all is going well, without ever getting in the way of your meal.

Among The Rowe's special events are off-season Sunday wine brunches, where a modest *prix fixe* brings a starter of eggs Benedict, a sumptuous buffet of such classics as *boeuf bourguignon*, and an array of wines for sampling. It's another of the ways the Rowe keeps us properly fed in winter (this is one of the few restaurants Up North that you will find open nightly all year long).

Westhoven has given the region something besides good food. He has given us talent as food; Tapawingo's Pete Peterson and Jim Milliman of Hattie's both were once chefs at the Rowe. And they, in turn, have developed new stars in their kitchens.

The Rowe Inn
East Jordan Road, Ellsworth
231-588-7351

www.roweinn.com

Tapawingo

Here is one of those restaurants to whom food lovers are inexorably drawn because of a reputation that transcends region. This is not just Northern Michigan's finest, some say, but the state's. To work in Harlan "Pete" Peterson's kitchen at Tapawingo is to court national attention, as Executive Chef Stuart Brioza did when *Food and Wine* magazine named him "best new chef" in America in 2003. Brioza left Tapawingo soon thereafter, but not to worry, for Peterson has a way of discovering and developing talent. The style might change a bit, but the quality never wavers.

Tapawingo is certainly pricey, but all good things come dear. Frankly, we pity the rich gourmand who dines there often simply because he can. Better, we say, to be an infrequent but appreciative pilgrim in search of a memorable meal.

The menus weave tales of unlikely romance in which down-home American foods and exotic, global preparations engage in a sinuous dance of exploration.

Yet no matter how richly complex and exquisite in both ingredient and preparation, Tapawingo's meals are as simple, elegant, and understated as true love. They're the product of a proprietor who is as much artist as chef. Indeed, Peterson was an automotive designer until he decided one day a score of years ago to pursue a higher calling (although that's rather like reminding you that Einstein was once a patent clerk).

Tapawingo is a charming, shingled cottage in the hamlet of Ellsworth, hidden from the road by a tangle of shrubbery. From almost every table, one looks out across green lawn at a peaceful little lake. For all the resort-country charm, however, Tapawingo's mystique is culinary and food is the focus of the dining adventure. We'd hazard a guess that if

you eavesdropped at random on ten tables, the conversation would be about food at eight of them.

Peterson draws from all over the world. No matter how "American" Tapawingo may be, its fare is rich with international surprise. Char-grilled beef tenderloin and pan-roasted Atlantic salmon comfortably share table space with tuna marinated in soy, ginger and garlic, or salt cod brandade from Provence. A principal dish of easygoing beef filet might follow a high-strung hors d'oeuvre of duck pâté, rabbit rillette, and rabbit liver mousse garnished with celeriac, a crouton, pickled red onion, a brioche and a cornichon.

You never know what surprises the menu will hold, but you can be sure it will tempt you. "We try not to specialize," Peterson once said. "What we try to do is build this trust in people that if we have something on our menu, whatever it is, they will like it."

A meal at Tapawingo is less a sequence of dishes than a culinary gestalt, a dining experience whose effect transcends mere description of its parts. One entrée we remember from a dinner there with a visiting sister was a dish of grilled duck breast that had been marinated with honey, lavender, molasses, cloves, and cinnamon. It came with wild-rice pancakes, a few sprigs of grilled baby asparagus, and some tender greens with figs and slices of red pepper. That is not a dish. It is an opus.

In like manner, Tapawingo is a sort of *sanctum sanctorum* of culinary adventure. Regulars here almost qualify as a sect; they receive Tapawingo's newsletter and accompany Peterson on culinary explorations abroad. They keep watch for annual feast days, such as herb luncheons each June, wine events, and the annual "chefs dinners" when Peterson's blue-ribbon colleagues from around the state and nation come to tiny Ellsworth to collaborate on a feast of feasts.

Through much of the off-season, lesser mortals collaborate in a sort of lay ministry, preparing their own feasts during Peterson's frequent cooking classes.

Tapawingo's magnetism is potent. While much of the regular clientele lives nearby, especially in summer, the people at the next table are equally likely to have driven from Detroit or Chicago just for dinner. Go there, and you, like them, you will be handsomely rewarded for having made the trip.

Tapawingo
9520 Lake Street, Ellsworth
231-588-7971   www.tapawingo.net

The Trillium

For some years, starting in the mid-'90s, the Trillium atop Grand Traverse Resort underwent more revisions in menu and style than the resort had management changes. It began as a pricey, white-tablecloth, destination restaurant. At one point it became a faux-rustic steakhouse. It has been year-round sometimes, and seasonal sometimes. For a time it was open only on weekends. Now, new owners with very deep pockets say they are committed to a comeback for the Trillium, and from what we've seen, they mean it.

Those new owners are the Grand Traverse Band of Ottawa and Chippewa Indians, whose gambling-supported empire of casinos, restaurants, hotels, and entertainment venues blankets the Traverse Bay region. The Trillium is the culinary capital of the realm.

For much of the '90s, during one of the resort's earlier incarnations, Sherri worked there. She so often went to the Trillium on business, we seldom went just for fun. Now it's a pleasure again. On our first visit after the GT Band took over, we found a restaurant with the same stunning view as always, with crisply efficient service, and with food that shows immense promise. The dishes were alive with well-matched flavors and textures, and were presented eloquently.

We're not alone in our assessment, either. At a charity-benefit "Chef's Challenge" cook-off event soon after the GT Band bought the resort, a panel of expert judges deemed the Trillium's team the best of the lot in a field studded with regional stars.

The Trillium is still a pricey restaurant, especially since all is à la carte. It is clearly a place to go either *before* you

get to the tables or after you win big. But the odds here certainly favor the food lover. We remember an off-menu special of lemon sole and scallops that were plated on a bed of lentils with a soft but savory, lemon-laced sauce that drew rave reviews around the table when we exchanged forkfuls for tasting. The rack of lamb, roasted to rare and tender perfection in a crust of kalamata olive and artichoke tapenade, also brought *oohs* and *ahhs* all around. It was served *au jus* atop goat-cheese whipped potato, and upright asparagus spears were placed interlacing the rack points. Now *that* is a full house of good food and presentation.

There has always been reason for cheese lovers to like the Trillium. Saga blue and mozzarella, for instance, appear in salads as well as in an appetizer of raviolis in herbed broth. Now you'll find good, Leelanau raclette on the menu as well. It is served as a starter, in a dish named for the Swiss-style fondue cheese it is made with. The cheese is heated on the block and scraped as it melts onto the plate, then served surrounded by fingerling potatoes and savory vegetable slices, a dab of grainy mustard and some toasted baguette chips.

It's nice to see such loyalty to regional produce, but hardly surprising, considering that the Trillium's owners have lived around here a lot longer than anyone else. The cellar also offers many Old Mission and Leelanau wines.

The Trillium's venerable signature dish, "Veal Boursin," remains on the menu, and the management recently revived another warmly remembered Trillium tradition by bringing back the Sunday brunch that once was so popular at the resort. They even added live jazz by the same, local musicians who play weekends in the lounge upstairs.

Service at the Trillium is expertly provided by a staff of experienced veterans who know the menu and the restaurant, and who stay attuned to guests' preferences. When someone at our table recently chose to omit an entrée and simply graze on soup, salad and two appetizers, the server meshed the little four-act meal seamlessly into the otherwise entrée-only script. The staff is graceful and adept, right down to bussers who silently whisk away empty plates and keep tables swept up throughout the meal.

And best of all, the view from the Trillium still reaches forever and offers panoramic light shows when sunshine washes the autumn landscape or lake-effect snow squalls dash across the bay under cold, blue skies.

Trillium

Grand Traverse Resort, 6800 US-31 N, Acme
231-938-2100   www.grandtraverseresort.com

Windows

Phil Murray's restaurant has long been famous Up North for its spectacular setting and outrageously scrumptious desserts, but anyone who patronizes Windows just for the sin of chocolate with a view makes a grave error of omission.

We don't go there often, partly because our newspaper agreed to Murray's request not to be reviewed. He's never told *us* why he's that shy, however, and we've no reason to change our view that his is one of Northern Michigan's top restaurants. A lot of people must agree, for it's a perennial favorite in those popularity polls newspapers and magazines are fond of.

Murray sets high standards for himself and his staff, and it shows in the polished service and opulent menu that enhance that sweeping view of West Bay.

Don't be surprised to find traces of Creole and Cajun here, for Murray's career began in New Orleans, where Paul Prudhomme was a mentor. Murray established himself quickly Up North with the likes of "Firecracker Pork," a dish involving pork tenderloin marinated with garlic and vegetables in oil,

cayenne pepper, and minced ginger. The tenderloin is then sautéed, simmered in rich stock, and served atop bow-tie pasta garnished with cashews. We've never known Murray to be exactly tentative about flavors.

Another dish with bayou roots that has delighted long-time patrons is "Veal Winn Dixie," a dish Murray says came to him one day as he sat pondering recipes outside one of the South's ubiquitous Winn Dixie supermarkets. As he once explained it, the dish calls for veal sautéed in jalapeño butter with shrimp, crab and mushrooms. Nothing wishy-washy about that, either.

Whatever you order here, however, keep your end-game in mind. The desserts are every bit as fine as you've heard.

And take time to enjoy the view, too. Accept its invitation to linger over an after-dinner drink while distant Traverse City turns into a necklace of lights as dusk falls across the water.

Windows
7677 West Bay Shore Dr., Traverse City
231-941-0100

Dining Out

Bistro Nights

When someone asks what our favorite restaurant is, we're always reluctant to answer lest they think we regard one place as "better" than another. "Best" and "favorite" are not at all synonymous. "Best" is absolute. "Favorite" is a matter of personal preference. We, personally, are very fond of what we'd call bistros (or, as defined by Barron's *Food Lover's Companion:* "small cafes, usually serving modest, down-to-earth food and wine"). Northern Michigan abounds in such places, and we love 'em. They're cozy, lively, and casual. We can go in jeans if we want, but coat and tie won't mark us as weird. The food is often as sophisticated as it is down to earth. These restaurants are modest, by and large, only in price and pretension.

So, now that we know you're not asking what we think the *best* restaurant is, we would probably tell you that our personal favorite is Amical in downtown Traverse City. Let us quickly add, however, that we live nearby and spend a lot of time in TC. If we lived somewhere else, our default destination might well be the Coho Café or Whitney's or The New York. These are the kinds of places we like to go for our busman's holidays — great food, cool atmosphere, no fanfare.

Their kitchens never just slap it down or crank it out, but they aren't showy, either. What they offer is sophisticated food that demonstrates serious respect for their customers' enjoyment, and at a price we can afford when it's not a special occasion.

Amical

This hip, urban bistro is a Traverse City favorite for all the right reasons. The name "Amical" means "friendly," and that's certainly appropriate. Since it opened a decade ago, Amical has made friends of every food-lover Up North with its informal charm, consistently lively cuisine and a versatility that borders on all things to all people.

The kitchen is so friendly, it's right there to greet you as you enter, behind nothing more than a patisserie display of tempting éclairs, tarts and cakes. Savory French-style cafe meals are prepared before your very eyes. Poultry and meats roast on spits alongside bowls heaped with the freshest of salads (including a simple, low-fat Caesar that is one of the best anywhere). In addition to the savory *rôtis* of lamb and chicken, you'll find quiches, pochettes, pizzettas, and pot pies hot from the oven. The soup list almost always includes a basil-tomato bisque

that does for cold northern days what hot neon does for cold city nights.

Amical has cool, coffee-house ambience with simple, old-brick walls adorned by a few canvases in ornate frames, and a cozy, three-sided fireplace flanked by tables that are perfect for intimate conversations on snowy winter days or romantic murmurings by summer candlelight.

The sidewalk café in front provides a place where you can linger over lunch on summer afternoons, watch the colorful parade of shoppers and tourists on Front Street, or spend an hour trading gossip over a cappuccino. The outdoor tables are sheltered from the elements and bathed in warm air from overhead heaters, so you can still eat al fresco in the chilly weather we sometimes have Up North.

The table service at Amical is friendly, efficient, expert, and knowledgeable, and the kitchen provides menus of simple yet sophisticated bistro fare. (While the evening menu is downright uptown, not much is lost at lunch.) We particularly remember a dinner of pan-seared duck sauced with lime and honey, but we'd never turn up our noses at their phyllo-wrapped salmon, braised lamb, or pan-seared sirloin — all stand-bys on the menu. You can almost always find rotisserie chicken here, as well. The fare also includes various pastas. Our personal favorite, when it's available, are ricotta raviolis in sun-dried tomato cream.

The evening menu's list of starters encourages grazing on such delights as crab cakes with a saucy chipotle remoulade, and "Olive Twists," a local favorite of charming simplicity — puff-pastry sticks twisted up with tapenade and feta.

At lunch or dinner, you'll find a wide assortment of wines — French, California and local — including a good selection available by the glass.

And on Sunday, there's table-service brunch from 9 a.m. to 3 p.m., which you order from a menu that's like none other in town. Folks who really want breakfast can have their sausage and eggs, their omelets and croissants, their Belgian waffles or *pain perdu* (oh, okay,

call it French toast if you must). The possibilities of an omelet with mild Italian sausage, tomatoes, basil and tomato sauce with a side of potatoes could make an early riser of anyone. Those to whom brunch means lunch will find a glorious assortment of pastas, crêpes, sautéed tilapia, chicken pot pie — and that steadfast rotisserie chicken.

Chef-owner Dave Dennison enlivens the winter months with a series of cookbook menus, taking a whole week to explore each new cuisine. These offer new variety to knowledgeable locals who appreciate it. Regulars enjoy getting into the spirit of accepting new culinary challenges right along with the staff.

Our favorite way to enjoy an evening at Amical is to park ourselves on the tall chairs at the tiny bar right inside the door, order up a bottle of wine, and have dinner right there where we can enjoy the atmosphere, chat up the acquaintances who seem invariably to appear, and people-watch the passing pedestrians outside.

Amical
229 E. Front Street, Traverse City
231-941-8888   www.amical.com

City Park Grill

New restaurants seldom spark the civic debate Bob and Mary Keedy did when they renamed the Park Garden Café, a venerable Petoskey landmark for 60 years. They were turning it into a new bistro but you'd have thought they were abolishing the bay itself for the uproar about tampering with tradition.

Happy endings: They honored history by keeping the old tin ceiling and massive mahogany bar, and what they've done to the menu has made just about everyone forget it was ever anything but the City Park Grill.

It's as lively a spot as it was in the 1920s when young Ernest Hemingway hung out there and it was known just as "The Grill." Hemingway is said to have used it as the backdrop for his 1926 Nick Adams yarn, "The Killers." Even back then, it was a relic; the décor is Gilded Age mahogany, with a giant mirror under a pillared arch behind the bar.

The Keedys are the folks who invented Roast and Toast, the deli-coffee house where so many locals enjoy their morning paper. At City Park Grill, they and co-owners Dick and Laura Dinon, have something altogether different: a bistro menu ranging around the world, from nachos and quesadillas to teriyaki and spring rolls. International, maybe, but it never strays so far as to make red-blooded Americans uneasy. You hear a Louisiana drawl in jambalaya and Creole gumbo, along with the Asian accents of grilled pork with coconut curry and plum sauce. A full menu section lists pastas, and you almost always find whitefish and home-made chicken noodle soup. At mid-day, there's a lighter (but still extensive) menu of tapas-like dishes, soups, salads and sandwiches.

The grill is entertainment central in Petoskey, too, from live music to improv and karaoke to comedy nights.

City Park Grill
432 E. Lake Street, Petoskey
231-347-0101   www.cityparkgrill.com

Coho Cafe

We like to spend time in summer along the Benzie coast, browsing galleries or hiking the National Lakeshore, and we often linger afterwards for dinner at Kim White's Coho Café in Frankfort.

We love restaurants with variety, and this is one of them. The cuisine ranges from classic pasta to Asian fusion, with an occasional seared whitefish or maple-glazed pork chop to make us feel at home. The lunch menu, too, sparkles with salads and wraps.

The Coho's cool, easygoing atmosphere is as interesting as its menu. A small deck in back affords a view of the river, but we like the funky, faux-industrial décor inside. It's as light-hearted as the food. The energetic, efficient young staff seems to have as much fun as the customers.

Kim's a Frankfort native who cooked at the Coho in high school when it was just a lunch spot. After culinary school out West she was working at a trendy bistro in Laguna Beach when her former employer called one day to say the Coho was for sale. Next thing anyone knew, she was a chef and owner, and was back in Frankfort planning menus.

On our first trip there, after biking the Betsie Valley Trail, we shared three appetizers—black-bean chicken quesadillas, grilled scallops, and shrimp spring rolls. The next time we had full dinners, and we had an awful time choosing. We passed wok-seared sesame shrimp (P. 190) in favor of Thai chicken curry, and had a classic vodka penne rather than herb-cheese raviolis with wild mushrooms in thyme cream. But it was *not* easy!

Before we could make up our minds, we were halfway through our bread and peppered dipping oil and were already looking forward to the next time.

Coho Cafe
320 Main Street, Frankfort.
231-352-6053

Lulu's Bistro

Forgive us for talking about art when we should be talking about food, but every time we get to Michael Peterson's Lulu's we check the walls to see what's hanging there. We like his taste. And one night we saw some paintings we really liked. So we found out the artist's name and got his phone number, and called him up the next morning as we sipped our second cup of coffee in the kitchen at home.

That's when we learned A) that the number was for his cell phone, B) that *he* was in California, and C) that we had roused him from sleep at 5:30 a.m.

He was very pleasant about it, however, once he found out why we were calling, and a few days later artist Richard Schemm was back home in Traverse City and in our living room, selling us two of his lively and colorful canvases.

Our point in telling you this story story is that when you approach food and art and life as adventure, you sometimes find your best adventures when you get off the road you had intended to travel.

Michael Peterson's food sometimes does that, too. It is very adventuresome.

Take corvina, for instance. Who Who would ever expect to find corvina on a menu in the land of whitefish? Yet there it was one day: "Roasted corvina with wild rice, watercress, bacon and white asparagus and a lemon-chervil butter sauce."

That's not just adventuresome, it's almost foolhardy. Corvina? When was the last time you saw that on a menu anywhere? Do you even know what corvina is? We didn't. We had to go look it up so we could tell you that it's sort of like drum or sea trout. Yet Peterson manages to carry this sort of thing off time after time. He's building a loyal following not only with good food and service in a very interesting place, but by regularly offering us an opportunity to swim once in a while out of the mainstream with the corvina.

Peterson is no stranger to the Northern Michigan foodscape. He first won notice as sous chef at Spencer Creek Landing in Alden, then wound up owning the place during the late 1990s with his brother Bill and Bill's wife, Kathy. They closed up there in 2000, and Michael took a couple of years off to design, remodel and open the bistro of his dreams in downtown Bellaire.

After a long gestation, Lulu's was a hit from the day it opened. It's an interesting place to look at, with its high ceilings and bare brick walls, hardwood floors and cool, spare, contemporary ambience (and all those lively and interesting paintings).

If you've not been there, don't let anything we've said put you off. No one will make you order corvina if you don't want to. Like any good Northern Michigan restaurant, Lulu's also has its share of beer-battered perch and fries. And Peterson serves up some of the best calves liver around—old-fashioned liver and onions with whipped potatoes and a little bacon. There is also a wide-ranging and comprehensive wine list.

One things that endears us to Peterson's fare is his knack for finding adventure in familiar things, like the salad on his lunchtime small-plates menu that's topped with sherried crabmeat baked with cheddar. Such small plates are a strength here, and grazing can be very rewarding when you enjoy such delights as baked duck confit with herb gnocchi, Gruyere and Dijon cream.

Bellaire itself is sort of off the beaten track, nowhere near I-75 or US-31. Like corvina, Lulu's was a risk for Peterson. But he has succeeded in making it far more than is just the best restaurant in Bellaire. It's among the greats in Northern Michigan — and certainly one of the most interesting.

If you have a shred of adventure in your soul, it's for you.

Lulu's Bistro
213 N. Bridge Street, Bellaire
231-533-5252

The New York

There's no missing The New York in Harbor Springs, prominent at Bay and State streets opposite the harbor in its classic, orange-brick, Victorian building. Owner-chef Matt Bugera has brilliantly achieved the "American Bistro" he once said he had set out to make.

The New York's clubby atmosphere engenders resort-town relaxation in surroundings whose etched-glass accents, brass fixtures, stamped-tin ceiling, and rich, dark woodwork provide a certain *fin-de-siècle* elegance. This place is the perfect companion for all those stately Victorian "cottages" along the shore nearby in the posh enclaves of Harbor Point and Wequetonsing.

The friendly staff is in no way formal or stuffy, but they know their menu and you can trust their recommendations. The fare is as American as the name and runs from burgers to rack of lamb.

The New York is a family operation. Matt's father, Bill, a retired AT&T executive and a serious oenophile, watches over an award-winning cellar and orchestrates frequent wine events.

Meanwhile, backstage, Matt performs feats of menu magic he learned at the Culinary Institute of America and has since honed to a keen edge in Harbor Springs. He came to The New York by way of a small deli he and his wife opened next door when they moved to town in 1983. In those days The New

York was a breakfast-and-lunch sort of place. The Bugeras bought it 1989, however, and transformed it into the bistro it is today.

One of our first adventures at The New York, almost a decade ago, was dining on char-grilled sturgeon steak, which Matt served with a piquant tomato-horseradish sauce. Although the fish had been pond-raised out West, we made note of its solid regional credentials as an ancient species once abundant Up North. A few remain in the wild, and anglers still occasionally bring one up through winter ice on Black and Mullet lakes

if they're lucky enough to get a license. It is such a rarity on American menus, however, that Matt was constrained to say, "A lot of people don't know you can eat them." Behind all that scaly armor, he showed us a delicacy. We have been discovering good food at The New York ever since, born of Matt Bugera's ingenuity and anointed by his home-grown herbs.

Sturgeon seldom appears these days. But whitefish always does— recently, broiled with a lemon-dill sauce, or sautéed, plated atop sautéed spinach and shiitakes, and sauced with a Champagne-mustard beurre blanc.

Like many Americans, The New York makes occasional excursions abroad with the likes of seared tuna in ginger-cream that comes plated with wasabi-mashed potato, or vegetarian canneloni stuffed with walnuts, chèvre and greens, and roasted tomato sauce. By and large, however, the menu sticks nearer home, with an all-American array of steaks, veal and lamb. We're fond, too, of Matt's crab-stuffed chicken breast (P. 180).

The New York's starter list is solid, but not extensive enough for serious grazing. You'll also always find two or three interesting soups, one of which is likely to be whitefish chowder.

In summer you'd best book ahead, because Harbor Springs is crowded and The New York fills early. In the off-season, when things slow down, year-rounders turn it into something of a hangout. Food lovers watch for off-season wine-tasting dinners and Valentine's or Mardi Gras events.

We enjoy The New York at any season, but our favorite is summer. We often land in Harbor Springs after a day's sail with our friends, Marj and Svend Teglhoj, and book for dinner as *Last Viking,* which is their boat. We like to arrive at the New York early and dock ourselves in the bright and elegant front room, whose broad windows lend a sun-porch air and an expansive view of street and harbor. We take our time about dinner and watch sun-bronzed resorters outside in transit from afternoons of play to convivial evenings of cocktails, dinner, and lively conversation about spinnakers and backhands.

This is a fine place for the Christmas season, too, after a day of shopping, or for a long, drawn-out dinner after an autumn day cycling the new trail to Petoskey and back. Leave time before dinner to browse the shops and galleries that make Harbor Springs such an interesting town.

We think this is one of Northern Michigan's top restaurants, and we enjoy returning there regularly—even when we're not working.

The New York
101 State Street, Harbor Springs
231-526-1904

www.Thenewyork.com

North Peak Brewing Co.

Maybe it's a stretch to apply the term bistro to a place as lively as this. Technically speaking, it is a microbrewery (one of three in restaurateur Howard Schelde's empire), so it's no surprise to find the gleaming brass and cop-

per brewing vats on display as you enter.

The restaurant occupies an old candy factory on Traverse City's west-side, Front Street, "Gourmet Row." The basics of the old industrial structure have been preserved in the remodeling, resulting in a barn-like shell of beams and struts, conduits and ductwork, trusses and maple flooring.

North Peak is a boisterous mix of good-but-casual restaurant combined with sports-bar scene. It's a hip after-work oasis for local suits, so don't be surprised to see neckties, but don't look for candlelight and white linens.

While they brew suds to serve on the premises, the main order of business is plainly food. It comes from a theatrical kitchen whose wood-fired oven takes center stage and where all but the dishwashing happens right out in front of God and everybody.

Wood-fired pizzas are prominent, and the rest of the menu often incorporates beer of some sort, such as cherry-porter BBQ sauce and white cheddar and ale soup. Those uncommon pizzas might be topped with Hvarti and dill, or salmon, wild mushrooms, grilled chicken, sun-dried tomatoes, artichoke hearts, and cherry-pecan sausage. We especially remember one with shrimp, pine nuts, and lemon zest. We sometimes attempt it at home, but it's never quite the same.

The North Peak menu has Tex-Mex for the nacho crowd, but we think the best efforts are pastas—rich, flavorful, and priced to keep any flint-hearted accountant happy.

The house beers, light and dark, are always fresh and have real bite. There's a perfectly adequate wine list as well and, for teetotalers, house-made root beer.

North Peak Brewing Co.

400 W. Front St., Traverse City
231- 941-7325
www.michiganmenu.com/np.html

Poppycock's

This place has been a restaurant throughout living memory, but never anything like Poppycock's. In the WWII era it was "Pete's," a family place whose motto on the wall read, "The fish you eat today slept last night in Grand Traverse Bay." Much of that original place remains, including the lunch counter (now the bar) and the booths (although they no longer have the jukebox consoles, with selections by the Dorseys and the Andrews Sisters). Pete Batsakis probably wouldn't recognize the food there today, either.

Mark and Josie Butzier brought the new name with them in the 1980s when Aspen grew too pricey for their tiny Poppycock's crêperie there. Locals and visitors alike greeted them enthusiastically in Traverse City, and their new Poppycock's was soon a favorite for its delightfully imaginative lunchtime salads, pastas and sandwiches. By the mid-'90s, it had blossomed into an interesting dinner restaurant as well, with everything made in-house, including fresh cookies, pastries and desserts.

Poppycock's luncheon salads are full meals encompassing the whole food pyramid, from salmon and chicken down through greens, fruits, herbs and condiments to grainy, earthy breads.

After dark, the menu expands to please a loyal, youthful, trendy, even theatrical clientele. The wine list is comprehensive, and the bar provides a hip array of martinis.

Whitefish in a peppercorn crust comes to mind as a dish we once enjoyed, garnished with fresh fruit and a kiwi-vinaigrette sauce. Ditto grilled duck breast with a blueberry-port wine sauce. Perhaps Poppycock's fish didn't sleep last night in Grand Traverse Bay, but then old Pete Batsakis never offered pan-seared salmon under a ragout of leeks, garlic, and mushrooms. The menu offers haven to vegetarians in ratatouilles, raviolis, and quesadillas that tempt even the carnivores.

When the line's long, you can read the chalkboard specials by the door and admire the décor, still a sort of work-in-progress after 20 years. Poppycock's adds late-night jazz and blues on weekends, with a limited menu after 9 p.m.

Poppycock's
128 E. Front Street, Traverse City
231-941-7632

Stubb's Sweetwater Grill

Until 1994, when Darren Hawley arrived in the kitchen, we'd stop in at this Northport tavern for soup and a burger, and maybe some fries and slaw, after a good day of hiking Leelanau State Park or Cathead Bay. Then, one day that year, we encountered a menu that offered walleye baked in a rich crust of basil-pistachio pesto and served with steamed, julienned vegetables and garlic-mashed white potato and yams.

We were more than mildly surprised, and by the time we finished our meal, we were also more than mildly delighted. That walleye was a long way from burgers and fries, and the presentation was stunning.

Imagine, we said to each other, this in a place where we'd only been looking for a burger. After finishing a wonderful apple-crisp dessert and two cups of perfect coffee, we had recovered enough aplomb to venture into the kitchen and find out what on earth had happened to Stubb's.

The answer, we now know, was Darren Hawley, then freshly graduated from the Culinary Institute. He has since established himself, of course, as one of Northern Michigan's most innovative and energetic chefs. Stubb's Sweetwater Grill, as it is now known, is still in many ways like the simpler eatery that preceded

Hawley's arrival. The décor is unpretentious but cheery, and the staff has an easy-going style that's conducive to relaxed conversation and informality.

From the start, Hawley was wise enough to keep in mind the old regulars who prefer things a bit simpler and more traditional, but for Leelanau's many culinary adventurers, he steers an inventive course. His kitchen follows much the same philosophy. He once described

his cuisine as "peasant gourmet," and said he enjoys preparing "simple dishes, but very good ones."

They might be simple, but Hawley's dishes are conceived, executed, and presented with considerable artistry. Darren obviously enjoys what he does and has fun in the kitchen. He's equally comfortable with the Mediterranean and Pacific Rim as with salmon, walleye, and whitefish. We are particularly fond of grazing on his invariably interesting appetizers.

Many people Up North also get to experience Hawley's work off the premises, for he has built quite a catering trade. Among his exploits each year are several exquisite wine picnics he puts on each summer at L. Mawby vineyards near Suttons Bay.

Our own personal favorite way to enjoy Stubb's is to go by water from Elk Rapids. It's 40 miles round trip but avoids a 95-mile drive around the bay. Granted, we need a very still afternoon, suitable for our little 17 footer, and even then there's an air of adventure about it, with Northport still below the horizon when we set out.

We go early enough to browse a few shops after we dock, and maybe check out the galleries before they close or enjoy a short hike to work up an appetite.

Then we conclude our stay with a leisurely dinner on the porch at Stubb's.

We might start with a couple of his delicate spring rolls and some savory, pungent dipping sauce, or a sampler of fried calamari, potstickers, and grilled shrimp. Then some walleye, perhaps, and a glass of good Leelanau white.

If we time it all just right, the sun will be setting behind us as we start back across the bay, and the full moon rising above the Antrim coast over our bow.

We'll throttle back and enjoy the scenery, and sometimes have the added treat of encountering the flock of swans that congregates out north of Old Mission.

We end these perfect, Northern Michigan summer days by homing in on the lights of Elk Rapids just after dark.

Much as we love the cruise, the meal at Stubb's is always an important part of the adventure. It's days like that, and places like this, that make us treasure life in Northern Michigan.

Stubb's Sweetwater Grill

115 S. Waukazoo St., Northport
231-386-7611

Whitney's

This classic waterfront bistro is a place we enjoy going just to hang out. We can listen to a little music, have good conversation and a few oysters and maybe some chowder.

It is rich with the patina of happy use, its paneled walls hung with nautical art and memorabilia that make us feel right at home after a day of adventure. Such charm is a miracle when you realize the place burned to the ground a few years ago and is actually brand new. In rebuilding, Gina and Chuck Whitney and their architect, David Kimble, somehow managed to re-create the original's look and feel right down to the massive bar, and tin ceiling.

In busy seasons there's a dining room upstairs and a deck above that. We like to stay downstairs, either at the bar or one of the tall tables up front where we can watch the ebb and flow of harbor and street.

In summer we go early, before the cottagers and yachtsmen fill the place with animated talk of shanked tee shots, unexpected wind shifts, and the rigors of scoring a good marina slip.

In winter, locals go there as to a social club, shelter from the elements in familiar surroundings where they can banter with friends over good food. We particularly remember one December evening there after a day's quest for a cut-your-own Christmas tree. We docked at the bar, on the lookout for a Margarita and something hearty to eat. A game was on the TV, and a guy in buffalo plaid down the bar was critiquing the new glass entrance to the Louvre.

Our hearts leapt at the sight of lasagne and seafood chowder on the menu, and within minutes Gina had a salad of spring greens and balsamic on the bar in front of us and was headed to the kitchen for a bowl of Manhattan-style chowder, with generous hunks of seafood, tomato, potato and corn, swimming in a savory broth. The lasagne was a boatload of ricotta, sausage, mushroom, and marinara sauce. It was just what a bistro meal should be: hearty, but not excessive; delicious but not pretentious; and served with an easy-going, friendly efficiency that reminded us not to wait for special occasions to go out for dinner.

Whitney's
305 Bridge St., Charlevoix
231-547-0818

Dining Out

On the Waterfront

For a place where water dominates the scenery, Northern Michigan has precious few places where we can go out to dinner by boat. We enjoy it so much, however, that we continually seek such places, and we have our favorites.

One of our treasured annual rituals is to launch our little runabout on Lower Lake Leelanau and cruise up through the Narrows, across the upper lake, and down the Leland River to dinner at the Riverside Inn. We can dock right outside the dining room, enjoy a lovely and interesting dinner, and maybe return back down the lake with moonlight on the water. We can even make an overnight cruise of it if we want, for the inn has guest rooms upstairs.

We spend a lot of time afloat on the Chain of Lakes, too, and we enjoy putting in at the Dockside in Clam River on a hot summer day. There, in the breezy shade on the deck, we can tuck into burritos and burgers and onion rings while we watch weekend skippers trying to dock downstream in the swift current. On Lake Charlevoix, the Landing at Ironton is equally casual, and beachcomber wannabes are welcome in shorts, tees and sandals.

The places we offer here, however, like the Riverside, start a notch or two up the food chain from burgers for lunch. They extend all the way up to the fine-dining elegance of the Pointer Room at Stafford's Pier in Harbor Springs, and the bright, cosmopolitan cuisine at Bay Harbor's Latitude.

Food-loving skippers and mates should remember that there are *many* more fine places which aren't right on the water, but still within an easy walk of the marina in any harbor town. Remember, too, that most towns' public harbors offer a few hours' free mooring at a "shoppers' dock" for folks like us.

So enjoy yourself. Please remember to go safely . . . and eat well.

Garrett's On Water Street

The lakeside setting at the foot of Boyne City's Water Street is so perfect for a restaurant that the opening of the new Garrett's On Water Street in 2003 was welcome news.

All the more so because the chef and owner, Garrett Scanlan, brought lively, new style to the menu while maintaining the good service that marked its predecessor, One Water Street.

Boyne City has become quite a restaurant town, and Garrett's enhances the scene. By the time we made our first visit, soon after the debut, it was already becoming a dining destination. This hardly surprises us, for Scanlan is well credentialed. He was chef for some years at Mahogany's in the Charlevoix Country Club. Many food lovers Up North enjoyed his fare there.

Barely ten days after the opening of his new place we found the kitchen already up to speed. The service, too, was pleasant, hospitable, and remarkably glitch-free for a startup.

Scanlan knows his stuff. He enjoys strutting it, too: The recipe he provided for this book was so incredibly complex we almost omitted it lest we discourage you. But we decided that if we're going to ask chefs for recipes that reflect their approach to food, we have an obligation to pass along what they give us. The one he offered (P. 186) is a remarkable dish of pan-roasted pheasant breast with blackcurrants, sweet potato, root vegetable puree, and herbed potatoes *Parisienne*.

While he excels at such culinary exhibitionism, and is quite willing to take risks in the kitchen on the patrons' behalf, Scanlan thoroughly understands

and appreciates comfort food. He takes pride and delight in simple cuts of black angus done perfectly on the grill.

His restaurant's menu is not overly complex, although even the simpler dishes sometimes convey a sense of adventure. Walleye once arrived at our table comfortably dressed in a robe of crisp potato crust and a cloak of sour-cream Hollandaise, but accompanied by some very homey, chive-laced, whipped potatoes.

The menu incorporates several favorites Scanlan brought with him from Mahogany's, such as Parmesan-sauced penne with tomatoes, asparagus and spinach. And (talk about comfort food!) he also brought with him his grandmother's meatloaf and mashed potatoes. We loved this dish in Charlevoix, and are happy to have it reappear in its new home at the other end of the lake. It's a meal that makes the perfect ending for a long afternoon of hiking on a crisp autumn day

Garrett's menu begins with a list of appetizers that makes tapas-style meals a pleasurable cinch. Choosing might be difficult, however, for the list overflows with such temptations as oysters Rockefeller, wild mushroom strudel with Parmesan cream, and roasted mussels with plum tomatoes, saffron and fennel. We particularly remember two knockout appetizers. One was a pair of lobster spring rolls on Asian slaw with a pineapple-laced sweet-and-sour sauce; the other was smoked salmon on a potato-leek cake, garnished with capers, sour cream and red onion. This restaurant is a grazer's delight, and the grazer can take comfort in knowing that the servers are adept in their timing. They know how to avoid the awkward moments that sometimes occur when grazers and traditionalists dine together.

Garrett's prices are part of the comfort, too, especially considering the variety of good food, the comprehensive wine list and that lakeside setting. There even are a few docks for waterborne diners and an outdoor bar where we can linger after supper to watch the sun set behind the hills across the lake.

Garrett's on Water Street

1 Water Street, Boyne City
231-582-1111

Latitude

Few developments have changed so broad a swath of Northern Michigan's landscape the way Bay Harbor has. It's hard to believe that less than a decade ago, those five miles of shoreline were pure eyesore—a rusting, crumbling, industrial ruin sprawled across a scrubby landscape and huge, abandoned quarries. Today it's a humongous, upscale, resort community with a hotel, deep-water marina, two golf courses, an equestrian center, and miles of waterfront mansions and bluff-top condos.

The development's shopping area, called the "Marina District," is an entire street consisting of the strangest architecture in Michigan. The designs echo styles that seem to range from industrial-age, steamboat boiler room to shingled, Low Country windmill. The entire development is still defining itself, in fact, and many of the new homes are unoccupied much of the year, so the Marina District's shops come and go.

One constant from the beginning, however, has been the upscale restaurant called Latitude down by the harbor.

Latitude is hardly a knotty-pine, Northern Michigan classic, but it is certainly one of the region's most interesting restaurants. One of four in Detroit's Epoch Group, it is sister to Birmingham's Forte and to Tribute in Farmington (and to a waterfront bar just around the corner called Knot Just a Bar.)

Latitude's fare, which is reinvented frequently, springs from the fertile mind of chef Rich Travis. Well-known Up North, he won his spurs in the kitchen at Tapawingo before moving to Bay Harbor to open Latitude. His output is as hard to define as the restaurant's funky, contemporary, nautical, industrial décor. It's hard to tell here whether you're being held captive in the hold of a Shanghai-bound tramp steamer or being beamed over the Internet to a birch forest on North Fox.

Thanks to a bright and playful staff and an interesting clientele of beautiful people, Latitude is often *very* busy, especially on summer weekends, so we like to go early and lay claim to a couple of prime spots on the back side of the bar. There we can sip a little wine and watch the bronzed and beautiful crowd ebb and flow, leaving it to management to worry about when we might find an open table. And if we don't, it's no matter, because we also enjoy eating right there at the bar. It's always fun to eavesdrop when a newcomer sits down and discovers that every other space at the bar has a private, tunable small-screen TV all its own.

Our favorite way to enjoy Latitude's food is to graze, tapas-style, by sharing three or four appetizers. The menu here is pricey, as befits a place with so serious a kitchen, but the portions are generous. Since that generosity extends to appetizers, we think grazing gives us more culinary bang for our buck by letting us enjoy a wider variety of what Chef Travis calls "contemporary, versatile, multicultural cuisine."

Grazing also lets us lavish our bucks on a bottle of good wine from a impressively comprehensive list that covers all points of the compass, from Leelanau to the Languedoc. It includes many half-bottle choices, too, which is nice. You'll find the bartenders here very up on their wines and keen on discussing the subject.

This is heaven for grazing, which is the way we like to experience Latitude. The appetizers are exquisite. Szechuan calamari and pizzettas of smoked salmon, onion, and capers, dart and veer like skiffs among higher-priced dreadnought entrees of, say, Moroccan BBQ chicken and tempura bonsai tuna. There's nothing wrong with those entrees, Lord knows, and Latitude certainly doesn't skimp on its entrée portions. But the entire menu is so good, that we'd rather have a little bit of a lot of things than a lot of just one of them.

As you might expect in a land where the waterfront gets chilly in winter, Latitude scales back in the off-season to dinner only, five nights a week. In summer it's flank speed all day, every day, and there's outside dining with glass screens to blunt the breeze on cool nights.

On weekends, don't be surprised if you find live music, too.

Latitude

795 Front St., Marina District, Bay Harbor
231-439-2750   www.latituderestaurant.com

Stafford's Pier

What better place for a restaurant in a harbor town than the harbor itself? And no restaurant is closer to the harbor than Stafford's Pier in Harbor Springs. The restaurant's Pointer Room once *was* the harbor. Actually, it was just the boathouse for the *Pointer*, a launch that ferried Harbor Point cottagers to and from town to save them a half-mile hike around the bay.

The *Pointer* itself is now part of the restaurant's resort-town ambience. Built 70 years ago in the Upper Peninsula Town of Hessel, the classic wooden launch was lovingly restored by restaurateur Stafford Smith and now spends its summers moored right outside the windows, a floating museum piece among the yachts in the marina.

The Pier, as you might expect, wears the town's yachting traditions on its sleeve. There's service outside in summer on "Dudley's Deck," which, roughly speaking, *is* the dock. Inside, varnished yachting paraphernalia adorns the walls. The restaurant's casual, bistro section is named the "Chart Room."

The Pier is almost as much of a tradition in Harbor Springs as the rule banning motor vehicles from Harbor Point. Tradition plays well in a town to which summer families return year after year expecting to find everything exactly as they left it the year before — if not exactly as they remember it from childhood.

Appropriately enough, the restaurant's menu leans toward seafood, and whitefish ranks high on the list. The Pier offers it many ways— baked with citrus butter, char-grilled with smoked-whitefish butter, or sautéed in white wine with lemon, shallots and capers. Perch may come flash-fried in a coating of seasoned flour, or finished in a sauté pan with sherry, garlic and butter.

Traditionalists adore the appetizers at the Pier — escargots, maybe, or oysters Rockefeller, blue points, and shrimp cocktail. There's a gratifying array of landlubbers' fare, too, from beef, lamb and veal to a yummy chicken on a bed of morel-sauced pasta. You might even find liver with onions, although they'll probably add a Grand Marnier sauce to convey a sense of uncharted waters.

Understatement counts in old-school resort towns, so if you see something on the menu that is casually labeled "Dijon mustard sauce," don't be surprised if it turns out to be a luxurious *duxelles* of onions and mushrooms, deglazed with sherry, reduced with cream and enhanced with mustards. No telling where on the menu it will show up, though—one night, perhaps, on chicken breast; the next on veal medallions or beef tenderloin.

The service here, of course, bears the stamp of efficient professionalism that marks all of the Stafford Hospitality properties.

The Pointer Room is a few steps up from the lounge,

high enough above water level to provide a commanding view of the harbor through panoramic windows, so you can keep track of arrivals and departures. Remember that in summer this is a very popular spot among locals, visitors, cottagers and the transient boaters who always flock here. It is always a good idea to book well ahead.

The bar area is a comfy lounge that makes waiting for a table a pleasure on busy summer evenings. The Chart Room is below decks, landward of the lounge, and offers informal quarters where the fare and ambience are easygoing and casual.

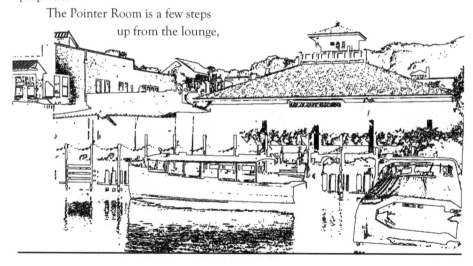

Stafford's Pier

102 Bay Street, Harbor Springs
231-526-6201

www.staffords.com

Riverside Inn

We will gladly confess to a really soft spot in our hearts for the Riverside Inn. Graydon remembers staying there occasionally as a lad in the 1940s, when innkeeper Blanche Schwarz would cheerfully make breakfast from any perch or bluegill her young guest caught. It was little more than a bed-and-breakfast then, although evening meals occasionally were available. The rooms were spare and simple and all guests shared the two baths, one at either end of the corridor. For fishing, there was always a boat rented from Blanche's brother, Jake, whose docks and sheds were across the river from the inn, where the Library now stands.

The original inn was built by their father, Jacob, who ran a floating sawmill business. When he died in 1917, Blanche and her sister Anna took over. The building burned down in 1924, but neighbors helped them get back in business by remodeling a neighboring dance hall, and that's what remains today as the core of the Riverside Inn.

The Riverside has seen many other incarnations in the decades since Blanche and Anna died, but we didn't rediscover it until we moved back to Northern Michigan in the late '80s. We were delighted to find we could not only still stay there, but dine there, too—and on food that's considerably more interesting than the simple, boarding-house fare of childhood.

In 1997, the Riverside got new owners again in Barb and Kate Vilter, a mother-daughter team, who have taken the menu to yet another level. In the bargain, the place has been remodeled into something Blanche wouldn't even recognize.

The Riverside's menu is a hard-to-classify culinary gazetteer of international proportions. The Southwest appears frequently, as in a spice-rubbed grilled salmon we enjoyed recently, which came plated with beans

and rice, tortilla chips and salsa, and cilantro crème fraîche. The vegetarian dish that night was corn and bean cakes, pan-fried and served on spinach and toasted pepitas. And beef tenderloin medallions were garnished with Spanish peppers and topped with Brie from France. Fans of the orient would have found a crunchy panko crust from Japan — on a filet of whitefish from Carlson's, the last of the real fishing operators in what Leland now calls "Fishtown."

Sundays bring brunch to the Riverside, when *huevos rancheros* with beans and salsa might rub elbows with Mediterranean omelets and eggs Benedict. The latter come in a variety of costumes, some orthodox, some not (think poached eggs on crab cakes, with Hollandaise on top and smoked salmon on top of *that*).

One thing unchanged from half a century ago is the charm of the Riverside Inn's setting on the grassy, shaded banks of the Leland River.

What once was the dining room (and originally was the dance floor) is now a lobby bar and lounge, a sort of tavern-in-the-round with 360 degrees of bar and space for the clientele all around.

The old side porch, once a reading room, is now a dining area, as is a pine-paneled porch overlooking the river that didn't exist in Blanche's day.

And for nice weather, there's a lovely deck in back from which we nostalgics can look across the river and imagine old Jake's docks and boat sheds.

The Riverside's Spartan bedrooms have been considerably improved as well, and modest rates make them very tempting for a romantic weekend getaway. Where once there were nine little rooms sharing two baths, there are now five, all with baths of their own. One is a two-room suite. We've stayed in almost all of them, and unless you need a suite load of space, we strongly recommend Room 5 — a quiet corner room overlooking the river. (Yes, you can book rooms on-line, and make a dinner reservation, too, while you're at it.)

Although closed in winter (except for special events), the Riverside is one of our most favorite places on earth during its May-December season, both for the nostalgia *and* the dining.

Riverside Inn
302 E. River St., Leland
231-256-9971   www.theriverside-inn.com

Scott's Harbor Grill

For a town with so much waterfront, Traverse City has precious few harbor side restaurants where skipper and crew can come ashore and walk to dinner, or nautical wannabes can lunch on deck and eye the yachts of their dreams. For our money, Scott's is one of the best of the genre, a bright and lively spot overlooking the slips of Traverse City's busy Harbor West.

There is nothing overly fancy about it; Scott's is about honest, straightforward, frill-free food. Make that *good* frill-free food. Throw in reasonable prices, friendly service, and an easy-going, convivial, waterfront atmosphere, and it's no wonder the place has a loyal, local following, even when the waterfront is frozen solid. In sailing season, of course, the choice berth is out on deck, with the view of the harbor.

The menu changes summer and winter, but it is always fully found and long on fresh fish, from walleye and perch to the obligatory broiled whitefish (seasoned, since you asked, with lemon pepper). For saltwater fans, Scott might lay on a few frills, such as citrus-rum butter on grouper, or ahi tuna soy-dipped and seared and served with wasabi. We particularly enjoyed blackened salmon there once that came on a bed of linguine topped with a red bell pepper cream.

There's a dry-land side to things, too — steaks and hickory-smoked pork ribs, for instance, or rotisserie duck with an orange glaze, as well as more casual tacos, burgers, BBQ beef brisket, and fish sandwiches for the hungriest foredeck crew. If they haven't had many sail changes and need no more than a snack, then there's a nice appetizer list with the likes of chowder, whitefish pâtee, fried oysters, quesadillas, and lime-marinated shrimp with chilies.

For weekend sailors who like to swap yarns at day's end over something tall and cold, the Margarita list will fuel a lot of yarn-swapping. And a short (but nicely varied) wine list includes several Northern Michigan whites and has a good variety of choices by the glass.

Scott's Harbor Grill

12719 West Bay Shore Dr. Traverse City
231-922-2114   www.scottsharborgrill.com

The Cove

In this land of spectacular views, the one from the Cove is unique, looking down on the picturesque Leland Fishtown docks and out over Lake Michigan and the Manitous. You can almost hear the *pocketa-pocketa* of the old fishing boats, the *Ace* and the *Etta*, the *Nu Deal* and the *Bonnie Lass*, returning with the day's catch, accompanied by flocks of raucous gulls.

We enjoy the Cove when the salmon are running, and we can sit by the window and watch them leaping up the old power-dam spillway in their reproductive frenzy. Alas, their frenzy always goes unrequited, for the spillway is screened.

Being somewhat higher up the food chain than Steelhead entitles us to frenzies all our own, such as The Cove's annual "Here Comes the Sun" party each May.

The Cove's menu is straightforward waterfront, seldom much fancier than seafood Alfredo, sautéed shrimp with crab and scallops, or whitefish and shrimp Creole. The Cove is very proud of a creamy chowder of crab, shrimp and clams, and of its garlicky, sautéed shrimp and escargots that come in a bread-loaf bowl. The kitchen also bakes "Campfire Whitefish" in foil with roasted onions and peppers. (Whitefish is offered many other ways, too — with lime vinaigrette, for instance, or crusted with crushed macadamias, or baked in garlic and Parmesan.) Naturally you'll also find the ubiquitous fried-fish platters with slaw and fries.

Some of these menu regulars are available at lunch, too, along with salads, burgers, wraps, sandwiches, and soups. In the evening, the menu swells to incorporate smoked chub, walleye, and whitefish, as well as black-angus filet mignon for landlubbers. Salmon, while unable to get past the old powerhouse dam, regularly find their way to table, grilled on a Caesar salad or roasted inside a crust of herbs and Stone House bread crumbs.

The Cove

111 River Street, Leland
231-256-9834   www.thecoveleland.com

Stafford's Weathervane

The Weathervane has one of the loveliest restaurant settings in the region, near enough to the water to give patrons a close-up view of the traffic on the busy Pine River Channel right outside the windows. Combine that with predictably solid fare and the sort of practiced, polite, well-drilled service that all Stafford Hospitality operations are known for, and you have a real winner.

The 'Vane is also an architectural landmark, one of the many quirky, Michigan-limestone structures designed half a century ago by Charlevoix Realtor Earl Young. None of them appears to have a single line that's square, plumb, true or level; the Weathervane's shingled roof resembles a gull's wing. Young built the restaurant on the foundations of an old gristmill, and a spiral staircase still leads down among the mill's old boulders and timbers and out to a seasonal deck along the river. Upstairs, a massive stone fireplace incorporates a 9-ton boulder that vaguely resembles the map of Northern Michigan. The interior is furnished with Young's nautical relics, and the bar is made from the planks of shipwrecks.

The kitchen makes the most of the region and its seasons. We remember an October evening there when the autumn menu featured apples in nearly everything—a potato soup starter garnished with leeks and apples, desserts of caramel-apple bread pudding, apple-cinnamon crème brulée, and apple strudel with crème Anglaise and raspberry sauce.

Needless to say, we had apples for dinner, starting with an exquisite apple-pheasant sausage that came thinly sliced and fanned on the plate with a light and savory mustard-cream sauce and apple garnish. It whetted our appetites for the main course of pork tenderloin stuffed with dried cherries, apples, leeks, mushrooms, spinach, and wild rice, and sauced with a cider demi-glace. The other meal that night was a classic "chicken Normandy," which we ordered out of an urge to compare it with a favorite dish we sometimes make for ourselves at home. We sear the breasts and then braise them for an hour with apples and mushrooms in cider, stock and cream. The Weathervane sautés them dusted with flour, deglazes the pan with cognac, and finishes the sauce with cider, apples, shallots, cream and thyme. Their version's flavors had more clarity than ours, and made us rethink our approach to chicken Normandy.

The portions are always ample, and the staff is quick to supply take-home containers for the excess. This not only allowed us to enjoy the dishes again, it let us have dessert in good conscience—a generous slice of house-made apple pie and some lovely cinnamon ice cream.

Our wine order that evening demonstrated why the Weathervane, like all Stafford's restaurants, has a fine reputation for service. The first wine we ordered had run out, so we ordered a back-up priced slightly higher. The poor server returned again somewhat sheepishly to say they were out of *that*, too, but brought with him an even more expensive bottle, and asked if it would be satisfactory for him to uncork it for the same price. Satisfactory? We almost exclaimed "Bravo!"

The Weathervane may be too big to be truly intimate, but it still swaddles diners in the comfortably homey atmosphere all Stafford's restaurants seem to have, and on that October night with a brisk wind blowing up-river from the lake, we were glad to be inside by the fire.

The 'Vane is extremely popular when Charlevoix swells with cottagers, so booking ahead is a good idea in summer. We enjoy going there most in the off-season, when the pace is slower and we have a much better chance of a table by the wall of windows overlooking the river.

It's fun to watch yachts go by in summer, but we remember an April night when it was equally nice to see the ice floes drifting by after the thaw. At that time of year we always need a little reassurance that summer will come again.

Stafford's Weathervane

106 Pine River Lane, Charlevoix
231-547-4311

www.staffords.com

All About Whitefish

Rare is the successful restaurant in Northern Michigan that serves no whitefish. This mild, white-fleshed, freshwater creature of 2-6 pounds is more than a local favorite. It's a staple, and has been since long before any Europeans came visiting. There is nothing new about food lovers' affinity for whitefish.

In ancient days, the original locals went out in their canoes and netted them in the Great Lakes. When the fish were running in the river at Sault Ste. Marie, the Ojibwa would descend en masse, make camp, and simply scoop them straight from the swift water. This fish, which they called *ticaming*, was a mainstay of their diet.

The Ojibwa smoked much of their catch to preserve it for winter sustenance. Their traditional way of preparing whitefish fresh, back before the French introduced the New World to the sauté pan, was to roast it on a slab of oak or cedar. Modern chefs still serve it "planked," traditionally surrounded by decorative duchesse potatoes. But that's hardly the only way. Whitefish is also regularly boiled, broiled, fried, baked, grilled, and sautéed. As a magazine called *The Outing* said in an article on Michigan in 1905, whitefish can be prepared any number of ways, but no matter which you choose, "one taste, and you are an enthusiastic admirer for life."

Early tourists caught right on to Ojibwa cuisine. A French explorer, the Baron La Hontan, wrote in 1793 of discovering a "white fish" so good that "all sorts of sauces spoil it." The French historian de Charlevoix agreed. Traveling the Great Lakes in 1721, he wrote, "Whether fresh or salted, nothing of the fish kind can excel it."

A century later, the Indian agent Henry Rowe Schoolcraft, scouting the Great Lakes on his famous expedition for Governor Lewis Cass, wrote in his journal that of all the fish in the lakes "the white fish is most esteemed for the richness and delicacy of its flavour." Schoolcraft, however, preferred it with sauce. "We can not agree", he wrote, "with the Baron La Hontan."

Chacun à son goût.

Dining Out

Back Roads and Hideaways

Northern Michigan is rich in cozy hideaways, sequestered on back roads and side streets and well-known to locals and veterans of many summers, while often overlooked by newcomers and tourists.

The most casual tourist can find the obvious places on the main highway, especially with the help of all those billboards along the roads Up North. But even some veterans of many cottage summers don't know about all our favorites, and some of them aren't on back roads at all, but in plain sight in the middle of town—like Chandler's in Petoskey or Terry's in Charlevoix. You have to know where to look.

Some of us think the best season for back-roading is autumn, when the landscape's in full color. It's a grand time of year to go poking around the countryside in search of new wines to taste or new roads to follow by bicycle through Technicolor forests.

The best back-roading days always end with a quiet dinner at a hideaway somewhere, far from city lights and noise. On the next few pages, we provide some naviga-tion aids to help you get off of your beaten path, to some of our favorite Northern Michigan hideaways.

Take along your GPS, though, so you can find your own way home.

Chandler's

This little hideaway is verifiable proof that good things come in small packages, but you'll not find it if you're in drive-by mode, even though it's on Howard Street in the heart of Petoskey's Gaslight District.

If you keep a good, sharp lookout, however, you'll spy it at the far end of a sort of alleyway that leads down a step or two down from the sidewalk, across from the back door of the wine store in the basement of Symons General Store around the corner on Lake Street. Got that?

The restaurant is the logical result of Symons' expansion a few years ago. The store has long enjoyed a reputation in the Petoskey area as a top-drawer purveyor of specialty foods and wines at retail. The growth of the wine trade in the 1990s sparked an expansion into the lower level with an entrance around the corner. Then Chandler Symons III, grandson of the store's founder, opened his new restaurant across the way.

It's an intimate hole-in-the-wall that is much favored for excellent lunches by locals and summer visitors on weekday excursions to downtown Petoskey. It is by night that the menu turns downright elegant, with dishes that range from exotic to earthy. We were smitten on our very first visit there by appetizers of wasabi-sauced duck roll and grilled langoustine in kaffir-lime broth.

This is serious food. We also have unusually fond recollections of a meal that began with an appetizer of smoked duck breast served atop linguine with garlic cream. There followed a salad of tender field greens with blueberry vinaigrette dressing and a Roquefort fritter as garnish. These were both exactly what starters should be: an elegant one-two set-up for a knockout entrée — in this case boneless breast of quail with a honey-Dijon glaze and a garlic-and-orange stuffing.

Keep in mind that what we just described was but one of our two meals. The other ended with a lamb chop with mint and apple chutney and a ragoût of mushrooms that came with those tender little flageolet beans that so often accompany lamb in classic French cuisine. This is not food to be trifled with, and we

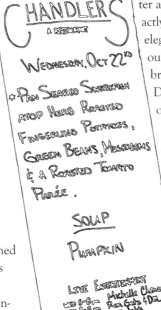

CHANDLERS

A RESTAURANT

WEDNESDAY, OCT 22ᴺᴰ

❖ PAN SEARED SWORDFISH ATOP HERB ROASTED FINGERLING POTATOES, GREEN BEANS, MUSHROOMS & A ROASTED TOMATO PURÉE.

SOUP

PUMPKIN

LIVE ENTERTAINMENT

strongly suggest that to get the full experience, you order all the courses. This might come as a surprise to readers who have heard us object to the unconscionable quantities of food some restaurants heap on our plates. At Chandlers, we are very pleased to say, we need not worry about overeating; this kitchen shows admirable restraint, serving appetizingly small portions that are as elegant as the restaurant.

While Chandler's is certainly much more than an adjunct to a wine shop, its wine list finds great strength in the connection. As you might expect, it is world class, as Symons is known for its extensive selection.

The prices here aren't elegantly dainty, however, but that's as you might expect. If you're a food lover in search of something new and interesting, we think Chandler's is a hideaway worth finding your way to.

Chandler's

215½ Howard Street, Petoskey
231-347-2981

Funistrada

The name of this place is quite literally a joke, but the restaurant is anything but. It is the source of some seriously good food.

The joke goes back to 1974, when the U. S. Army commissioned a survey of GIs to see what mess-hall chow they did and didn't like. Among the 350-odd menu items listed were some made-up names the surveyors tossed in to see if the troops actually paid any attention to their food. They called one of these totally imaginary foods "funistrada," and to everyone's surprise, it was extremely popular. The 53,000 GIs surveyed said they liked it better than lima beans, eggplant, instant coffee, beets, apricot pie, and even grilled bologna.

Literally translated, Funistrada would mean something like "rope road," which is apt enough for a restaurant at a bend on a winding road east of the causeway on the south side of Big Glen Lake. It may be remote, but it has made a lot of food-lovers quite happy in the few years it has been open. A hideaway, to be sure, although the path to the door is becoming quite well worn.

Tom and Holly Reay opened their Trattoria Funistrada in mid-2000, in a building that for many years housed a restaurant called the Glen Lake Inn. Funistrada bears no resemblance, however, to its predecessor.

Tom Reay had something of a local following before he and Holly opened their new restaurant, having been both chef and bartender for some years across the lake at Art's tavern in Glen Arbor.

In his new kitchen, he offers considerably more than tavern food, however. Funistrada's menu plays to the food lover whose idea of good Italian cooking transcends seasoned tomato sauce on pasta. Tom does a bit of that, too, but we'd urge you to try something more along the lines of his white clam linguine, or some penne with asparagus tips sauced with lemon-asparagus cream. We particularly remember ending a day of fall hiking with a wonderfully autumnal dish of portobello raviolis in a creamed corn-and-squash sauce. Each meal here begins with savory *antipasti* on a bed of greens. Several imaginative appetizers are always on the menu to get things going after that.

His changing list of entrees often includes such conventional, Italian mainstays as veal piccata and chicken Marsala, but Tom is just as happy to go adventuring with some cream-sauced tilapia or baked salmon *puttanesca*.

Funistrada is cozy and intimate with limited seating and a small staff, so it is a very good idea to call ahead and let Holly know you're coming. She runs the front of the house, where the staff, small or not, is cheerful and deftly expert on even the busiest of nights. Funistrada is gently priced and so is its Italian-accented wine list, which has a wide selection that is offered by both bottle and glass.

Off-season deals include some unusually reasonable pasta dinners for two, *prix-fixe*, including a bottle of wine.

Before we go, we can't resist adding that in the Army's survey, they also asked the troops what they thought of a few other fake foods, such as "braised trake" and "buttered ermal." The GIs liked those, too, but they said they liked funistrada a lot more.

We like Funistrada a lot more, too. There is nothing fake about it.

Funistrada
4566 MacFarlane Rd. (C-616), Burdickville
231-334-3900

Fischer's Happy Hour

Unless you know the territory, Paul and Lori Fischer's Happy Hour Tavern is the sort of place you might sail right past, thinking it just another cottage. But sometimes, even in the off-season, the waiting line goes all the way out the door. Don't be put off; people flock there for good reason.

Any food-lover who spends much time in Leelanau will eventually tell you about Fischer's burgers, but don't stop there. This old-time, family-operated roadhouse offers gracefully efficient service at even the busiest of times, and a time-tested menu that also includes hearty soup, fresh local fish, generous salads with homemade dressings, and Lori's own pies. Many regulars swear the best of all is fried chicken.

The Fischers devote tireless attention to detail, and their hospitable and well-drilled team will never rush you or make you wait too long.

Fischer's informal atmosphere evokes the days when it was a saloon, before Paul's father made it into a family restaurant in 1971. Booths and tables flank the bar at one end of the paneled front room and the pool table at the other. A dining room in back has room for whole families. The ambient sound is of animated conversations over good food.

Fischer's follows the seasons closely. In spring, the fresh asparagus soup is awesome. The only time Lori makes cherry pie is when she can use cherries fresh from the tree. The same goes for other fruits, in their turn. Whitefish is on the menu only when Paul can get it fresh from the Carlsons in Leland. The rest of the year, look for perch. As to those burgers, let's just say they start with a third of a pound of good beef, grill it as you ask, and adorn it on request with grilled onions and the cheese of your choice — Swiss, cheddar, American or blue. Your burger gets tucked into a grilled, over-sized sesame bun and delivered with an array of additional condiments and options. And with a burger like that, you just have to have some sweet, crisp, evenly done onion rings, too.

Fischer's Happy Hour
7144 N. Manitou Trail W., Northport
231-386-9923

The Fish

At first blush, The Fish doesn't seem aptly named. You'd expect it to be at least somewhere near water instead of at a rural crossroads with no water in sight. Once inside with menu in hand, however, you understand the name; aside from an occasional, polite reference to a four-legged creature—lamb, perhaps—the menu relies on things that swim or live in shells.

The "fresh catch" list changes at least weekly and covers a lot of latitude. It's the only restaurant where we've ever seen alligator, shark, and Arctic char on the same menu. You'll find whitefish, walleye, and perch in season, and shellfish are always evident—shrimp tempura, say, or grilled Maine lobster, or roast Dungeness crab. Imagine, on a snowy February night, enjoying grilled scallops with a pineapple glaze and spices from the sunny Caribbean. (Think of the air fare you save!) The Fish makes a specialty of creamy New England clam chowder, and its oyster stew will warm up any winter night.

Even the salads come from the sea—tuna Niçoise, say, or Caesar, with shrimp or salmon. We offer you the recipe for their "Warm Shellfish Salad" (P. 142). It's a satisfying mélange of mussels, shrimp, and calamari that's sautéed in oil and lemon juice with herbs and garlic and plated on tender greens with white beans as a relish. It's a meal in itself.

Friday is "sushi night," and on Sunday, it's open season on shrimp.

This is one of three restaurants operated by Northern Michigan's Magnum Hospitality. All stick to a specific cuisine, and The Fish is pricier and a tad more sedate than its sisters, the Red Mesa Grill and Pearl's New Orleans Kitchen. The décor is cleanly contemporary, and the staff is knowledgeable and attentive. A solid wine list spans a gratifying array of domestic, imported, and regional labels.

In a few short years, The Fish has established itself as a favorite in the summer-resort and ski country around Petoskey and Harbor Springs. Go there in mid-summer and you can expect a wait. But it's worth it, fish-lovers. It's worth it.

The Fish
2983 S. State Rd., Harbor Springs
231-526-3969

La Bécasse

Peachy and John Rentenbach's little 40-seat restaurant offers a sense of discovery to the food adventurer who finds it for the very first time. Ensconced at a wooded crossroads called Burdickville, on the south side of Big Glen Lake, it provides rustic French fare in a simple, country setting that somehow seems a perfect fit Up North.

The proprietors certainly brought their own sense of adventure to the place. After eating there as visitors to the area in 1987, they returned home downstate only to get a letter from the owner offering to sell the restaurant. Next thing anyone knew, Peachy and John had chucked their day jobs and moved Up North as restaurateurs.

"Some start!" she remembers. "We moved in the middle of a blizzard. On our very first night at the restaurant I curdled the crème brulée and the roof in the men's room sprang a leak." With characteristic aplomb, she simply took crème brulée off the menu and alerted guests to use the ladies. On their first New Year's Eve, she recalls, the chef skewered a hand carving pheasant and went off with John to the hospital, leaving Peachy flying solo in the kitchen. "There I was," she said, "with nothing ready and 120 people coming for dinner. All I could find was a list that said 'leek, potato, shrimp.' Luckily, they got back in time to save me."

The kitchen today is far more placid, but no less adventuresome, thanks to the skills chef Greg Murphy applies to Peachy's classic notions of French country cooking. It is rich with Gallic consommés, remoulades, and ratatouilles; timbales, pâtes, and galantines. Here you'll find grilled *escalopes de veau*, tournedos of beef in red wine, chicken

breasts with basil mousse in *croustades* of potato. La Bécasse even manages to give Great Lakes whitefish a French accent that old-time gill-netters would never have recognized, by baking it in bread crumbs with black olives, herbs and lemon *beurre blanc*.

La Bécasse's frequently changing menu often includes game, and the kitchen delights in accommodating special orders. Peachy told us about a customer who invariably called ahead and asked for elk venison.

Bécasse means "woodcock" in French, but it is also a slang term for a naive, gullible woman. What that has to do with anything is beyond us, however, for Peachy is certainly no gullible neophyte. Not only did she once run the state restaurant association, she was a food columnist for the *Free Press* and a recipe tester for Kraft. Early on, she herself took to making desserts—profiteroles, white chocolate mousse and raspberry sauce, and hazelnut pudding with *crème Anglaise*.

The atmosphere at La Bécasse is as simple and austere as the frugality of French peasant life, with walls of whitewashed masonry adorned by a few simple paintings. It might pass for a simple *ferme auberge*, and the food matches the ambience in its earthiness.

Le Becasse's cellar, favoring the regions that gave us classic "French" cooking, is rich with Beaujolais and Burgundies. There are clarets from Bordeaux for balance, however, and a few Californias and Leelanau wines as well. Most important, we have found that Mme. Rentenbach is quite reliable when it comes to suggesting wines to pair with the food from her kitchen.

To demonstrate that his kitchen has managed to maintain momentum, Chef Murphy strutted proudly a year or so ago in a major charity-benefit cook-off at a Leelanau winery. The judges accorded Murphy, Peachy and their crew a virtual dead-heat silver medal against an all-star field, a close second behind a team from a huge and exceptionally well-financed resort.

Leelanau food lovers are proud of "their" restaurant, and La Bécasse has loyal local following.

La Bécasse
9001 S. Dunn's Farm Rd., Burdickville
231-334-3944

Monte Bianco

This is one of those hidden gems that we treasure about Northern Michigan. It may be in plain sight on the Charlevoix-Boyne Road only a few miles west of Boyne City, but is so low-key in appearance that we have to watch carefully for the sign, even though we *know* where it is.

Of all the restaurants in our first guide, in 1996, this is the one readers most frequently thanked us for telling them about.

It seems an unusual fit in this land Up North — an Italian restaurant in an old roadhouse, run by Irish proprietors from San Francisco. But from the start, it has been a lovely match. John and Mary Kelly know what they're doing and pour heart and soul into it. In the decade since Monte Bianco opened, they've built a steady, devoted clientele by quietly running one of the most reliably good restaurants in the region and letting word of mouth do the rest.

Once a year or so we head there for the reassurance of a touchstone, and we're never disap-

pointed. Our most recent dinner there was as pleasant as our first a decade ago. Mary runs the front of the house with calm efficiency and watches over a polite, energetic, and efficient young serving staff. John presides with taciturn dignity over the bar.

As soon as you're seated (with your basket of hot, fresh, herbed bread), you'll see from the menu that Monte Bianco does not rely on cutting-edge razzle-dazzle, but on solid execution of a menu so immutable that four of the five recipes the Kellys gave us in 1995 for the first edition of *The Connoisseur Up North* are still offered regularly. Immutable, maybe, but certainly not boring, and we'd still recommend just about anything on it. The menu begins with such *antipasti* as carpaccio with oil, black pepper, and mustard sauce, and a pizzetta with garlic and Cambozola. There is Minestrone, of course, and salads of fresh, crisp greens even in winter.

We're suckers for good pasta, and we always find it difficult to choose among the

Kellys' various fish, seafood, and veggie dishes with their pesto, curry cream, and tomato sauces. Often, it's penne *"Casalinga,"* tossed in oil and garlic with chicken, tomato and olives. When we're not in a pasta mood, *vitello Monte Bianco* catches our eye. A house specialty of veal piccata—filets sautéed in butter with lemon, parsley and mushrooms—it demonstrates the timeless virtue of simplicity.

For hearty appetites, Monte Bianco's *vitella all'Parmigiana* might be the ticket; the veal is coated with seasoned breadcrumbs and baked under cheese in a marinara sauce. One of those recipes from 1995 that we still often enjoy at home is *rollatini di Pollo*, with figs, mozzarella and prosciutto rolled up in butterflied chicken breasts and baked in Gorgonzola cream.

There's room to graze as well, on such appetizers as pizzetta, baked mozzarella, grilled prawns in mint vinaigrette, and beef carpaccio with lemon, oil, mustard, capers, basil, and Parmesan. There is almost always a fish special of one sort or another, depending on season and availability. And the fully à-la-carte menu has minestrone and a seafood soup, as well as two salads: mixed greens in house-made vinaigrette and a classic, garlicky, Caesar salad with egg and anchovy — just as the great Cardini himself prescribed 70 odd years ago.

Another reason we think Monte Bianco will never disappoint you is that the Kellys treasure their good name. This stood them in good stead their very first summer when their chef left at the peak of the season. They could have faked it for a while for the sake of cash flow, but they're managers, not cooks, and they know it. Rather than compromise quality even for a few days, they closed the doors until they could find a good new chef.

Good food and service aside, Monte Bianco is just a convivial place to be. You won't find silent couples staring at the walls, but animated families and groups enjoying lively conversation over good food. And that is something we always treasure in a restaurant.

Monte Bianco
2911 Boyne City Rd., Boyne City
231-582-3341

Old Mission Tavern

If your next trip here is your first, you probably won't believe us when we tell you the place once was a Dairy Freeze. That was in 1980, however, and the tavern has undergone a few changes. It has evolved, in fact, into a fine roadside tavern and restaurant that is also a sort of art colony.

Although it is plainly visible alongside a major state highway, we think of it as a hideaway because it is so far out on the scenic Old Mission Peninsula that it's easy to miss unless you're actively looking. It's one of our very favorite places, for its atmosphere, its food, and for the interesting art that accompanies every trip there.

Proprietress Verna Bartnick is a sculptor whose works of wood, bronze, and welded metals adorn several local landmarks. She moved to the site of the restaurant in 1976 and set up a studio next door, and that Dairy Freeze helped her avoid becoming one of those starving artists you're always hearing about.

One thing led to another, and today's restaurant is a much higher life form—a remarkably fine restaurant with classic Up North charm and an adjoining gallery where Verna displays the work of fellow artists from near and far.

The food has artistic merit on its own, especially if you like a broad palette. Butter, cream, and cheese figure prominently in the cuisine, but the kitchen turns out some very full-flavored lighter fare as well.

An artist's eye for elegant simplicity appears in the fish preparations, which are among the reasons we enjoy the tavern so much. You'll generally find whitefish, perch, and walleye, in any of three ways: herb-crusted, Parmesan-crusted, or Provençal style. All are flavorful and light. The way this kitchen does fish is one of the reasons we love going here for dinner. As you might expect of a place with an artist in charge, much about the OMT has a creative flair and conveys a sense of simple elegance.

One such recipe is for beef tenderloin medallions, pan-seared and then sauced with a red-wine pan reduction that's been thickened with blue cheese. A bit more blue cheese gets sprinkled on top as garnish. It's a favorite among the tavern's regulars, which also helps explain why this place *has* so many regulars.

Verna herself might suggest you try her artichoke chicken, which is a sort of signature dish of butter-sautéed breasts covered with a white wine and cream sauce that's laced with scallions, shiitake mushrooms and garlic. Cream sauce or not, it, too, is one of the lighter dishes here.

Plenty of the tavern's food is in the hearty range (as you might sense from that blue cheese with the beef medallions). The richer end of the spectrum came up once when Verna was telling us about a dish she had just added to her repertoire called "Blue Cheese Spinach Pasta with Bacon." We said we thought that sounded pretty good, and the next thing we knew, she had a sample in front of us. We discovered what a knack she has for understatement. The dish didn't stop with blue cheese, pasta and bacon. Parmesan and mozzarella were in there, too, and it came with a trencherman's hunk of good sourdough bread. Frankly, it was delicious, but we'd never tell our cardiologist we tried it.

Ambience-wise, there's a bit of something for everyone at the OMT. The gallery allows a little browsing and intellectual conversation before or after dinner, and the tavern part of the restaurant is a sort of neighborhood watering hole. Adjoining that is a pleasant sun porch where the romantically inclined can hold hands and enjoy the bucolic view.

This is a grand place to end a long autumn hike on the trails of the park at the peninsula's tip, or a bike tour among the orchards and vineyards and lovely scenic views. But exercise really hard, so you can enjoy this good food in equally good conscience.

Old Mission Tavern
17015 Center Rd., Old Mission
231-223-7280

Terry's Place

Every bit as good as it is modest in appearance, this bijou of a restaurant is sequestered on a side street off the main drag in downtown Charlevoix. It is well known among locals and gives visitors who find it a real sense of discovery.

The fare is proof of the virtue of simplicity. It would delight our friend Sally Adamson, who is proud of her repertoire of dishes with no more than three ingredients. That's a bit drastic, but Terry's has built a fine reputation on much the same credo. Proprietor Terry Left goes beyond three ingredients, of course, but not very far. Aside from the whitefish in his signature dish, he uses only capers, parsley, shallots, and lemon juice, plus a little butter to sauté it in. Okay, salt and pepper, too. He calls the method "Grenoboise," and the directions are equally simple: "Sauté whitefish. Combine other ingredients in saucepan and cook over medium high heat until butter has melted. Pour over sautéed fish and serve."

Left is something of an institution in Charlevoix, a local lad whose first job was washing dishes at Grey Gables at the age of 13. He knew at 15 that he wanted to be a chef, and after training at the Culinary Institute of America and earning some stripes in Miami, he came back home. Now, years later, he is one of the region's hardiest and most successful restaurant veterans.

His flagship establishment, The Villager, is on the main drag, Bridge Street, while Terry's is relatively inconspicuous around the corner. Inside, a few steps down from the street, plain brick walls adorned with artwork surround a dozen or so white-covered tables.

The fare, as we said, is classic simplicity. His perch, whitefish and

walleye come in four different costumes. The preparation he calls "à la Robinson" is sautéed in oil with garlic and parsley. Fish "almondine" is sautéed, sauced with lemon butter, and sprinkled with toasted almonds.

"Whitefish Grenoboise" is what he says he'd serve a king, should one walks in and ask for a dish that's fit for him.

One of us is very fond of his whitefish "Grenoboise," and one generally prefers the even simpler *meunière* style— lightly floured and sautéed in drawn butter.

Whitefish is a sort of culinary fetish with Left, and however it's prepared, it will be fresh, flaky, and sauced to enhance every bite. Portions are generous but never overwhelming, and entrees come with fresh, seasonal vegetables.

Salads, too, are fresh and crisp, and the balsamic vinaigrette house dressing richly thick and well-balanced.

Terry's is hardly one-dimensional. There is much besides fish. Steak with mushrooms and Marsala reduction is always a temptation, as are the rack of lamb, roast duckling, shrimp Provençal, and morel-sauced veal that frequent the menu.

Appetizers are as varied, and almost always include classic Burgundian escargots and baked onion soup, plus excursions into such interesting territory as steamed mussels Provençal and Marsala-sauced wild-mushroom raviolis.

Terry's relaxed pace and quietly efficient service make it perfect for a conversational rendezvous with friends. This is one of those places we enjoy going in any season. With the town's cinema right next door, it's the perfect spot for dinner before a show in winter. And in summer, it's always nice to go somewhere that's not likely to be overrun by casual tourists just passing through.

Terry's Place

101 Antrim Street, Charlevoix
231-547-2799

Little Traverse Bay Golf Club

This clubhouse restaurant is hidden away on a hilltop with a commanding view of Little Traverse Bay that will leave you breathless if you take the time to find it. On a summit east of Harbor Springs, it is approached up a long, lovely drive that offers nary a hint of the spectacle awaiting you. Only after you have entered the building up some stairs from the parking lot, and passed through the paneled lounge and into the dining room, does the full sweep of the view appear.

The dining room consists of a big, bright, wrap-around sun porch, and it surveys the bay from end to end. Every table can enjoy the view.

The menu is as straightforward as meat and potatoes, but it is hardly mundane. Like the view, it covers a lot of familiar territory, from pasta to planked whitefish and walleye by way of Leelanau Chicken—sautéed breast with local cherries and apples, deglazed with brandy, white wine, and honey. Like any good golf club, this one also has solid steaks—both filet mignon and strip sirloin—and rack of lamb. The brief but respectable wine list is as reasonably priced as the menu.

Luncheons run to soups, salads, and a satisfying variety of sandwiches, burgers, fries and such. Golfers congregate at the bar in the anteroom.

The restaurant is open from the first golf in spring until the last difficult lie has been replayed one final time as color season ends. It's so far off the main drag, we'd better tell you that from the Harbor-Petoskey Road you want to go east on W. Conway, then quickly north on Clayton to the end. A right on Hideaway Valley lets you follow the sign to the club up on top of the hill.

Little Traverse Bay Golf Club
995 Hideaway Valley Rd.,
Harbor Springs

Blue Pelican

This new restaurant's menu of crab cakes and crab legs, oysters and clams, shrimp and scallops, cod and sea bass, is the stuff we in Michigan associate more with spring break than Torch Lake. The Blue Pelican comes by all this saltwater fare honestly, however. Owner Chris Corbett is a Marylander, and is as passionate about his part of the world as we are about ours. That includes both the fishing and cooking up the catch.

While the fare is the stuff of a really good crab shack, the atmosphere is slightly more sedate. Think of it as a swept-up crab shack with carpeting and good insulation. The walls display beach-combers' treasure, plus a sign proclaiming the Chatterbox — the place that used to occupy the site.

Naturally, crab cakes are a house specialty. Corbett delights in describing them as "all lumpy and loose," made of nothing but moist, lump crabmeat, Old Bay seasoning, and a little mayo. Lightly browned, they're thick and rich and come with snappy tartar sauce and fresh salsa. Two make a satisfying main course, but suggest having just one as an appetizer and then moving on to some steamed snow- or king-crab legs as a main dish. Either that or some charbroiled sea bass and a side of baked beans.

Heck, if you like seafood, it's all good. We ordered char-grilled bass once and got blackened by mistake, and after tasting it, we didn't care a bit.

The bar's longest suit is a humongous list of draft and bottle beers. The wine list is short, but its prices are low enough to make us gasp.

Inland chauvinists can get perch, cat-fish and walleye, but the menu relies heavily on salt water cod, tuna, sea bass, shark, and salmon—all available char-broiled, blackened, or sautéed.

The appetizer list fills a whole menu page: crab cakes seared tuna with wasabi, fried clams, mushrooms, onions and tuna-bites, and house-made soups that include crab-and-corn chowder and a white-bean chicken chili.

There's often live music (a limited bar menu is available until midnight), and summer brings outdoor dining.

Blue Pelican
Old State Rd. & E.Torch Dr., Central Lake
231-544-2583 www.thebluepelican.com

Mustard at Your Bech and Call

Elk Rapids may not be world famous as a culinary capital, but it's the source of two products well known among food lovers Up North: Bech's Mustard and Zagolli's feta cheese dips.

Zagolli's savory dips are made by a fellow named Scott Zagers, who owned a local deli and butcher shop until he closed it to make his dips full-time. He started making them just to augment his store's specialty foods, and now they're in supermarkets and food stores all over the Midwest.

Bech's is a somewhat longer story, about a Dane named Johan Bech who emigrated to the U. S. in 1961 and built a successful business in Michigan with his House of Denmark furniture stores. His business may be furniture, but his passion is mustard, and he never found any here as good as the mustard back in Denmark. When he finally tired of bringing cases of it back from visits to the old country, he decided to make his own. He chose a site on the river in Elk Rapids, where he lives, and built a factory that preserved the scenery by not looking at all like a factory. It is so unobtrusive that when strangers ask directions and someone says to turn at the mustard factory, they ask, "What mustard factory?" Fortunately, Bech's mustard is far more visible than the place where it's made. He calls it "Mustard with Authority," and his secret is Swiss seed mills. They keep the newly ground mustard fluid and moving so it won't overheat and damage the delicate oils that carry the flavor. That, Bech says, would rob the mustard of its tangy essence. Bech's Mustard is a smooth, thick, sharp — not what Bech calls "moody mustard . . . of the sort that will bite in unfamiliar surroundings." It works on chicken as well as burgers, and is terrific in rubs for grilling. Maybe it's not an exact copy of that Danish mustard he used to love, but Bech thinks it might be better.

One night at the Bechs' home, he grilled us a rack of lamb slathered with a mustard rub (P. 168) Linda made, and it had *awesome* authority!

Bech's, PO Box 667, Elk Rapids
231-264-5080
www.mustardwithauthority.com

Zagolli's, 114 River St., Elk Rapids
231-264-9969

Dining Out

Resort Country Classics

More than 120 years have passed since the first tourists landed on Mackinac and the first trains arrived in Traverse City and Petoskey with summer visitors from Chicago, Detroit, Grand Rapids, and points south. By 1890, Northern Michigan was a popular summer destination for families seeking relief from the Midwest's notorious heat and humidity.

Some of the region's restaurants have roots that go back almost that far; a few of them hark back to the dawn of the tourist trade itself. Over the years, they have become institutions unto themselves, landmarks without which Northern Michigan just wouldn't be the same. Places like the Bay View Inn and Grand Hotel are classics among Northern Michigan's restaurants. They were there in our grandparents' day, and our grandparents would still feel right at home were they to return to them today. In some cases—Leland's Bluebird, for instance—the establishments may have changed in appearance, but they are still owned and operated by the families that founded them. These are all places known throughout the region.

It's no accident that three of our "classics" are inns where you can book a room as well as a table. In the old days, visitors often came to spend their vacation time at an inn that set a good table. These still do.

One of our "classics" isn't ancient at all — at least not as a restaurant. Bowers Harbor Inn, however, has more history than most establishments, for it is the home of a ghost that's been haunting the premises almost as long as there have been cherries on The Peninsula.

All of these classics have about them an air of the sort of easygoing, summer-resort comfort that makes Northern Michigan so delightful a place to live and visit.

Stafford's Bay View Inn

This Victorian establishment still has every ounce of the charm it has acquired in the half century since the legendary Stafford Smith started his career here, working summers as a college student.

It is the sentimental centerpiece of his regional hospitality empire and a landmark in Bay View, the quaint resort town of gingerbread, period-piece cottages north of Petoskey.

The past is preserved in every room and in the warmth of polished woodwork and plush settees. The Roselawn Porch dining room bathes its guests in restful, summery pastels of peach and green, and well-trained waitresses swirl efficiently.

All this charm is genuine, and if it evokes romance, credit the owner; Smith is something of a romantic, and this is where his romance blossomed.

Built as "Howard House" in 1886, the inn was the Bay View by the time Smith took his summer job there in the 1950s and fell in love with another summer employee named Janice.

They married in 1961, bought the old inn, and soon began adding such modern touches as whirlpool baths. But they adhered strictly to Victorian decor and furnishings, and there phones or TVs sully the guest rooms even now. It is no stretch when the company likens the inn to "Great-Grandma's House," even if Grandma didn't have 31 bedrooms.

The kitchen is more up to date, and its reliably good food is downright comforting in an era of noisy, staccato upheaval. It leans to regional favorites, such as broiled whitefish, baked trout, and grilled pork with apple-smoked sausage.

The traditionalist is comfy here with the creamy Great Lakes chowder and Granny Smith apple pie. Wine lovers, note: Bay View is a church-affiliated association and frowns on alcohol. The inn is unlicensed, although guests can bring their own wine to table with them. Resorters love the Bay View's monumental brunches, when eggs Benedict share the stage with Sunday dinner, and Smith himself still stands watch at the griddle or carving station.

Stafford's Bay View Inn
2011 Woodland Ave. , Petoskey
800-258-1886 www.thebayviewinn.com

Bowers Harbor Inn

Dining at Bowers Harbor is like visiting an interesting old friend who lives in a stately country manor with a stunning bay view. Only thing is, your old friend is a ghost.

She's been around since the 1880s, when the place actually *was* the stately manor. It was built by a Chicago lumber baron named Stickney, whose wife, Genevieve, was somewhat eccentric. She made delicious fruit brandy, then buried the bottles in the yard. Some are whispered to be there to this day. Well, Genevieve took ill and Stickney hired a nurse, who soon became his mistress. When the old goat died, the nurse got all his money. Poor Genevieve inherited only the house. There, in despair, she hanged herself. It is said she still goes about after hours slamming doors, dousing lamps, pulling paintings from the walls, and moving furniture around.

Don't let this keep you away from a fine mealtime adventure. On some nights, you can even enjoy haunting dinner music by a local, classical guitarist.

Ghost and all, Bowers Harbor Inn has long ranked high in the esteem of locals and visitors. It combines the trappings of classic elegance and the delights of old-fashioned American comfort food. The menu mixes stand-bys such as lamb, beef and whitefish sauced with béarnaise and hollandaise, with occasional non-trad' surprises from the Pacific Rim or Southwest, and some venison, pheasant, and salmon.

A house specialty is "fish in a bag," in which fish, crabmeat, lobster, and shrimp are cooked with sauce *en papillotte*. Hardly our favorite dish, but it's a Traverse City tradition almost as entrenched as the Cherry Festival, and a manager once vowed it will be on the menu "until the building burns down." Well, the media keeps speculating that the place *will* soon be razed and subdivided, but owner Howard Schelde, who lives nearby, insists he'll be serving that fish in those bags for a time yet.

Schelde displays neighborhood loyalty by featuring wines from nearby vineyards, whose quality, for all we know, is favorably influenced by old Genevieve's buried brandy.

Bowers Harbor Inn
13512 Peninsula Dr., Traverse City
231-223-4222 www.michiganmenu.com

The Bluebird

Leland is one of those tradition-steeped resort towns to which loyal cottagers have been returning for generations, and the 'Bird is such a tradition that few remain who remember watching outdoor movies there on Saturday nights.

Boatbuilder Martin Telgard and his wife Leone opened their Bluebird Tea Room in 1927, and it is one of the traditions for which whole generations of cottage families keep returning to Leland. Martin died in 1961, but Leone presided over the kitchen until the 1970s. Today's Bluebird is run by their grandson, Skip Telgard, who greets regulars from his station it the bar just as his parents, Jim and Nancy, did.

The modern Bluebird Restaurant and Bar evolved in stages, from tea room and sandwich shop, to bar, to restaurant. No wonder the place has a sort of dual personality: The spacious, 180-seat dining room in back, added on Jim's watch in the 1960s, is the more elegant half, with wide picture windows overlooking the gentle Leland River. The bar up front is all pine-paneled casual, with sequestered booths by the windows and the ubiquitous tavern pool table on the far side of the bar. Friendly banter among the regulars marks it as the town's unofficial community center, and in season you're sure to find the game du jour on the numerous TV screens.

Ever since tourists discovered Leland and its indescribably quaint Fishtown in the 1960s, the Bluebird has become such a busy place in summer that you probably shouldn't even *think* about dinner in the restaurant without a reservation. In the bar it's okay just to show up and hope, and if you find yourself in for a bit of a wait, it's no matter, because you'll quickly be

deep in conversation with others who are waiting with you.

The 'Bird can sometimes seem just as crowded in the off-season when only the bar is open.

Frankly, dining in the bar is our favorite way to enjoy the Bluebird at any time of year. The menu leans to burgers and fries, soup and sandwiches, chicken and steak. The 'Bird also makes a specialty of fried smelt, which is as regional a dish as you'll find anywhere.

The treat we home in on, however, after a day of biking or skiing in the lovely Leelanau countryside, is a platter of perch or whitefish with fries and slaw. The Telgards might not have invented the whitefish platter, but the Bluebird kitchen has as much practice with it as anyone, and nothing counts like experience. The "Bluebird style" whitefish is a classic—dusted with seasoned flour and fried in clear, light oil.

The main restaurant has a more extensive and sophisticated menu and a somewhat more genteel air. (We should point out here that when the Dining Room is open, you can order from its menu even if you're in the bar.)

The Dining Room cuisine is not exactly what we'd call "haute," but it's always well and thoughtfully done. A salad bar still keeps traditionalists happy, and the menu invariably has whitefish blackened, or broiled and sauced with citrus butter. The most complicated dish you're likely to encounter is something like baked mushrooms stuffed with onion, squash and Creole-seasoned breadcrumbs.

The restaurant also still serves the magnificent, pillowy, cinnamon rolls that Leone started making about 60 years ago. Until a bigger oven was installed in the 1990s, the rolls were rationed one to a customer. Now you can not only get seconds, but buy a dozen to take home.

The Telgards reward year-round regulars with off-season "Ethnic Nights" on Wednesdays and Thursdays. These popular events are mileposts on Leland's winter social calendar. The bar gets dressed up in candlelight and white tablecloths, and chef Steve Schwarz conducts tours of the regional specialties of China, Thailand, Mexico, Italy, Greece, New Orleans and New England.

The Bluebird Restaurant and Bar

102 E. River St., Leland
231-256-9081

www.leelanau.com/bluebird

Grey Gables Inn

I t's easy for the casual, passing tourist to overlook this unobtrusive little place on Belvedere Street, but locals and veteran cottagers keep it busy even on snowy winter nights because they appreciate what the chefs and co-proprietors, Darren and Kelly Romano, do in the kitchen. The charming, Victorian house might be quaint and old, but the menu is a modern marvel.

In the decade since they took over the venerable Grey Gables Inn, Darren and Kelly have solidly anchored their reputations with a wide range of interesting fish and seafood dishes and a whole roster of such inland classics as barbecued ribs, rack of lamb, lamb shank, and steaks.

"It might be a little rich," Darren once told us, "but I believe in giving value."

He also believes in giving variety. After a visit to Hawaii turned him on to sushi, Darren began doing sushi at Grey Gables on Wednesday nights.

We think some of the best value at Grey Gables is at the top of the menu; Darren's appetizers are a such a trove, grazers can go whole meals here without venturing into entree territory. You might start, say, with a bowl of mushroom bisque or sherried five-onion soup, and follow that with a classic Greek or Caesar salad. Then you'd round things out with an order of escargots wrapped in phyllo, or with sautéed scallops, crab and shrimp, finished with cream and baked with Swiss cheese in a pastry shell. That's enough to satisfy even a trencherman. The extensive appetizer list often includes *saganaki* — the traditional Greek dish of sautéed kasseri cheese, sprinkled with lemon juice and flambéed at tableside with brandy.

The menu makes plenty of concessions to lighter appetites. John Cross Fish Market is practically across the street, so whitefish, perch, and walleye appear regularly on the menu. Darren can wax downright rhapsodic when it comes to whitefish. Besides the usual sautéed or broiled versions, he might bake it stuffed with shrimp, spinach, pine nuts, and mustard sauce, or sauté it in a crust of hazelnut and mustard seeds, and sauce it with a dark-rum pan reduction.

Just between us, however, don't let too many visits pass without trying those escargots, maybe as a starter before some house-sauced baby back ribs. Darren sautés the escargots with ripe tomatoes in garlic-chive butter, then wraps it up for baking with herbs and roasted pine nuts in a delicate phyllo envelope.

The other star of any meal at Grey Gables shows up right at the opening curtain, in the form of a basket of Kelly's sweet, little crescent scones and lovely French bread. And even at the risk of overdosing on carbs, spud-lovers should save room for Darren's whipped potatoes. They may be the best you'll find north of the 45th parallel, and if they don't come with whatever you order, you can always have them à la carte.

The Romanos are very versatile, and have lately launched a catering business in addition to the restaurant. They offer everything from complete sit-downs and buffets to cocktail-time hors d'oeuvres and wedding cakes.

And should the long drive home daunt you after a long evening of good food and wine, you can consider booking a room next door at Grey Gables Inn's alter ego, the Inn at Grey Gables.

Grey Gables Inn is not fancy and showy, or right out there amongst the tourists, but it's worth the excursion a block or so off the main drag, especially on weekends, when you'll find live music in the lounge.

Grey Gables Inn

308 Belvedere, Charlevoix
231-547-9261

www.greygablesinn.com

Leelanau Country Inn

Our first meal ever at John and Linda Sisson's Leelanau Country Inn, oddly enough, was a continental breakfast. It was back in the 1980s, after we'd spent a night there while enjoying a summer weekend's cycling. We still remember sitting in the morning sunshine in Linda's magnificent perennial garden and looking out on quiet Little Traverse Lake as we breakfasted on warm, buttery croissants and the freshest of fruit.

We decided that anyone who can make a continental breakfast that pleasant must be special, so we went back and had another memorable meal there that evening. A lot of other people must think the inn as memorable as we do; on midsummer evenings, it is generally a very busy place.

The inn has so much to offer that dinner is often memorable for the time spent deciding what to have. The appetizer list overflows with choice—Cajun shrimp, perhaps, or escargots baked in garlic sauce. And there is always Swiss onion soup, a fixture on the menu since the editors of *Gourmet* featured it a decade ago.

The specialty here is seafood, which is only logical; John's restaurant career began with the late Chuck Muer's Charley's Crab restaurants downstate. He knows his seafood. He buys the inn's freshwater fish from Carlson in Traverse City, and has an arrangement with Northwest Airlines to fly in the fresh North Atlantic catch every day. The offerings vary with the seasons — cod, scrod, tuna, whatever. Almost always you'll find several preparations of whitefish. (The one we'd urge upon you is stuffed with Chesapeake Bay crab and sauced with béarnaise; it is a very happy geographic blend.) Scallops frequent the menu, too, as do North Atlantic lobster and frog legs. Nor is there ever a dearth of beef, lamb, pork and poultry for the landlocked appetite.

A bit of culinary legerdemain is required to transform this abundance into artful meals. John relies on skillful mixing and matching of entrees with an array of

The *Leelanau Country Inn*

Your Dining & Lodging Destination

such basic, old standby sauces as lemon-butter, pecan-butter, and sherry-cream. He once told us that he found seven different uses for a certain Provençal sauce.

The Leelanau Country Inn has been there more than a century, but it was the Sissons who made it into the landmark it is today. They bought it in 1984, and now they and their inn are both as much a fixture in Leelanau County as the sand dunes.

It's an association they are proud of, and they're not shy about it. Their wine list honors four Leelanau wine-making pioneers—Mawby, Good Harbor, Boskydel, and Leelanau Cellars. A Leelanau artist, Peggy Core, illustrated their first *Leelanau Country Inn Cookery* book, and winemaker Larry Mawby edited it. (He's such a friend, he once named a wine after one of the Sissons' dogs, and they reciprocated by naming their next dog after "Moira," a Mawby wine.) The Sissons' first book was so successful, they've published another.

Books are not the Sissons' only sideline. They also have an on-line store where they sell their own vinaigrettes, dressings and marinades. And the inn still has rooms—four simple bedrooms available in season on a B&B basis. The Sissons are quick to say, however, that theirs is "a restaurant with rooms, not an inn that serves food."

Another thing they are quick to say is that the no one at the inn may ever refer to patrons as "customers," but only as "guests." That explains much about the success of this lovely country inn.

Leelanau Country Inn

149 E. Harbor Hwy. (M-22), Maple City
231-228-5060   www.leelanaucountryinn.com

Stafford's Perry Hotel

When we tire of things rustic, we often head for Petoskey and Stafford's Perry Hotel, for it is the home of some of Northern Michigan's most civilized dining.

This sort of urge seems to hit us most often in the off-season, particularly in the late autumn when we begin to yearn for an elegant, urban evening. At times like that the well-mannered shelter of the Perry's H. O. Rose dining room is particularly welcome. We always enjoy weekends, when live dinner music invites guests to dance.

The Perry, built in 1899, is rich in elegant *fin de siècle* décor that warms guests the moment they enter the lobby. The main dining room is laid out so that diners enter through a lounge. In fact, the lounge is where we like to begin our evenings, taking time to examine menus over cocktail. The staff will be happy to take your order there and, in the manner of a well-bred English country hotel, summon you to "go through"

when your table and meal are ready. Once at your table, you'll find your first course waiting for you, along with a basket of hot, fresh bread and fragrant, rosemary-infused dipping oil.

From the warm greeting on arrival to the genteel thank-you as you leave, the service at the Perry is as old-world and gracious as the hotel itself.

Among Stafford's Hospitality's restaurants, the Perry seems to lead the way with new and interesting dishes. Yet there's no dearth of comfort foods, either. When they find something good, they have the sense to hang on to it. We've been enjoying the "Perry salad" of Bibb, berries, scallions and nuts for years, and the rich, flavorful, seafood chowder is much the same as the one whose recipe has been in our books since 1996.

Meals at the Perry start with a little

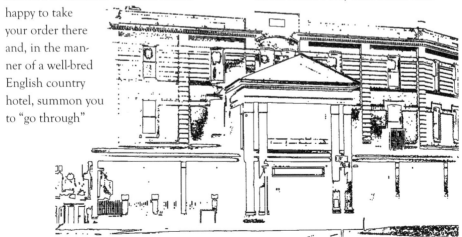

amuse-bouche the chef sends out. Our favorite recently was a generous and savory roulade of smoked whitefish and lettuce with shrimp sauce.

The Perry's kitchen always manages to do interesting things with those comfort foods. You're likely to find something like the beef-tenderloin medallions we had once that were draped in a pan reduction and rested against a cushion of mashed potato, flanked by a succulent lobster claw and a tidy cup of drawn butter. Alongside all this lay neatly sliced ranks of crisp, buttered vegetables. That same evening, our other entree was an equally comforting half of a roasted chicken with a tangerine-sage glaze.

The Perry — both the hotel and the dining room — makes a perfect base for a day or a weekend of shopping in Petoskey's charming Gaslight District, which is right outside the door. We don't consider any Christmas season complete without a pilgrimage to Petoskey and the Perry.

The hotel is particularly smashing in summer, when flowers overflow the planters on the massive front porch, making it a delightful spot for breakfast or lunch on bright, sunny days. There is something special, too, about lunch on the Perry's breezy, sequestered Veranda with its sheltered conservatory, charming perennial garden, and expansive view of the bay.

It is in summer, too, that the Perry peculiarly evokes a more leisurely and innocent time when resorters from Ohio and Indiana journeyed north for "the season" on the Pennsylvania Railroad's daily "Northern Arrow." When the train pulled into Petoskey's Pennsylvania Railroad station, the new arrivals would step across the street to the hotel for breakfast before heading off on the "dummy" train to spend the summer at their cottages on the bay.

The hotel was built in 1899 by a dentist named Norman Perry. Twenty years later, two doctors bought it and proposed turning it into a hospital. But the city fathers persuaded them otherwise, and a hotel it remained through two more owners.

Today, the Perry bespeaks a genteel sort of 19th-century elegance that had all but vanished from Northern Michigan until Stafford Smith and Co. bought the lovely old hotel in 1989 and restored it to a state of grace and glory.

Stafford's Perry Hotel
Bay and Lewis Streets, Petoskey
231-347-2516   www.theperryhotel.com

The Morel of the Story

While hardly unique to Michigan, the morel mushroom has a huge fan base here and is a big in regional cuisine. It is also a major source of sport for devotees who hunt morels in May the way others cast for trout. Two whole towns, Mesick and Boyne City, have morel festivals, and whole websites are devoted to the succulent fungus (e.g., *www.morels. com*). Competition is fierce in organized hunts for cash prizes and bragging rights, and business reputations are at stake for professional morel guides.

If you're an inexperienced mushroomer, such a guide might keep you from eating the wrong kind, such as an amanita. Just one of them can make you very sick, or even very dead. (Nausea, vomiting, abdominal pain, diarrhea? Get thee to the ER fast!)

Morels pop up when daytime highs hit the 60s and it stays over 40 by night. Look for a sunny day after a good rain. (Don't ask where to look; go find your own!)

As fungi go, morels are a recent arrival, having evolved from yeast as the glaciers were melting. Biologically undeveloped, they are fragile, succulent, and hard to grow commercially. That's why we hunt them in the wild and carry them in mesh bags, so spores will spill out and grow more.

Most good restaurants Up North use morels in their cuisine. The Rowe Inn has its own morel week in May, and makes a specialty of pecan-stuffed morels. Tapawingo does things with morels that dazzled even Martha Stewart. The May menus at Walloon Lake Inn and Hattie's brim with stuffed morels, morel-stuffed veal, morel soups, morel raviolis, and morel sauces. Black Star Farms takes guests morelling by kayak and cooks a feast with what they find.

Want to keep your find for later? Here's what Tapawingo's Pete Peterson suggests:

Wash morels gently to remove debris from the wrinkles. Dry thoroughly, then sauté quickly in a lot of butter over high heat, stirring until they're fully coated but not shriveled. Spread them on a foil-covered baking sheet to freeze, then seal them in plastic bags. They'll keep in the freezer for months.

Dining Out

Down by the Lake

Wherever you go in Northern Michigan, you're never more than a few minutes from a lake. And we're not talking about the Big Lake. We're talking, too, about the myriad other lakes that punctuate our landscape of dunes, orchards, and forests. Some are major bodies of water in their own right, stretching so far in some cases that you can't see one end from the other. Some are barely bigger than ponds. Collectively, they help define the landscape and the region.

One of the main reasons people have been coming up North for so many years, whether to live or just visit, is all this water. No wonder so many enjoyable restaurants are on the water, too.

Some, like the venerable Walloon Lake Inn, were places where little passenger steamers landed in the days before automobiles and paved road, when people used the lakes for transportation as well as scenery. Other lakeside restaurants, such as Garrett's in Boyne City and Timmerin in Beulah, are by the lake because that's where it all happens in a resort town.

Few things about life Up North are as soul-satisfying and civilized as enjoying a good meal on a warm summer evening in one of those little places by the lake where you can watch dusk settle gently on the quiet water. If it's a still evening and you're very lucky, you might even hear a loon.

Douglas Lake Bar

This rustic charmer is on the shores of one of the loveliest little lakes around, tucked away in a corner of Emmet County so remote, you almost have to look up to see out. The casual tourist might never find it. This might be just as well in the eyes of the locals and resorters who flock to their beloved "DLB" on summer evenings and midwinter ski weekends alike. Whatever the season, this place is likely to be lively.

Ambience-wise, Steve and Copland Rudolph's DLB is a North woods classic, with dark paneling, a big stone fireplace topped by an antlered trophy. Naturally, there's a screened porch overlooking the lake.

But don't be deceived by architecture or name. This is not your basic, rustic steakhouse. Go here expecting only steak and burgers and you might be surprised to find yourself feasting, instead, on pan-seared Indiana duck breast finished with a Zinfandel glaze, or rack of New Zealand lamb, or coriander-dusted salmon garnished with a gooseberry puree.

Of course, there are steaks, too. We particularly remember a steak *au poivre* we had there some years ago — a butter-tender filet mignon, perfectly grilled so it was lightly crusted outside but still almost molten pink within. This has since become the house specialty known as the "DLB Steak," but it still comes sauced with the same, light, Dijon-Cognac cream. Washed down with a robust Zin from a wine list that's not long but covers a wine range of good California wines.

This steak alone places the DLB head and shoulders above the ordinary, run-of-the-mill, roadside steakhouse. But the

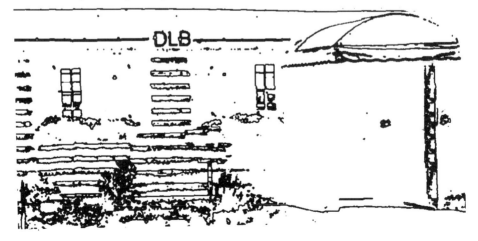

credentials hardly stop there. There's grilled salmon with a cherry glaze, for example, and big baked shrimp, stuffed with crab, wrapped in bacon, and sauced with Hollandaise. If you like your shrimp done more simply, try them roasted with a tomato-fennel tapenade.

There's always something for the vegetarian; not even the fanatic vegan would go hungry here (quite a concession for a steakhouse, we think). As steakhouses go, the DLB is also a pretty good place for grazing, with appetizers such as a wild mushroom strudel that incorporates Spanish manchego cheese and a sauce of roasted shallot cream.

It's easy to see why the DLB is favored by locals in the Petoskey-Harbor Springs neighborhood, cottagers around Burt and Crooked lakes, and skiers from the slopes at Nub's or Boyne.

This is also a virtual community center for its close neighbors on Douglas Lake, including folks at the University of Michigan Biological Station.

Those of us who live farther south find it a terrific place to land for dinner on the way back from an excursion to Mackinac or the U.P. We particularly enjoy summer evenings there, when we can seek out a table on the porch, close enough to the water to put us on almost intimate terms with fishermen.

In colder seasons, it's nice to tuck in by the fireplace. This is the season when the DLB feeds visiting skiers very well. Winter also brings periodic special events for the loyal locals, such as cooking classes, wine dinners, and the bigtime sled-dogging that comes to Douglas Lake each February. The DLB serves as headquarters for mushers and spectators alike. Check the DLB's website for events, and the live music schedule as well.

Regulars may hate us for telling you that you'll find this magic little spot two miles east of US-31 on Douglas Lake Rd., which turns off just opposite the airport in Pellston.

Douglas Lake Bar & Steakhouse
7314 Douglas Lake Rd., Pellston
231-539-8588   www.douglaslakebar.com

Freshwater Lodge

Since Traverse City restaurateur Howard Schelde opened Freshwater Lodge in 2000, it has become known to locals and visitors alike for straightforward, solid fare and dependably good service. The concept was so successful, in fact, that Schelde built a twin just outside of Detroit a year later.

Right across the road from the water, TC's Freshwater has the look and feel of an Up North sportsmen's lodge, even if it is almost downtown in TC. There's plenty of Great Lakes fish and game on a menu, too, along with the prime rib, steaks and seafood.

West Bay is on wide-angle display outside an entire wall of windows, and mammoth stone fireplaces provide an antidote to snow days. The servers wear outfits you might find on a game warden, and the walls are adorned by rods, reels, creels, kayaks, and oars.

Schelde and his brother-in-law partner, Bob Kowaleski, take good service so seriously that all new hands get two weeks' training before taking the first order. Nothing ruins well-prepared food faster than bad table service, and nothing wrecks good service faster than bad food, so new hires are also cross-trained by a "faculty" of chefs and head servers who emphasize the importance of good team-work between kitchen and floor. Once on the job, servers meet with the chef before every shift to taste and discuss the day's specials, and to learn about any new wines that might have appeared on the list.

You'll be greeted with hot buttermilk biscuits almost as soon as you're seated, and you can expect intelligent, helpful answers to your menu questions. If you're clearly not in a hurry, no one will rush you, but if you have a plane to catch, they'll see you make it. Whenever we've ordered, say, a glass of wine to share or a salad to split, it came to us already divided into two very generous "halves." In short, this place makes its

guests feel like, well . . . guests.

When we go to Freshwater Lodge, one of us often orders perch. It's a personal weakness we share, especially when it comes, as it does here, as a classic, Michigan-style platter with slaw and fries. The Lodge's perch are beer-battered and, like the fries, are invariably crisp, golden and well drained. The slaw is creamy without being heavy or sweet. One of us also usually winds up having Freshwater's gratifyingly flavorful clam chowder, which is chunky and flavorful and, like all Freshwater's soups, made in-house from scratch. It's an especially rewarding dish when you need to brighten up a dreary, off-season day.

Freshwater Lodge, as you might expect, makes something of a specialty of freshwater fish, although there's no dearth of steaks, ribs, sandwiches, pastas, or shellfish. Berry-glazed salmon, maple-glazed walleye, and pan-seared trout with bacon also grace the menu along with the perch and whitefish. Tourists from salt-water country can get

grilled tuna if they must. The kitchen will fix any fish however you want it — broiled, sautéed, fried, whatever.

Graydon remembers catching perch by the dozen in the bay, fishing from a pier that was practically across the street from where the lodge stands. The restaurant's perch, however, are likely to have been farm-raised, because those yellow lake perch just aren't available in sufficient quantities any more. Freshwater's whitefish, however, come straight from the ice water of Lake Superior.

The menu here is the same at lunch and dinner, except that portions and prices of some specials are smaller through the early-bird hour. At any time of day, your budget won't ever get into very deep water.

The place is also big and well staffed enough that you'll seldom have to wait for a table — except, of course, at peak summer hours, when long lines can form.

Freshwater Lodge

13890 West Bay Shore Dr., Traverse City
231-932-4694

The Boathouse

In 1995, John Bailey masterfully remodeled the old Bowers Harbor general store into a waterfront restaurant that is as airy and easygoing as it gets Up North. Today he and his young chef, Jim Morse, provide their appreciative patrons some of the region's most interesting food in one of it's loveliest waterfront settings.

There's a see-and-be-seen bar up front with a cushioned window seat, and in the dining room, picture windows thoughtfully provide a dramatic, wide-angle view of Power Island, Neahtawanta, and West Grand Traverse Bay. Beyond them, of course, lie those nice Michigan sunsets.

Seafood has always played a major role at the Boathouse, and Morse lists his fish dishes among his proudest culinary achievements. He describes his fare as "French Mediterranean and some Asian," and says he likes working with tomatoes and olives, soy and ginger.

Another thing of which he is proud is his vegetables, which says much about his attention to all aspects of a meal and all tastes. He, himself is a vegetarian. His recent menus included a light fried asparagus tempura appetizer served in an Asiago cheese cup with smoked tomato coulis.

The Boathouse menu changes seasonally, but certain items tend to be carried over. Another regular in the cast is an appetizer of warm, walnut-crusted goat cheese medallions on Belgian endive with a pear-ginger chutney and beet dressing. You'll find the recipe in this book.

An entrée you're likely to find any time of year is what he calls "Chicken Wellington," a breast stuffed with mushroom, spinach, corn, and Gruyere, and baked in a pastry blanket.

Morse is a local lad who trained in Northwestern Michigan College's fine culinary arts program and as an intern in the kitchen at Crystal Downs Country Club. His first job out of college was at the Boathouse as sous-chef. When his predecessor moved on to a place of his own, Morse took over.

His appetizer menu invites grazing on a solid lineup of starters. It's likely to include that asparagus tempura and those warm goat cheese medallions *(P. 149)*. The list also offers grilled lamb chops

with Moroccan spices and a caramelized reduction of mint and onion. Another recipe you'll find in this book is one for an appetizer of seared sea scallops, wrapped in prosciutto and served with asparagus coulis, sun-dried tomato ratatouille, and a balsamic reduction.

A changing gardenscape of salads ranges from the obligatory Caesar and a "Boathouse Salad" of mixed greens, mozzarella, and tomato, to warm spinach salad with goat cheese, and a nice Niçoise. Some salads come in both dinner and side versions.

The Boathouse is a far busier place, of course, in summer, when it operates daily for lunch and dinner. In the off-season, the pace slows to evenings only, and the restaurant closes a couple of days a week. Owner Bailey, like many Northern Michigan restaurateurs, closes his Boathouse much of March and April to regroup for the onset of the season.

Summertime lunch menus in recent years have run to salads, wraps and sandwiches, including Reubens and black Angus burgers that come on Kaiser rolls with bacon and Gorgonzola. (And yes, as you might expect, there's a vegetarian wrap of hummus, avocado, feta, carrot, cucumber, tomato, and romaine.)

Service at the Boathouse is as crisply expert as the view is restful, and the prices are well inside the "moderate" range, especially when you consider the spectacular view.

Yachtsmen should note that despite appearances, the Boathouse is *not* affiliated with the private marina right outside the door, and the marina's proprietor does *not* welcome transients unless they pay for a slip — if one's available.

Boathouse
14039 Peninsula Drive, Traverse City
231-223-4030

Timmerin

Every Northern Michigan water-side town should have a restaurant like this, a harbor of quiet civility on a sea of tourist tumult. It's especially nice when the restaurant's most prominent feature, even *with* the lovely view, is the food.

Timmerin's owners, Mike and Donna Malecki, bought the place in 1990 when it was just another old cottage. They lived there a decade or so while transforming it into the Beulah Beach Inn, which opened in 2002.

Timmerin is the inn's restaurant. Its eponymous name stems from Tim and Erin White. Erin, Donna's daughter, is Timmerin's general manager and pastry chef, and her husband, Tim White, is the executive chef. They met at the New England Culinary Institute.

As Northern Michigan inns go, this one is quite new, but first-time visitors to the area might think the inn and restaurant had been there for decades. The building is so lovingly refurbished that everything about it has

the placid look of a long and well-lived life.

Timmerin, in short, has immense charm. It also has some of the best food in Benzie County, which is saying a lot when you consider the culinary renaissance that area has enjoyed the last few years.

Timmerin's menu varies frequently, but always has a solid roster of familiar and comfortable fare on which Tim White puts his own remarkable culinary spin. The molten beef tenderloin we once enjoyed with a Port wine reduction is about as straightforward a dish as you'll find. The focus is on fresh, seasonal ingredients and preparations that let natural flavors come through clearly.

Tim is a technique-oriented chef who

regards process and product as inextricably bound together. Indeed, he admits he had to reach a bit to offer recipes for this book. "So few of our dishes require them," he pleaded.

A recipe he did share with us is one for the wild duck confit (P. 189) that Timmerin regulars often praise. "It can be used with every season's accompaniments," Tim said. "It pairs perfectly with fruit sauces and gastriques, and can be shredded and added to white beans or wild rice." It's a long process, he said, but worth the effort. "Like all things comforting and soulful," he added.

The method outlined in his recipe, White said, works equally well with other poultry, such as chicken or goose.

Tim White is plainly passionate about food. When he speaks about his work at Timmerin, the conversation regularly strays to his kitchen at home. When he makes the cure for his duck confit, he said, "I sometimes omit the sugar and use the excess to season steaks for the charcoal grill at home." And when his sous-chef Sarah Moseler devised a simple new vinaigrette, it not only found its way onto Timmerin's spinach salad (with walnuts and blue cheese) but onto the king salmon or chicken he grills at home.

Timmerin has a classy wine list, as well as fine food. One of the fondest memories we have from our many Benzie coast outings is of sharing a bottle of crisp, cold Sancerre over dinner there one sultry summer evening after a long afternoon's hike.

Timmerin's atmosphere is restful and elegant, perfect for a quiet end to a busy day. In high summer, the meticulous landscaping lends an air of elegance, and the white-wickered porch overlooking the lake is the perfect spot for dinner on a pleasant evening or for after-dinner coffee with a sunset. If the breeze has a bit too much chill in it, the dining rooms inside are cozy as it gets.

As far as we can judge, the only thing wrong with Timmerin from the food-lover's perspective is that it closes for a time in winter. But we look at it this way: Their reopening in spring only makes us appreciate that lovely season all the more.

Timmerin

173 Lake Street, Beulah
231-882-5523

www.beulahbeachinn.com

Walloon Lake Inn

David Beier's Walloon Lake Inn could serve as a prototype for restful, easy-going lakeside dining. Almost any seat in the house offers a view of the placid, blue-green lake just steps away under a canopy of pine boughs.

Like Walloon Lake itself, the inn is a place where tradition counts a great deal. We once asked owner-chef David Beier to characterize his cuisine, and his reply was an anecdote about Andres Soltner, the founding chef at New York's Lutece. He told us that when a reporter once inquired about new and exciting dishes he was doing in his restaurant, Soltner replied, "I am not doing any things that are new. I am happy to work on getting the old ones right."

Accordingly, although Beier makes occasional excursions into new terrain such as, say, the Pacific Rim, his Walloon Lake Inn is always rich in the tried and true. One of the familiar, tried and true things is the building itself. It was erected in 1890 as "Fern Cottage," an inn where arriving summer resorters could stay while their nearby cottages were opened and readied.

A rich and literary sort of history is conferred on Walloon Lake by Ernest Hemingway, who spent youthful summers (and set his early yarns) in the neighborhood. Beier's menu still nods in homage to Papa with his "Trout Hemingway" (P. 194), browned in butter then baked, and sauced with sautéed shallots and mushrooms laced with lemon juice and brandy.

Beier has had the inn since 1981, and admits he struggled a bit at first to introduce his style, which he once described to us as "very, very French and very, very simple." There is almost always a veal dish, whose preparation varies daily, and a satisfying soup. Another menu regular is "Three Kings," a fish trio of whitefish, walleye, and Beier's choice of the day. Wine plays a prominent role in the cuisine, as in poultry simmered in Côtes du Rhone, beef in Madeira, or duck in Burgundy.

Beier's cuisine is now as firmly rooted among local traditions as Hemingway, but it wasn't always so. Back when he took over the inn, local diners were so accustomed to having their whitefish either fried or planked they couldn't understand why Beier did it any other way. "We were char-grilling whitefish and couldn't sell it to save our souls," he says. Now they like things his way. "I changed the sauce one year," he remembers, "and people screamed."

Gone are the days when the inn was a mere stopping-off place for summer resorters. It's open the year around now, seven days a week, a practice that keeps the staff intact and in good form. And it is still an inn, with five cozy rooms upstairs, all with private baths, and a continental breakfast that's as good as the dinner the night before. It's a terrific place for a weekend getaway for folks from Traverse City or Leelanau.

Serious food lovers know to keep an eye out for periodic special events, and for 4-day residential cooking schools almost every other week in the off-season. Beier offers small groups serious, hands-on instruction in everything from menu planning and kitchen organization to prep and presentation, with special attention to sauces. Lodging and food are included in the tuition, and each day's lunch is the students' own work. (There's even a "commuter rate" discount for locals who don't board at the inn.) What a great way to immerse yourself in the nuances of menu, methods, and *mis en place.*

Walloon Lake Inn

4178 W. Walloon Lake Rd., Walloon Lake Village
231-535-2999   www.walloonlakeinn.com

Dining In, Dining Out

Dining Out

Island Dining

There's something mysterious about an island when it's visible only as a shape on a hazy horizon. Few visitors spend much time in Northern Michigan without gazing at one of them and wondering what's out there, but we're amazed by the number of people who live here and have never gone to see for themselves.

Oh, most have probably been to Mackinac, and some might even have taken a day trip on the Manitou ferry. But far fewer have ever been to the state's largest island, Drummond, or the most populous, Beaver Island, and fewer still to Bois Blanc. So we urge you to put an island on your personal to-do list. Trust us: We've been to them all, and we assure you that going there won't diminish the sense of mystery one bit the next time you gaze at them across a hazy lake. Moreover, you can eat well on most of our islands.

We'll give you our general take on the island-dining scene first, and then provide more detail about three special island treats.

Mackinac Island, of course, is a thing unto itself, right up there with Sleeping Bear as a national treasure. And from a food lover's perspective, the sheer number of visitors it draws makes it the island most awash in eats. Fudge is the national dish there, and the island produces enough fried food to warrant a weekly oil change. But there's only so much anyone can do to whitefish, potatoes, and chicken wings in a deep fryer.

Three of the islands, we are happy to say, have some very pleasant exceptions to the prevailing, deep-fried cuisine.

We think the best island restaurant, bar none, is the **Carriage House** on Mackinac, which serves as the dining room at the island's Hotel Iroquois. It certainly is our favorite, with its superb food and service, and a truly sublime view from every table.

The other must for Mackinac Island visitors is the Main Dining Room at **Grand Hotel.** The food is quite good, considering the size of the operation, but the real attraction is the sheer spectacle of it all. Grand Hotel's Dining Room is as much theater as restaurant.

Our other island-dining delight is on

Beaver Island, where food lovers love **Nina's** at the Beaver Island Lodge. It's an easy walk from the ferry, the food is upscale, the service excellent, and the view stunning.

Beaver Island locals hang out at the **Shamrock Pub** in St. James. It's one an Up North classics: part family restaurant, part saloon, and part community center. The meal to have there, if you can swing it, is the annual wild-game benefit supper on Opening Day, when islanders bring in their best covered-dish renditions of elk, venison, 'possum, 'coon, rabbit. In good years there might even be something green.

Drummond Island, a short ferry ride from Detour at the eastern end of the U. P., is one of the few islands where winter is a high season. The restaurant to head for is **Bayside.** You'll find

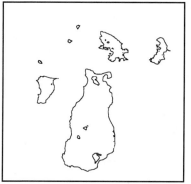

dishes such as pan-seared halibut with grape tomatoes, wild mushrooms and pancetta, or roast duck with cranberry balsamic. And that's the *winter* menu. Bayside is operated by Drummond Island Resort, a rustic, year-round lodge where you can golf in summer and rent snowmobiles in winter.

For even higher adventure there's Bois Blanc, the big, mysterious island just east of Mackinac whose name is pronounced "Bob-lo" by the locals. Several

hundred hardy cottagers pass the summer there in blissful seclusion, and 50-odd year-rounders sometimes rustle up a few pupils for the two-room schoolhouse. Once Curt Plaunt's ferry from Cheboygan gets you to there, you can go east or west on the island's only serious road. West takes you to the **Hawk's Nest General Store**, an establishment that is all things to all people here: grocery, deli, ice-cream parlor, video store, real estate office, and restaurant. Go east and you'll find the **Bois Blanc Tavern.** The island also has a post office, firehouse, town hall, church, and grass airfield, but is otherwise mostly just trees surrounded by water. The tavern has a few rustic cabins, but if adventure isn't your middle name, finish lunch in time to catch the ferry back. Bois Blanc makes great summer and fall hiking (at least, until deer season brings people with weapons). But it isn't exactly a happenin' place, even in July. We remember a conversation between the waitress and the cook one morning at breakfast in the tavern:

"Not much traffic this morning," said the cook, gazing out the window at the island's only paved road.

"Oh, I don't know," replied the waitress. "Jim went by in his truck a while ago."

Carriage House

If you have only one evening to spend on Mackinac Island, our advice would be to head for the Carriage House at the 100-year-old Iroquois Hotel. In fact, we think it's one of the top restaurants in Northern Michigan, and worth the ferry trip over and back just for dinner. Not only is the food outstanding, everything else about the Carriage House is, too.

The McIntyre family, which has owned this hotel for generations, has an uncanny knack for recruiting bright and personable young staff and training them very, very well. The kitchen offers thoughtful, balanced menus and exquisite dishes built from scratch of the freshest seasonal ingredients. The clean, simple décor that won't distract you from the scenery beyond the huge windows. Indoors, or on the waterside patio, every table has a wide-angle view of the straits and the full sweep of Round Island Passage. Gigantic lakers pass dramatically close, and busy passenger ferries swoop and swirl on their way to and from the mainland.

The menu has the elegance that so often accompanies simplicity. Smoked Scottish salmon and icy shrimp with wasabi curls tug gently at your appetite, competing politely for attention with chilled gazpacho, tuna maki with sweet ginger, and a polenta gratin with portobello ragout and foie gras. After a chilled gazpacho cools you off, you get to consider seared scallops with ginger, lemongrass and frizzled leek, or sherry-marinated salmon.

And all this is accompanied by non-stop piano music from the lounge bar, where we can never resist lingering for a nightcap after dinner. The Iroquois is an oasis of civilized dining in a sea of fudge, a place to unwind after a day immersed in hiking, cycling, history, and all that wonderful tourist kitsch.

The Iroquois is right on the water, at the south end of the main street. Turn left from your ferry landing and it's just a short walk. The Carriage House is tucked in back, down a lilac-bordered walk alongside the hotel.

Carriage House

Iroquois Hotel, Huron Street, Mackinac Is.
906-847-3321   www.iroquoishotel.com

Grand Hotel Dining Room

What food lover can possibly visit Mackinac very often without a meal in the cavernous Grand Hotel Dining Room? It is Michigan's most theatrical restaurant, with a menu that covers all the bases, and food that's about as good as food gets when produced in such prodigious quantity. First and foremost among our reasons for sending you there, however, is the sheer spectacle. The Grand is truly grand, with its fabulous gardens and liveried staff. The Dining Room is said to seat a thousand, and its impeccably drilled Jamaican waiters plain blow you away with panache.

Grand Hotel is also one of the most civilized places in Northern Michigan. Their hotel is the region's only establishment that still requires gentlemen to wear a coat and tie after 6 p.m. In an era when backwards baseball caps and muscle shirts are acceptable in many "casual fine dining" restaurants, Grand Hotel's dress code is downright courageous. Bravo to the Musser family for preserving standards!

Ladies (who hardly need a dress code to prompt them) also get all fancied up for dinner here, and the Dining Room provides a veritable fashion show when all those well-turned-out guests parade along the main, center aisle to their appointed tables. It's the way we imagine it was in the dining salons of fashionable ocean liners in the Roaring Twenties. The glow remains after dinner, when the guests repair to the Parlor for coffee, and then on to the Terrace Room to dance the night away to Grand Hotel's house orchestra. The only way to make your Grand Hotel experience complete is by starting with cocktails in the Cupola Bar up on the roof. There, along with your favorite beverage and some light entertainment, you'll enjoy one of the most breathtaking views in the world. There's no place in Michigan like it.

A caveat: Grand Hotel is an American-plan property, so guests have priority in the dining room. If you propose to go just for dinner, be sure to book ahead.

Grand Hotel

Mackinac Island
906-847-3331   www.grandhotel.com

Nina's

One of our favorite annual adventures is an overnight cruise with sailing friends from their home port of Charlevoix to Beaver Island. Whenever we go, we make a point of booking ahead for dinner one night at Nina's. This is the fine (but seasonal) restaurant at the Beaver Island Lodge. Beaver Island is a very laid-back-and-barefoot sort of place, as close as Michigan gets to Caribbean informality, and Nina's is always a pleasant surprise. It's not just "good, for an island," it could hold its own anywhere.

The lodge is a small and simple resort on the north shore, only half a mile's walk from the ferry landing at St. James. In pleasant weather, try to dine on the patio. You'll not only have a view of the sunset but can gaze from mysterious Beaver Island at the even more mysterious Garden and High islands, uninhabited, it is said, except for a mysterious old Odawa medicine woman.

Indoors or out, the service at this family-staffed resort is friendly and efficient, and the food is outstanding. There is a grazer's bonanza of appetiz-ers—a brie torte, for instance, drew our eye recently, filled with cherries and pecans. So did a tomato bruschetta and some classic escargots *Bourguignonne*.

Main dishes, although predictable, are exquisitely prepared. Grilled salmon, for example, comes with a savory basil-lime garlic butter; whitefish is poached in bouillon and sauced with a lemon vinaigrette. The meat lover can have prime rib, strip and rib eye steaks, and butter-tender filet mignon.

As you might expect, when Beaver Island's population swells with summer residents, Nina's is a popular place. So book ahead.

Nina's at Beaver Is. Lodge
Beaver Lodge Rd., St. James
231-448-2396

www.beaverisland.org/ninas

Dining Out

Ethnography

We aren't fad dieters or vitamin poppers, but prefer variety as our path to health, longevity and maximum enjoyment.

Consider the French. No steady diet of same-old, same-old for *them*. Instead, they go for moderation and variety, a little bit of a lot of really good stuff. Despite their reputation for rich cuisine and good wine, they have healthier hearts than we do. Scientists call it "The French Paradox."

Maybe it's not a paradox at all. Trendy *Salon* magazine once exclaimed how those pesky French "eat all the butter, cream, foie gras, pastry and cheese that their hearts desire, and yet their rates of obesity and heart disease are much lower than ours." That's just baloney! The French do *not* eat "all that their hearts desire." While they vary their diet widely, they serve portions most American restaurants would call tiny. Restaurants in France do not automatically bring every patron a Styrofoam box to take the excess home in. The French are less likely to be couch potatoes, too — not surprising, considering that their TV programming is even worse than ours!

So give us variety!

Other people's ethnic foods are a great way to relieve the *ennui* of our own ethnic dishes of whitefish, cherries, salmon, and morels. It's much easier these days: Ethnicity has blossomed Up North. Why, we even have Thai carryout in Bellaire and Japanese *donburi* in downtown Petoskey. We can get Cajun in Elk Rapids, and home-cooked Mexican on South Airport Road. At this rate, who knows? We might all live happily ever after.

Some ethnic cuisines have been with us so long we hardly think of them as ethnic any more—Italian, for instance.

Northern Michigan has some very nice Italian restaurants, but none is quite so, well . . . *Italian* as Alex Czinki's **Villa Ristorante Italiano** in Petoskey. Czinki enhances a

classic menu with a truly remarkable wine list and a savvy staff that offers a cheerful *"Buon Giorno"* when you arrive and a pleasant *"Arrivederci"* as you depart. In between you can all but hear the accordions and violins and operatic tenors. Czinki, who started his restaurant 28 years ago as a pizza parlor, has built a wide following with a classic Italian menu that's laced with marvelous pastas, smooth cheeses, and glorious tomato sauces. He still bakes pizza on stone, Napoli style, but the menu has a score of less casual main-stays. There's all manner of *pesce, pollo* and *carne*, from *tagliatelle alla Bolognese* and chicken Marsala, to veal scalloppine, *saltimbocca* and *ossobuco*. We like his gnocchi with porcini in a portobello cream sauce. Czinki has the region's definitive Italian wine cellar, too, with unusual finds from his annual missions to the old country. Even the grappa list is extensive. (*Villa Ristorante, US-131 S, at Pleasant St., Petoskey; 231- 347-1440.*)

Mexican food, especially in its Americanized "Tex-Mex" form, has been around as long as Jimmy Buffet and his Margaritas. How else to explain the popularity of such places as the laid-back **Roadhouse** in Benzonia and its spin-

off **Roadhouse on the River** in Manistee?

We think the **Red Mesa Grill** in Boyne City is about as good as the genre gets Up North, with pan-American cuisine covering latitudes from Argentina (skirt steak) north to the Tex-Mex territory of tacos, enchiladas, and wet burritos. Red Mesa takes the Margarita trade to new and encyclopedic heights by offering a tequila list the way others might offer a wine list (even providing instructive menu text about the botany of the agave plant whence tequila comes). The relaxed, informal tone is set by Toltec symbols painted large upon the walls, inside and out, and a concrete floor reminiscent of a cantina. Folks come here to relax. That, too, can fend off heart-busting stress. *(Red Mesa, 117 Water St., Boyne City, 231-582-0049.)*

If you're a purist seeking food Mexicans themselves do, you want Miguel Osorio's **Taqueria Margarita**. There's nothing "Tex" about it. This is the real, unhyphenated thing. It's so Hispanic that Spanish is the official language and there are flyers on the counter for classes in English as a second language. The language of good food is universal, however, so plenty of food-loving Anglos find their way here. One of them is Tapawingo's Pete Peterson, who tells us this is where he heads when he takes a holiday from his own kitchen. Each day brings a special soup and plate lunch to augment the regular lineup of tacos, quesadillas, and tamales, *bistek encebollado*, and pork ribs in red sauce. The *chiles rellenos* are properly stuffed, battered and fried. The quesadillas are lightly filled with soft, mellow, white cheese. The tacos, of flour or corn, come with any of seven fillings: pork, chicken, steak or chorizo for the less adventuresome, and *tripas* or *lenguas* for the truly serious fans. Every meal comes with a flavorful tomato salsa that is only mildly hot, and a smooth, creamy *salsa verde* of avocado puree, lime juice, and oil. Breakfast is served all day here. Think *huevos rancheros* with tomato, onion, garlic and peppers. Or *chilaquiles* of sautéed tortilla pieces tossed with eggs and meat. The service at Taqueria Margarita is swift and friendly, and the prices are downright thrilling. They have carry-out, too. *(Taqueria Margarita, 1319 W. South Airport Rd., Traverse City; 231-935-3712.)*

We often call food "ethnic" when what we mean is "foreign," but there's nothing foreign about the Louisiana bayous, where good, ethnic Cajun cuisine comes from. The best example Up North is **Pearl's New Orleans Kitchen** in Elk Rapids. When Pearl's first opened, we had a hard time mentally mesh-

ing jambalaya with an Up North life-style, so we feared for its future. Silly us! Folks from all over the region quickly took to flocking there, even in midwinter, for foods seldom found north of Baton Rouge, such as alligator steak, crawfish cakes, and etouffée. It fits right in with the restaurant's ambient throb of jazz, blues and zydeco. Cajun isn't our own favorite cuisine, but Pearl's has persuaded us that a fine way to ward off winter's chill is to hang at the bar with Margaritas that come in a jar and enjoy a batch of crawfish cakes and some jambalaya. *(Pearl's, 617 Ames St., Elk Rapids; 231- 264-0530.)*

Having lived so long in Cincinnati, let us not overlook German, the heritage more Americans share than any other. Should our friends Detlef und Melitta come to visit, we'd probably take them to **Schlang's Bavarian Inn** on old US-27 south of Gaylord for some schnitzel or sauerbraten mit spaetzle *(517-732-9288)*. But if it's wine they want, however, we'd point out that **Brookside Inn** has the region's definitive German-wine cellar *(115 US-31, Beulah; 231-882-9688)*.

There's no dearth of oriental fare Up North, either, with numerous classic "Chinese" restaurants. Many in Traverse City swear by **Golden Chopsticks**, on Munson Avenue near Acme, which of-

---

Road Food: Eating Outside of the Box

Much as we like it here, we do travel, so we've developed some alternatives to Interstate chain food — much of it ethnic. Dinner at **Franzisi's** is worth the trip to Canada all by itself (256 Bruce St., Sault Ste. Marie; 705-253-1500). In Grand Rapids, we're torn between **Tre Cugini** downtown (100 Monroe Center; 616-235-9339) and **Tuscan Express,** hidden in a strip mall at 6450 SE 28th St., a mile _east_ of I-96 (616-956-5522). Both are rich in authentic, elegant Italian cuisine. If you stay in Grand Rapids at the Amway Grand Plaza, be sure to dine at the **1913 Room,** the hotel's exquisite French-American restaurant (616-774-2000). Our favorite suburban Detroit hangout is **220** in Birmingham, just off Old Woodward at 220 Merrill St. (248-645-2150); it has great food with Italian accents and a hospitably efficient staff, and the sea of suits on the prowl at happy hour makes fine people-watching. In Ann Arbor, _everyone_ knows Zingerman's and the Gandy Dancer; we gravitate to the **West End Grill,** at 120 W. Liberty (734-747-6260) for American bistro fare with touches of Pacific Rim. If you stray as far as Marquette, trust us on **Vierling's** at 119 S. Front St., downtown (906-228-3533); it's busy all the time and there's a very good reason. Stray even farther, to the magnificent wilds of the Keweenaw, and you have to keep going to Copper Harbor for dinner at the **Harbor Haus** (906-289-4502). While you're there, pick up some "Poorrock Abbey" thimbleberry jam from the **Jam Pot,** the roadside shop at Eagle Harbor run by monks at the monastery across the road. They sell by mail and Internet, too *(www.societystjohn.com/jampot.jp)*.

fers a pan-Asian menu ranging from sushi to Szechuan, by way of Thailand. Little **Panda North** in Traverse City's Logan's Landing shopping center is another favorite of many locals.

Two relatively new Asian places offer food of a somewhat different sort. One is the improbably minuscule **Indo China Express** in Bellaire, which isn't a restaurant at all, but a carryout behind an insurance office. The take-out counter is in a cubicle so small that only the aromas tell you you're in the right place. But our first order—shrimp *gang ped* curry from the Thai side of the take-out menu and sesame chicken from the Chinese side—was all the evidence we needed. The menu is almost

bigger than the place, with a wide array of pad, Thai and Chinese dishes, curries and stir-frys. The dishes marked as "hot" *are,* so take care, and if you don't tolerate heat, ask for less incendiary preparation. Carryout meals include rice and a generous serving of mellow egg-drop soup with a hint of sweetness that went with the sweet-sour sauce on tender, deep-fried, sesame-crusted chicken. *(Indo China Express, 634 Willow Dr. at M-88, Bellaire; 231-533-4300.)*

Petoskey's **Tokyo** is perhaps the most "authentic" ethnic restaurant Up North. It is certainly the only Japanese restaurant. Owner-chef Masahiro Ohkawa adheres faithfully to his ethnic roots with the quick, delicious sort of fare the Japanese look for in their donburi shops. It's fast food in a bowl — rice topped with meat, fish or vegetables, and a savory broth. Ohkawa augments this with a wider menu of delicate soup, savory teriyaki and sushi, and crisp, flavorful, tempura dishes. It is inscrutably delicious food. Equally interesting are the mauve walls and electric-purple leatherette dinettes left from the days when a Coney Island stand occupied the place. Masahiro's fare is just as bright, but far more thoughtful, subtle, and tantalizing. He works his magic behind the counter and his wife, Naoka, provides service with a quiet grace that goes well with the soft, classical background music. *(Tokyo, 307 Petoskey St., Petoskey; 231-439-3268.)*

Dining Out

Taking the Bar Exam

We once took issue in a newspaper column with someone who suggested that "bar food" is an oxymoron. Hold on, we said. What's more satisfying on a cold winter evening than a juicy cheeseburger or gyro, and maybe some fries, in a home-town tavern where we feel right at home in boots and Polartec? The good news is that some of our saloons have gotten way beyond burgers lately.

Much depends here, of course, on how you define "saloon." We're pretty relaxed about that. There needn't be sawdust on the floor to make it a "saloon." What counts is motive: These are places where we'd be welcome if all we wanted was a drink. That's seldom the case, however, so we like our saloons to have some appreciation for food.

This may smack of slippery-slope reasoning, but it helps us introduce you (in case you've not had the pleasure) to such diverse watering holes as Art's Tavern in Glen Arbor and The South American Lounge in Bay Harbor.

But let's start with a favorite of another sort, **The Beacon Lounge.** That's the rooftop bar at Traverse City's Park Place Hotel. Some locals still call it the "Top of the Park" because of the long-defunct restaurant next door by that name. Whatever you call this place, however, it is not primarily an eating establishment, and we would never go there solely out of hunger.

We go there to have a drink or two, and to enjoy the marvelous view of the city and the bay, and to hear some good music and enjoy good company. And later on, if we get hungry, we might order a pizza or two.

This is a very fortuitous confluence, for the Park Place has some of the best pizza in Northern Michigan. Like everything on the bar menu at the Beacon Lounge, it is hand-delivered from the main kitchen ten floors below.

The thing about this pizza, aside from house-made sauce, is that it has a thin, crisp, cracker-like crust that doesn't in any way distract you from the vivid, intense flavors of the fresh and inter-

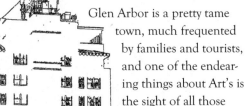

esting toppings. This pizza is not weighed down by thick, chewy dough. The best nights are when the Beacon Lounge gets into jam mode. We remember one night when pianist Tom Kaufman got into an impromptu duet with the bartender, who tapped out "I've Got Rhythm" with swizzle sticks on the bottles behind the bar. Kaufman, who keeps her glassware tuned, said she prefers single-malt Scotch bottles "because the glass is heavier and gives a truer sound." You don't hear talk like that in a place that serves thick, spongy pizza. *(Beacon Lounge, 100 State Street, Traverse City; 800-748-0133; www.parkplace-hotel.com.)*

Then there's **Art's Tavern.** Every town Up North has its local pub, and this is Glen Arbor's. Local pubs often reflect something of the communities they serve, and Art's is no exception. For all the booted feet and Buffalo plaid, the locals aren't the rough-hewn rustics they sometimes appear to be.

Glen Arbor is a pretty tame town, much frequented by families and tourists, and one of the endearing things about Art's is the sight of all those baby-booster seats stored under the pool table. We'd never let that distract us from the real reason we go there, which is to have a cold draft or two and one of their bleu-cheese burgers, or a grilled salmon salad — the fish trimmed of all traces of fishy fat and bearing picture-perfect grill marks. *(Art's Tavern, 6487 W. Western Ave., Glen Arbor; 231-334-3754.)*

Burgers are almost a regional ethnic specialty, and locals in almost every town will tell you about the great burgers at their local tavern.

Our local pub in Elk Rapids is **The Town Club,** and of course *we* think it has the best cheeseburgers in the Midwest. We hasten to add, however, that when we go there, it is almost always as much for the Margaritas as the food.

We'd probably patronize the Town Club even if the burgers weren't served on grilled buns big enough to contain all the onion, tomato, pickles, and lettuce, and the thick layer of good Swiss that comes with them. (If that description daunts you, remember that owner Brendan Burke is also a master of grilled-chicken gyros and tzatziki.)

Dining In, Dining Out

The Town Club has enough TVs so that everyone to watch the sporting event of his or her choice, and the usual pool table lurks in back. The atmosphere here is almost tame in summer, when the harbor fills up with cruising yachtsmen from effete places like Wisconsin. (*The Town Club, 133 River St., Elk Rapids; 231-264-9914.*)

The **South American** is something else altogether. We doubt they've ever served tzatziki, and there certainly isn't a pool table. This is the cocktail lounge and grill off the marble-floored lobby of the Inn at Bay Harbor, and it is probably Northern Michigan's classiest saloon. It is so classy it doesn't just have atmosphere, it has *ambience*. That ambience includes a polished bar and a big, warm fireplace; comfy leather chairs and plush sofas; expansive cocktail tables and huge doors opening to a terrace that overlooks Lake Michigan. This is hardly the place for a shot and a beer. Better make it a champagne cocktail with Courvoisier and a dash of Angostura, or a very dry Tanqueray martini, stirred, not shaken, up, with a twist. Do they have burgers? You bet! They are described on the menu as follows:

Grilled Black Angus Ground Round
French Fries
Nine

See? We told you it was classy. You can enjoy a nice little meal here even without burgers if you want. Start, say, with chilled shrimp cocktail, which comes with ancho chile oil (*ten*). Or, if you've overspent on Courvoisier, there's chicken satay with peanut curry ginger sauce (merely *six*). Or bucatini pasta tossed with olive oil, garlic, sun-dried tomatoes, artichoke hearts and toasted pine nuts (*eight*). You can add roasted salmon if you wish (only *six more*). On the walls, you'll find a splendid and detailed portrait of the Great Lakes luxury steamer for which the lounge is named, the fabled *South American*. It carried tourists from Chicago to the resorts Up North until the 1960s. (*South American, 3600 Village Harbor Dr., Bay Harbor; 231-439-4000; www.innatbayharbor.com.*)

Only one Northern Michigan watering place rivals the South American's sheer civility. That's the **Cupola Bar** on the roof of Mackinac Island's Grand Hotel. If you spend more than a night or two on your next island visit, you will disappoint us terribly if you don't make your way up there for cocktails sometime. It's not easy to do, mind you. Besides that ferry ride to the island, it means paying a fee to enter the hotel if you're not a guest there, and on top of that you have to dress properly. No matter what you have in your glass, drink in the breathtaking view of the Straits and enjoy the cocktail music before returning to *terra firma* for dinner. *(Cupola Bar, Grand Hotel, Mackinac Island; 906-847-3331; www. grandhotel.com.)*

Sleder's in Traverse City is one of the few places Up North older than Grand Hotel. A Bohemian immigrant named Vencel Sleder built it in 1882 as a saloon for his neighbors in Slabtown, where people built homes of leftover "slab wood" from the sawmills. Sleder's is one of the few saloons Up North that survived Prohibition. That's because Vencel's grandson, Louie, took good care of any cops or revenuers who came around—such good care, in fact, that they came around rather often. Their favorite beverage was Louie's root beer, which came in teacups and tasted remarkably like good Canadian rye. Sleder huge, original bar remains, and historical photos and signs adorn the walls. It is more restaurant than saloon today, although newcomers are still urged to kiss the moose over the back door. The specialty is a burger of buffalo meat, but they also have a long menu of sandwiches, salads, burritos steak, ribs, cod, smelt, walleye, and whitefish. *(Sleder's Tavern, 717 Randolph St., Traverse City; 231-947-9213; www.Sleders.com.)*

Apache Trout Grill in Traverse City is more restaurant than bar, too, although one of its popular features is the waterfront tiki bar. The restaurant always seems full of people who are just

happy to be here—even if they're *from* here. Go early in the day and you can arrange some charter fishing, and then have the restaurant cook up your catch for lunch. *(Apache Trout Grill, 13671 S. West Bay Shore Dr., Traverse City, 231-947-7079.)*

In Leland, the local saloon is the **Bluebird.** Although it has a pool table and the game on TV every night, it morphs into a restaurant so often that we've treated it extensively elsewhere, although we think the place to dine at the 'Bird is in the bar. In Northport it's **Woody's,** where not much has changed, although Woody doesn't own it any more.

The cuisine at these places might not always be haute, but there's no denying cholesterol sometimes. This, in fact, might be the *real* ethnic American food.

Dining Out

Let's Go to Lunch

Why do they call it "lunch hour?" We're so harried as a nation that we're lucky if we end up with 30 minutes. And we are such creatures of habit, we hardly think about where to go. Day after day, we follow our regular route to the same old, same old lunch.

When Graydon worked in downtown Traverse, he went around the corner to Cousin Jenny's four days in five (although he'd have gone all the way across town in any event, just for their tortellini salad). Sherri always seemed to land at the Taste of Traverse in Acme.

Now, 10 years later, half of those places are gone. Lunch is a very competitive business Up North, where little deli-counter soup-salad-sandwich shops sometimes seem to open, close and change hands overnight. We just hope all the places we tell you about here are still in business when you get there.

Our old lunch-hour friend, **Cousin Jenny's** will be. It's such an institution that it's hard to believe Nick and Jerilyn DeBoer started it, a block away, as a mere hole in the wall. While we still like tortellini salad, you might prefer the house specialty, the Cornish pasty. These hand-made, sandwichy things are what miners in Cornwall used to carry in their pockets to have for lunch underground. Their wives (known as "Jennies") made them of meat and veggies and potatoes, all sealed and baked in a softball-sized bread-shell. It made a wholesome cooked meal a guy could eat between tons, in the dark. Miners brought the recipe with them when they emigrated to the Upper Peninsula to dig copper in the 19th century, and it's still practically the national dish there. We bet those miners would sometimes have liked a little tortellini salad, too, but the pasty is the best self-contained lunch we know of that comes with such interesting history. Cousin Jenny's also has a fine array of home-made salads and soups, including some of the best chili north of Cincinnati. Rushed regulars know the counter service won't keep them long from their desks. For the leisure classes there's seating inside and at sidewalk tables in summer. (*Cousin Jenny's, 129 S. Union, Traverse City; 231-941-7821.*)

That little hole in the wall where Cousin Jenny's began may have magic. Pretty much the same thing happened to the next occupants, Brad and Alice Campsmith. After opening Good Harbor Coffee Co. there a few years ago, they went on to create **Crema,** a hip, cool, trendy, urban place a few blocks away at Front and Park. The day there starts with coffee, cappuccino, espresso, muffins, and scones. From mid-morning until late evening they do deli fare. Their interesting sandwiches are on house-made focaccia—ham and artichoke, for instance, or chicken, cheddar, basil and tomato; or tuna with avocado, tomato, cucumber, and lime-

ginger dressing. What we'd steer you to is the crisp-crusted, open-hearth, flatbread pizza—a house specialty, with toppings that both traditional and unexpected. (*Crema, Front and Park Streets, Traverse City; 231-922-9311.*)

Quite different is **The House,** which is as simple, homey and un-

adorned as the old house it occupies at the far west end of Front Street. Here, Michael Bauer and Joni Capling make a fetish of regional farm products and vary the menu to incorporate whatever's in season locally. They can get you started with a hearty breakfast of, say, blueberry pancakes or a bacon-and-Gruyere egg sandwich. Lunch hour's salad or soup will be laden with seasonal local produce, although they often go farther afield for seared tuna with fruit relish on soba noodles, or Brie on roast turkey with an apple relish. (*The House, 826 W. Front St., Traverse City; 231-929-4917.*)

For star treatment in TC, it's **Mustard's**. Order at the deli counter and you get a card bearing a celebrity's name — Mel Gibson, maybe, or Renee Zellweger. When your order's ready, they holler the name and you hoist your hand to identify yourself to the server. Graydon swears he'll never go back if they ever make him answer to "Barbra Streisand." Until then it's a terrific source for hefty sandwiches with funky names and a deli-lovers' paradise of pastrami, Swiss, liverwurst, roast beef, and sprouts on top-drawer breads. Burgers too, plus shrimp fritters, fries, salads and split-pea soup. (*Mustard's, 202 E. State, at Cass, Traverse City; 231-929-9700.*)

Turnover can be so swift in this business that **Burch's Bayside Grill** was the third deli-café in about five years to occupy the same storefront, but we're optimistic, for Scott and Kim Burch made it a perfect fit for the 30-minute lunch hour. Order a BLT and salad at the counter and you'll have them in front

of you in five minutes—the sandwich on golden toast evenly painted with mayo, with plenty of crisp bacon, fresh lettuce and tomato. The menu bulges with wraps — tuna, ham, olive, veggies, and chicken, plus brats, chilidogs, corned-beef on sourdough, and pastrami and Swiss on pumpernickel. *(Burch's Bayside Grille, 149 E. Front St., Traverse City; 231-935-1000.)*

Another place enjoying reincarnation is Wally Green's **Green House,** which carries on a long association of that address with good soup. That, plus good salad and good service make it *very* busy at lunch. *(Green House, 115 E. Front St., Traverse City, 231-929-7687.)*

Visitors are often baffled when they ask directions to **Another Cuppa Joe** at Grand Traverse Commons, because locals still call it "Building 50." You just have to live here to know that it is the historic state mental hospital, now being rehabbed into a mix of condos and restaurants and things. Another Cuppa Joe is as interesting as the place it occupies. *(Another Cuppa Joe, 1200 W. 11th St., Traverse City; 231-947-7730.)*

A chef we know has a pet theory to explain why these little deli-soup-salad-sandwich-lunch-hour places keep popping up. He thinks it's because they are precisely the sort of operation that every over-worked, haute-cuisine restaurateur and chef in America secretly wants to own. "Think about it!" he said. "Simple food. Low overhead. Small payroll. No liquor license. And you get to go home at night."

Is that what Derek Boyer had in mind when he bought the tiny **Harbor Café** in Elk Rapids? He caused quite a stir in town because he'd been sous chef at Tapawingo, but the café is pretty much the same friendly little 20-seat hole in the wall, only it has some *really* good soup. Not a speck of foie gras, though, and Boyer *does* get to go home at night. *(Harbor Café, 129 River St., Elk Rapids, 231-264-8700.)*

Chef Charles down the street is another of those places whose owner-

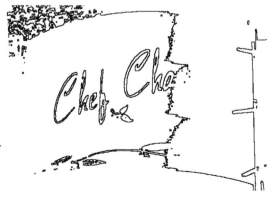

chef, Charles Egeler, traded in a life of haute cuisine for a secret dream. His was fine pizza, and we're glad he traded. He also makes terrific sandwiches, a mean Greek salad, and proper, home-made pesto, by the pint, to go. Chef Charles is so good, they don't have to deliver, so his place is a busy hang-out much of the time for teens and families (and, in summer, hungry boaters up from the harbor). Alas, however, he stays open so late that he does not always get to go home at night. *(Chef Charles, 147 River St., Elk Rapids; 264-8901.)*

Every town has its HQ eatery where locals get gossip. Elk Rapids has three. Grab a fresh salad or some home-made soup and a wheat-bread sandwich at **Java Jones,** and you might miss the news making the rounds at the Harbor Café or next door at T. J. Charlie's. In addition to that good, fresh food, Java Jones has Internet access. But you don't need the Internet for entertainment when the mayor and his pals are in for lunch and enjoying some midwinter putting practice on the snow-rug inside the door. *(Java Jones, 139 River Street, 231-264-1111.)*

Don't go to **T. J. Charlie's** for golf or data. Go for pie. Dessert pies are Denise Heeke's *forte,* and if John is making chicken pot pie,

snap some up to take home because it'll fill a crowd. John rocks when he fires up his sidewalk barbecue for the Wednesday-night street parties. The rest of the time he gets to go home at night—except when he's doing some of the catering the locals know him for. *(T. J. Charlie's, 135 River St., Elk Rapids, 231-264-8819).*

Ask about lunch in Leland and we'd send you straight to **Stone House Café.** If the name's familiar, it's because the café was Stone House Bread founder Bob Pisor's way of recycling his original bakery when he moved production to Traverse City. Chef Martha Ryan designs imaginative sandwiches, soups and salads that we bet the kids wish she'd given them in *her* old haute-cuisine job as the local school lunch lady. Naturally, the café also sells Stone House breads and specialty cheeses and foods. *(Stone House Café, 407 S. Main St., Leland; 231-256-2577.)*

Up north in Petoskey and Harbor Springs folks have their fair shot at a fine 30-minute lunch, too. **Roast and Toast** is where people in Petoskey like to go for morning coffee with their *New York Times.* At lunch

Dining In, Dining Out

it provides classy soups and a salad-sandwich menu that embraces all the favorite deli stuff. *(Roast and Toast, 309 E. Lake St., Petoskey, 231-347-7767.)*

Julienne Tomatoes (cleverly named for its principals, Julie Adams and Tom Scheffler) has a very eclectic menu, and appears as well to have been furnished with treasures from a dozen garage sales. Rough charm also oozes from ancient brick walls that

bear evidence of the building's long history as feed store and print shop. Julie, the pastry chef, always has fresh, house-made croissants, éclairs and other goodies ready for the morning folks. At lunch, this is classic deli. You order from a blackboard, find a table, and await your food. Each day brings a new soup, along with crunchy salads (including a magnificent Cobb-like platter with julienne ham, turkey and Swiss, plus tomato, cucumber, onion, and boiled egg). The sandwich list leaves us gasping with indecision—peppered turkey club or maple-cured

ham and Swiss? Tuna salad with onion, celery, lettuce, tomato, parsley and mayo on a fresh croissant, or roast turkey and cranberry with cream cheese and romaine on whole wheat? Lord, it's hard! *(Julienne Tomatoes, 421 Howard St., Petoskey; 231-439-9250.)*

Gelato is a cute, seasonal café in Petoskey operated by American Spoon Foods, whose local retail outlet is next door. A bright place, with broad windows onto the park, it will first sell you a nice luncheon sandwich or salad, some terrific pasta, or maybe some soup. *Then* comes the specialty, the gelato made by American Spoon. This Petoskey-based company, a nationally known maker and marketer of specialty foods, uses nothing but natural stuff in the smooth, creamy Italian-style ice creams and sorbets. *(Gelato Café, 413 E. Lake St., Petoskey; 231-347-7004.)*

Like most resort towns, Harbor Springs shrinks a bit when the cottagers and tourists drain away south in fall. But locals stay connected all through winter at **Woolly Bugger,** an Internet café where they can read e-mail over morning coffee, and then Google away lunchtime while enjoying a quiche or wrap and a salad. Owner Darrell Lavender is fond of saying that good coffee, like fishing, will "separate you for a moment from ordinary things." That explains why the café is named for a trout-anglers' streamer bait. *(Woolly Bugger, 181 E. Main St., Harbor Springs; 231-242-0592; www. wbcoffee.com.)*

Juilleret's, while somewhat less progressive, is a true landmark in Harbor Springs. Its owners claim their family invented planked whitefish five generations ago. The Indians who cooked whitefish that way might differ. But who's to say? Juilleret's goes back almost as far as they do. The original, 19th-century ice cream parlor was a pine plank on sawhorses. They have a real building now, where they make fluffy breakfast waffles and cinnamon French toast, and then serve planked whitefish and other stuff until closing time at night. It's about the only place Up North where Graydon can indulge his passion for a club sandwich and a chocolate soda. *(Juilleret's, 131 State St., Harbor Springs, 231-526-2821.)*

Horizon Shine Café at Horizon Books in Downtown Traverse City is not only Wi-Fi equipped for Googlers, it offers food adventure with a menu of homemade soups and salads; veggie, chicken or tuna wraps; pizza, even quiche with a cornbread crust. All the usual bookstore espressos, lattes, and cap-

puccinos live here, too. *(Horizon Shine Cafe, 243 E. Front St., Traverse City; 231-946-7290; www.horizonbooks. com.)*

Borders Books Café in Traverse City also lets you surf wirelessly as you sip your latte or home in on the fresh-daily salads, soups, and sandwiches and (of course) some good, bookstore coffee, latte and the like. The café here also features a rotating display of interesting work by local artists to go with the good food. *(2612 Crossings Circle, Traverse City; 231-933-0412; www. borders.com.)*

On the road downstate we always try to fit in a stop at **Blue Heron Café** in Cadillac, where locals flock for downright fascinating sandwiches on some of the North's best deli bread. Their big, chewy, chocolaty, nutty, crunchy cookies alone make us glad we live within 50 miles! *(Blue Heron Café & Bakery, 304 N. Mitchell St. Cadillac; 231-775-5461.)*

Cunningham's in Mackinaw City is a locals' favorite where an occasional tourist wanders in by mistake. We go deliberately, however. Graydon became a fan the first time he ate there 30 years ago and lost his heart to the good meat loaf, green beans, mashed potatoes and gravy. He still wouldn't dream of lunch anywhere else in town. *(312 E. Central Ave., Mackinaw City; 231-436-8821.)*

Chefs' Cookbook

This "Chefs' Cookbook" section has two purposes, reflecting the nature of the book as a guide both to restaurants *and* to resources for the stay-at-home chef.

As in the original *Connoisseur Up North*, chefs' recipes are our way of giving food-lovers a glimpse of what to expect from restaurants we profile. It's one thing to read that a restaurant serves, say, Chilean sea bass, but far more illuminating to read the recipe and know exactly how it's prepared. Even if you're not a serious cook yourself, this enhances your appreciation of the food, and the restaurant.

Our second purpose is to let the serious cook enjoy making at home some of the culinary delights our region has to offer. With this in mind, we are including for the first time numerous recipes that are *not* from restaurant chefs but from the farms and markets that provide Northern Michigan's food lovers with an increasingly wide variety of good, fresh produce, wine and cheese, bread and dairy products.

We are immensely pleased, for instance, to bring you the recipe for Grandma Julia Altonen's apple pie. Altonen Orchards is one of the many roadside markets Up North where farm families sell their produce, and we're grateful to our neighbor, Kristi Altonen, for providing the recipe.

Almost all the 130-odd recipes in this book are new. A few are repeats from *The Connoisseur Up North* that readers have said they enjoyed or (in a few cases) that we just like a lot.

Trends come and go, and we've noticed some shifts in the culinary trade winds since we began collecting and testing chefs' recipes in 1995. We see less Middle Eastern, Cajun and Southwest influence (except in kitchens specializing in them). "Comfort food" surged in the wake of 9/11 and the dot-com debacle, and now we notice heightened interest in Asian food beyond Szechuan and Thailand.

While we delight in our region's easy acceptance of global cuisines, we also hope to convey a greater appreciation of Northern Michigan's own rich and varied agricultural output. (Hey, if we enjoy foods of the Pacific Rim, what's to keep cherry cheesecake from making it abroad as a delicacy from the "Lake Michigan Rim?")

A few of our chefs' recipes call for unusual or uncommon ingredients, and we've tried to do some footwork for you. The spicy, South Asian condiment, sambal oelek, for instance appears in two recipes, and we tracked it down at Esperance in Charlevoix. Miso was elusive until we found it at Oryana in Traverse City (thanks to Kris Elbert of Torch Lake, a keen-eyed scout for our columns who provided valuable assistance on this book). Specialty food stores are good starting places for your treasure hunts, although supermarkets stock more sophisticated ethnic foods all the time.

Many of these recipes are startlingly simple, and we're sure you'll enjoy trying them. A few, on the other hand, are so stunningly complex, we almost omitted them. But, we decided, if a chef wants to strut, so be it.

Inevitably, some chefs sent recipes for immense, commercial quantities, and we had to do the math to cut them down to readers' size. We hope we got it right. (When our math yielded awkward results, such as 5/8 of an egg, we tried to check to be sure.) If we didn't get it right, please let us know about our error at the address below.

Since these are the chefs' recipes, we have left the instructions in *their* words when possible. We hope you take the same delight we do in their different styles. Some are control freaks, who specify what size spoon to stir with. Others are free spirits who simply say,

"Make a pan reduction," and trust you to know how. Whatever their styles, we are grateful to all who provided recipes. These are their trade secrets, and they have been *very* generous. When you dine in their restaurants, please thank them for us. We are thankful, too, for recipes received but not used. The reason was always editorial: We got six recipes, for example, for squash bisque, and decided two was all we needed.

We hope above all that we inspire you to take more time for good food, and to make room in your busy lives to enjoy it with friends and family. Life is short and we live it too quickly. Food doesn't need to be fast any more than cars need to be tasty, and meals shouldn't be an interruption of life. They *sustain* life! (Check the website *www.slowfoodusa.org;* if you can get past the politics, you might appreciate the message.)

Whether you wade right in and start whisking away in your own kitchen, or are content simply to let these recipes heighten your enjoyment of your favorite restaurant, we hope our Chefs' Cookbook will inspire you to go forth, eat well, and love life.

—*Sherri & Graydon DeCamp*
Elk Rapids, Mich., May, 2004

We acknowledge that error is not only possible, but likely. (We still laugh at a place in our first book where we dropped the slash and called for 12 cups of butter in turkey stuffing rather than ½ cup!) If you encounter error, please forgive us, but please let us know at PO Box 549, Elk Rapids, MI 49629, or by e-mail to DINING@BAYSHOREBOOKS.COM

Starters, Soups & Salads *

Latitude
Morels Stuffed with Ham Duxelles

Yields 25 Stuffed Morels

25	morels	½ C	sherry wine
2 T	butter	¼ C	flour
½ C	onion, finely diced	½ C	heavy cream
1 t	minced garlic	½ C	chopped parsley
12 oz	ham, finely diced	Taste	salt & pepper

Wash morels by immersing briefly in salted water. <u>Do not soak</u>. Agitate and drain. Remove and chop stems. Check insides of caps for insects and debris. Melt the butter over medium heat in a large skillet and add the onions and garlic and cook until onion is translucent, about 8 minutes. Add the ham and chopped morel stems and cook over brisk heat until mushrooms are tender. Add the sherry and reduce slightly. Stir in the flour and cook until it is absorbed. Add the cream and mix until smooth. Remove from the heat, cool, and add parsley. Adjust seasonings with salt and pepper. Pipe the mixture into morels, then bake in a flat pan at moderate heat until warmed through.

---

* *Many of our "salad" recipes are actually only recipes for dressings; we leave it to the reader to figure out what sort of greens are fresh and available and what sort of salad fixings they like.*

Folgarelli's
Fried Stuffed Olives
With Blue Cheese

Serves 6

36	**Sicilian olives stuffed with blue cheese**	**½ C**	**Progresso Italian bread crumbs**
½ C	**Folgarelli's imported olive oil**	**2**	**eggs (beaten well)**

Dip olives in egg and roll in bread crumbs. Heat olive oil in a large skillet and fry until lightly brown. Drain on paper towel. Serve warm in a wine glass, six per person.

Pearl's
New Orleans Style BBQ Shrimp
With Garlic Butter

Serves 4-8

Garlic Butter

¼ Lb	**butter, softened**	**¼ t**	**hot sauce**
1½ T	**parsley flakes**	**½ t**	**lemon juice**
¼ t	**salt**	**1½ T**	**minced garlic**
1 t	**Worcestershire sauce**		

Combine ingredients thoroughly. *(Use as needed; surplus may be kept refrigerated as long as any butter).*

Shrimp

16 Lg	**(21-25 ct) shrimp, shell-on**	**1½ T**	**unsalted butter**
1¼ C	**Worcestershire sauce**	**¼ C**	**white wine**

Heat a medium sized saucepan until hot, melt 1 T garlic butter, add Worcestershire and wine, and reduce to about one cup. Add shrimp and cook until opaque. Remove from heat and let sit about a minute, then stir in unsalted butter until smooth and serve immediately.

The Fish
Warm Shellfish Salad
With Bean Relish

Serves 18 to 24

Bean Relish

1 C	great northern beans	1 T	chopped parsley
2	cloves garlic	1 T	chopped chive
1	sprig each of rosemary, thyme	1 t	chopped rosemary
2	bay leaves	1 t	chopped thyme
5	black peppercorns	2 T	canola or other salad oil
2 T	diced red bell pepper	2 T	white balsamic vinegar
2 T	diced yellow bell pepper	1 t	salt
2 T	diced green onion	Taste	fresh ground black pepper
2 T	diced poblano pepper		

Sort beans, looking for stones. Rinse, then soak overnight in plenty of water. Make a sachet of garlic, rosemary, thyme, bay leaves and peppercorns wrapped in cheesecloth (or coffee filter) and tied closed with twine. Put beans, sachet, and plenty of fresh water in pot. Cover pot, bring barely to a simmer (but never a boil) and simmer until beans are just soft. Discard the sachet. Drain the beans and cool them in the refrigerator. Toss cooled beans with remaining ingredients and refrigerate overnight. (*It's okay to use canned beans, but do not substitute dried herbs.*)

Salad

1 Lb	mixed greens	1 Lb	calamari, sliced
1 T	chopped parsley	1½ Lb	pound shrimp
1 T	chopped chives	1¼ C	lemon juice
1 t	chopped rosemary	½ C	good olive oil
1 t	chopped thyme	1 T	minced garlic
1 Lb	mussels	Taste	salt and pepper

Sort and rinse mussels, discarding any that are open. Sauté garlic in olive oil for one minute over low heat. Add mussels and cook for one minute, until they just begin to open. Add shrimp and cook for 1 minute. Add lemon juice, increase heat to high, and add calamari. Place mixed greens in serving bowls and top with bean relish. Check shellfish for doneness (the calamari needs only to warm up). Discard any mussels that do not open. Add chopped fresh herbs and season to taste with salt and pepper. Pour over greens and serve immediately.

Leelanau Cheese Co.
Anne's Croute au Fromage

Serves 8

½ t	olive oil	8 oz	raclette cheese, grated or
2	eggs, separated		thinly sliced
1 C	milk	1 C	dry white wine
1	clove garlic, minced	2	Lg. slices day-old dense
Pinch	salt, pepper, nutmeg		bread

Preheat oven to 425°F. Grease 8 x 8-inch baking dish with olive oil. Blend egg yolks in a bowl with milk, garlic, salt, pepper, and nutmeg. In another bowl, beat egg white until firm. Fold egg whites and cheese into yolk mixture. Pour wine into a shallow dish or pie plate and very lightly soak the bread, then put bread in bottom of the baking dish. Cover with egg-cheese mixture and bake 10 to 15 minutes until slightly puffed and golden on top. Serve immediately.

Chef Nancy Allen
Grilled Shiitakes on Skewers

Serves 4

16	large shiitake mushrooms	1½ T	mirin *
3 T	toasted sesame oil	1½ T	lemon juice or rice vinegar
3 T	shoyu or light soy sauce	2 T	toasted sesame seeds

* *Mirin is available at Esperance in Charlevoix (or substitute dry vermouth).*

De-stem the mushrooms and brush dirt from the caps with a damp paper towel. Mix the oil, soy, mirin, and lemon juice, and put in the mushrooms to marinate 30-60 minutes at room temperature. Grill the mushrooms until tender on each side. Sprinkle with toasted sesame seeds and drizzle with more of the dressing. Serve on individual skewers.

Hattie's

Thai-Style Scallops

with Cucumber Relish

Serves 8

24	fresh sea scallops (abt. 1 Lb)	6	cucumbers
3 T	olive oil	2 T	fresh cilantro
¾ C	rice vinegar	½ C	lime juice
½ C	sugar	1 T	jalapeños, diced
½ t	red pepper flakes	½	medium lemon
½ C	water	½ T	salt

Peel and seed the cucumbers and dice into half-inch pieces into a metal pan. In a saucepan, combine vinegar, sugar, red pepper flakes, water, and cut up lemon. Bring to a boil, then strain out solids and pour hot liquid over the cucumbers. Stir in the peppers and lime juice and chill overnight in the metal pan. Sauté scallops in olive oil and serve plated on top of cucumber relish.

Leelanau Cheese Co.

Leelanau Cheese Fondue

1	clove garlic, peeled and halved	14 oz	raclette cheese
		4 T	Kirsch
½ C	Riesling or other dry white wine	½ t	cornstarch
		Pinch	nutmeg
1 t	lemon juice	2 Lb	baguette or other crusty white bread, 1-inch cubed
8 oz	Swiss Emmental cheese, chopped		

Rub the inside of a stainless steel fondue pot with the garlic halves, then discard them. Add wine and gently heat about 5 minutes. Add the lemon juice and the cheeses and bring to a boil, stirring constantly. When all the cheese is melted, stir in the Kirsch and cornstarch. Season with black pepper and nutmeg. Stir to blend thoroughly. To serve, place the fondue pot over a flame and provide tongs or skewers for dipping bread in melted cheese. Stir as you dunk, to keep the fondue creamy.

Coho Café
Salmon Cakes
with Mango-Tomato Salsa

Serves 6

Mango-Tomato Salsa

2	mangos, chopped	2 T	chopped fresh cilantro
3	Roma tomatoes, chopped	2 T	minced jalapeño
¼	red onion, finely diced	2 t	honey
½ C	lime juice	Taste	salt and pepper

Blend all ingredients thoroughly and let marry, covered, in refrigerator for an hour.

Salmon Cakes

2½ Lb	poached salmon	2 T	diced red onion
4 oz	smoked salmon	2 T	chopped fresh cilantro
3 C	mayonnaise	2 T	Dijon mustard
1½ t	minced jalapenos	½ C	lime juice
1½ t	puree of chipotle pepper	¼ C	diced red bell pepper
1 T	minced garlic	1 t	salt
¼ C	chopped green onion	2 C	tortilla crumbs

Crumble salmon in a bowl and make a filling mix by blending all the other ingredients except the tortilla crumbs. Slowly add just enough filling mix to hold the crumbled salmon together. Blend thoroughly to make a uniform mixture of filling and salmon. Create cakes and dredge in tortilla crumbs to coat them. Sauté cakes until golden brown and warmed through. Serve with salsa on top or on the side.

North Peak
Cheddar-Porter Dip

Serves a Crowd

1 Lb	shredded cheddar	1 t	chopped jalapeños
12 oz	cream cheese	1½ t	green chiles
1½ t.	garlic powder	1½ t	chipotle
1½ t	onion powder	1½ t	parsley flakes
1½ t	white pepper	4 oz	porter

Blend all ingredients and mix well.

Red Mesa Grill
Black Bean Cakes
On Jalapeño Cream & Roasted Red Pepper Cream with Roasted Corn Salsa

Serves 12-15

Red pepper cream

2 C	heavy cream	½ t	salt
½ C	diced red bell pepper	pinch	cayenne pepper
2 T	vegetable stock	1 t	Worcestershire sauce

Roast diced peppers 30 minutes at 350°F, then puree in blender, adding a small amount of vegetable stock if necessary. Combine pepper puree and all other ingredients in a saucepan, bring to boil, reduce to simmer and cook until slightly thickened. Place in storage container and cool.

Jalapeño cream

2 C	heavy cream	¼ C	sliced jalapeños
½ C	green chiles	½ t	salt

Combine ingredients in a saucepan, bring to a boil, reduce to a simmer and cook until sauce begins to thicken slightly. Puree in a blender until smooth. Cool.

Salsa

1 Lb	fresh or frozen corn	¼ C	olive oil
1	red bell pepper, diced	2 t	Worcestershire sauce
1	green bell pepper, diced	2 t	Tabasco
3	small green onions, thin-sliced	¼ C	chopped fresh parsley
2 t	minced garlic	½ t	salt
2	limes (juice only)		

Spread corn on a baking sheet and toast at 350°F until golden brown. Let cool, then blend with other ingredients in a mixing bowl.

Cakes

1 qt	cooked, drained black beans	2 T	Worcestershire sauce
1 oz	minced garlic	¼ C	chopped cilantro
¾ t	salt	5	green onions, sliced
2 T	cumin	2 C	bread crumbs
¼ t	cayenne pepper	¼ Lb	butter, for frying
2	eggs		

Combine all ingredients except bread crumbs, and puree in mixer or processor. Add enough bread crumbs to make a stiff mixture, and blend. Form into 2-ounce patties on a tray of dried bread crumbs, and pan fry in butter until golden. Serve atop red bell pepper cream and jalapeno cream. Garnish with roasted corn salsa. (*These cakes can also be a main dish. Adjust portions and quantities accordingly.*)

Latitude

Portobello Fries

With Spicy Soy Dipping Sauce

Serves 8-10

Portobello Fries

4 Lg	portobello mushroom caps	Taste	salt and Szechuan pepper
2 C	rice flour		peanut oil for frying
4 C	club soda		flour for dusting
2	eggs		

Fill a fryer or heavy-gauge pot one third full of peanut oil and heat to 300° F. In a large bowl whisk together the flour, soda and eggs; don't worry if it's slightly lumpy. Cover and let rest 20 minutes. Slice away the mushroom stems and remove the gills with a spoon. *(Reserve the stems for another use!)* Cut each mushroom into 1-inch fries, toss them lightly in flour to coat, then dip each in the batter. Fry 3 or 4 fries at a time in the oil for one minute on each side, or until the batter sets. Remove with a slotted spoon and let drain on a paper towel. When all have been fried once, increase the temperature to 375° F and again fry each piece, 3 or 4 at a time, until golden brown. Remove and let drain on paper towel and seasoning generously with salt and Szechuan pepper. Keep warm. Serve with spicy soy dipping sauce.

Spicy Soy Dipping Sauce

1/3 C	soy sauce	1/3 C	sliced scallion
1/3 C	rice wine vinegar	1 T	sesame oil
1 inch	ginger root, peeled & thinly sliced	1 T	sambal oelek *
		½ T	chile oil

> * *Sambal oelek is a South Asian condiment—a paste of chiles and salt mixed with some combination of oil, vinegar and/or brown sugar. It is available at Esperance in Charlevoix.*

Combine all ingredients.

Pond Hill Farm
Escargots Au Champagne

Serves 6

18	canned snails, drained	1 t	minced shallots
2 C	Champagne or white wine	1 T	minced chives
18	large mushroom caps	1 T	minced parsley
½ C	butter	Taste	salt and pepper
1	Lg. garlic clove, minced		

Marinate snails in Champagne in a glass bowl, 3 hrs to overnight. Reserve marinade.

De-stem mushrooms and scoop out gills. Stuff each mushroom with one drained, marinated snail and enough butter to fill cap. Place in a covered dish with reserved marinade and bake at 350°F for 15-20 minutes. To grill, place three filled mushrooms on a foil square. Moisten with 1 T marinade, fold foil over into a triangle and crimp edges. Grill packets for 15 minutes. Serve with bread. (*Says Pond Hill's Sharon Spencer:* "*What makes this recipe special is that you do not need snail shells, plates or as many escargots per person. And if you have a snail-hater at home, you can substitute chicken.*")

Stafford's Weathervane
Smoked Whitefish Spread

Serves a crowd

4 oz	smoked whitefish	24 oz	cream cheese, softened
2	green onions, coarsely chopped	2 T	horseradish, squeezed dry
		Dash	lemon juice

Bone whitefish thoroughly, and coarsely chop flesh. Process in a blender or processor with green onion until fish is finely ground. Place mixture in mixing bowl and add cream cheese, horseradish and lemon juice. Blend until smooth. Chill in a bowl and serve with crackers.

Boathouse
Walnut-crusted Goat Cheese Medallions
On Belgian Endive with Pear-ginger Chutney and Beet Dressing

Serves 8

Pear-Ginger Chutney

4	pears, peeled, cored, small diced	3½ oz	crystallized ginger
½	medium red onion, minced	¼ C	granulated sugar
¼ C	golden raisins	½ C	apple cider vinegar
¼ C	dried cherries	1 t	ground cinnamon
		¼ t	ground nutmeg

Combine all ingredients in a medium saucepan and cook over medium heat, stirring occasionally, until most of the liquid has evaporated and the pears are tender but not mushy (30 to 40 minutes).

Goat cheese Medallions

2	goat cheese logs	2	eggs, lightly beaten to make a wash
2 C	ground walnut meat		
4 t	flour	4 T	vegetable oil, for frying

Cut goat-cheese logs into ½-inch discs (*use taut monofilament fishing line*). Toss them in egg wash, then coat with ground walnut mixed with the flour. Chill the coated discs, then lightly pan-fry them in vegetable oil until they soften. (*The Boathouse garnishes the plate with endive leaves tossed in an emulsion dressing of boiled beets, rice wine vinegar, honey, Dijon mustard and olive oil.*)

Pearl's

Andouille and Cheddar Grits

With Collard Greens

Serves 8-12 as appetizer

Cheddar Grits

2 T	butter	2 C	milk
¾ t	salt	1½ C	water
¼ t	pepper	½ t	chicken base
¾ t	dried thyme	¾ C	grits
3 T	minced shallots	¾ C	Cheddar cheese

Sauté butter, salt, pepper, thyme and shallots for 2 or 3 minutes in medium sauce pan. Add milk, water, and chicken base and bring to a boil. Add grits, stirring constantly, and cook until mixture is smooth and creamy (about 20 minutes). Add Cheddar cheese, and stir until melted. Keep warm.

Sausage and Collard Greens

1	bunch collard greens	3 C	water
4 oz	bacon, cubed	1 T	chicken base
¼	Lg. yellow onion	4 T	garlic butter *
¼ C	sugar	½ Lb	andouille sausage, bias-sliced
1½ T	Louisiana hot sauce		

  * *Garlic butter recipe on P. 141*

Trim stems from greens and julienne the leaves into half-inch strips. Crisp the bacon in a medium saucepan, then add the onion and cook until soft. Add sugar, hot sauce, water, and chicken base, and bring to a boil. Add the greens and cook until tender (about 35 minutes). Drain well. Melt garlic butter in a large skillet or sauté pan, add andouille slices, and cook until juices start to release. Add the collard greens and cook over medium heat until completely heated through. Reheat grits if necessary and divide onto small plates. Top with collard greens and Andouille. Serve immediately.

Chef Nancy Allen
Salmon Shao Mai

Makes 30 to 35 dumplings

1 Lb	salmon, cleaned, boned and cut in ½-inch chunks	2 t	soy sauce
1 T	sesame oil	2	scallions or chives, minced (incl. half the green part)
1 T	minced pickled ginger (or 2 t grated fresh ginger root)	2 T	cilantro leaves
1 T	Chinese rice wine or sherry	2 T	black sesame seeds (optional)
		50	3-in. round wonton wrappers

Pulse salmon in the processor with the sesame oil, ginger, rice wine, and soy sauce until it's almost smooth. Scrape into a bowl and mix in the scallions, cilantro and sesame seeds. Place a tablespoon of the filling in the center of a wonton wrapper and bring the wrapper sides up, pleating it and pressing it a bit like an empire waist. This is an open-faced dumpling so don't close it off entirely. Keep the dumplings covered with plastic wrap so that they don't dry out. Set a steamer basket into a wok and fill wok with water to within one inch of the bottom of the basket. Pull the basket off and heat the water to boiling. Meantime, lay bits of cabbage or other leaves onto the steamer basket and arrange the dumplings on top of them. Place the basket onto the wok and cover it. Steam the dumplings for about 6 to 8 minutes. Serve with a dipping sauce made of soy sauce, molasses and rice vinegar.

The Rowe Inn
Pecan Stuffed Morels

Serves 8

1 Lb	morels	½ t	black pepper
½ C	butter	½ t	paprika
1 C	chopped onion	5 C	dry bread crumbs
1 t	salt	½ C	coarsely chopped pecans
1 T	melted butter		

Clean morels, trim and set stems aside. Melt ½ C of butter in large, heavy skillet and sauté onion, celery and chopped morel stems until tender and transparent. Stir in seasonings, bread crumbs and pecans. Stuff morels and set with points up on a buttered baking sheet. Drizzle with 1 T melted butter and bake 20-30 minutes at 350°F. Serve upright on chopped parsley or other greens.

Tapawingo
Scallop Ceviche
with Citrus Vinaigrette and Avocado

Serves 8

1 Lb	sea scallops, sliced thin (preferably hand-harvested diver scallops)	½	lime, juiced
		1 t	each of minced garlic, ginger and shallot
1	lime, peeled, juiced, chopped (reserve juice)	1 t	Dijon mustard
10 T	extra virgin olive oil	1 t	soy sauce
1 T	each of diced cucumber, red and yellow pepper, red onion	1	avocado
		As needed:	
1 T	each of rough-chopped basil and cilantro		salt and pepper; baby lettuce; thinly sliced radishes for garnish
1 t	minced jalapeño		
1	tangerine, juiced	**Opt.**	salmon or trout roe

Combine the scallop slices, chopped lime and its juice, diced vegetable, herbs and jalapeno. Mix in 4 T olive oil and season with salt and pepper. Keep very cold and let marinate 10 minutes. In a small sauce pot with 1 T olive oil, sweat the minced garlic, ginger and shallot until tender. Add the tangerine juice and bring to a bare simmer, then immediately chill. Put the cold, infused tangerine juice in a small blender with the mustard, soy sauce, and the remaining half a lime's worth of juice. Blend on low speed, then slowly drizzle in the remainder of the olive oil to form an emulsion. Season with salt and pepper. Dice the avocado and mash with a spoon, season to taste.

To plate
Use cold plates. Place three slices of marinated scallop in the center of each. Spoon about 1½ teaspoons of mashed avocado on top of each trio of scallops and offset another slice of scallop on top of the avocado. Scatter the diced vegetables on, among and around the scallops. Spoon the citrus vinaigrette around scallops and garnish with a few small lettuce leaves and radish slices. If you have the salmon or trout roe, spoon it liberally on and around scallops (*its saline flavor is a wonderful contrast to the tartness of the ceviche*).

Stubb's Sweetwater Grill
Grilled Shrimp and Seared Scallops
With Tropical Citrus Melon Salsa

Serves 6 or more as appetizer

12	sea scallops	2	limes
12	lg. shrimp (16-20/lb)	1	orange
½ C	finely diced fresh pineapple	1	red bell pepper, finely diced
½ C	finely diced cantaloupe	¼ C	roughly chopped cilantro
½ C	finely diced honeydew	1	jalapeno, minced
1	lemon		salt to taste

Peel, seed and chop lemon, orange and one lime. Starting with pineapple in a bowl, add chopped citrus, juice of the other lime, the diced melons, peppers and cilantro. Mix thoroughly and let the flavors marry 1 hour. Peel and de-vein shrimp. Wash and drain shrimp and scallops. Slice each scallop in half horizontally. When ready to serve, heat a lightly oiled, non-stick pan over high heat until very hot, and sear scallop pieces on both sides (keep finished ones warm if done in batches). Periodically wipe pan with a clean cloth. On the hottest part of a preheated grill, mark the shrimp on both sides then transfer to cooler part of grill to finish. Arrange shrimp and scallops on plates and serve with salsa spooned alongside.

Authors
Smoked Salmon Bisque

Serves 6

2 T	unsalted butter	1 C	Peninsula Cellars Pinot Gris
1	Lg. onion, coarse-chopped	3½ C	fish or clam stock
1	fennel bulb, ½-inch diced	1 C	half-and-half
1	Med. celery root, peeled, ½-inch dice	Taste	salt and black pepper
½ Lb	smoked salmon,* 1-inch pcs.		lemon slices for garnish

   * *At Sonny's Torch Lake Market*

Sauté onion, fennel, and celery root in butter on medium heat until crisp, (8-10 minutes). Stir in salmon, raise flame to high, stir in wine, and reduce liquid to about half a cup (6-8 minutes). Add stock and bring to a boil, then reduce heat and simmer, covered, until vegetables are tender. Strain out solids, reserving broth. Puree solids in batches in a blender, adding broth as needed for a smooth puree. Transfer to a clean pan, stir in cream, season to taste, and simmer 5 minutes on low heat. Serve in soup plates, garnished with very thinly sliced lemon rounds and sprigs of parsley.

Stafford's Bay View Inn
Great Lakes Chowder

Serves 10-12

1¼ Lb	walleye	5 C	cream
½ Lb	whitefish	6 C	diced white potato
¼ Lb	smoked whitefish	2 T	clam or fish base
½	leek, diced	1	bay leaf
½	Med. onion, diced	8 T	flour
4	strips smoked bacon, diced	Taste	salt, thyme, white pepper,
¼ Lb	butter		coriander, Old Bay

Skin, de-bone and dice fish. Mix base in 2 quarts of water to make stock and bring to a boil. Add potatoes and cook until just done, then remove, drain and set aside. Poach walleye and uncooked whitefish in the water, then remove and set aside. Add cream to poaching liquid and reserve. In a separate pan, crisp the bacon, add butter, leek and onion and cook until vegetables are transparent. Add flour and stir to mixture and cook at least 3-4 more minutes to make a roux. Bring cream-stock mixture to a slow simmer (keep heat low so cream doesn't break). Add roux mixture, a little at a time, to thicken the mixture. Add potatoes and fish. Season to taste.

Rowe Inn
Morel and Wild Rice Bisque

Serves 8-10

3	strips bacon	6 C	chicken stock
½ C	wild rice	Taste	salt and pepper
½ C	diced onion	½ t	thyme
½ C	diced carrot	1½ C	heavy cream
½ C	diced celery	1 T	minced parsley
¼ C	flour	1 oz	dried morels

Chop the bacon and sauté until crisp. Remove the cooked bacon and reserve. Add the rice and vegetables to the bacon grease and sauté until crisp but tender. Add the flour and stir and cook for one minute, then add the chicken stock and thyme. Bring to boil, and reduce heat, then simmer covered until rice is barely tender, about 30 minutes. Reconstitute the dried morels and drain and slice. Add the morels to the soup, and then the cream and heat through. Add the parsley, reserved bacon and salt and pepper as needed.

Stone House Cafe
Butternut Squash Bisque
With Asiago Croutons

Makes 5½ quarts

1	bunch celery, chopped	2-3 Lb	potatoes, peeled, ½-inch cubed
4	Lg. Carrots, peeled and chopped	2	pepperoncini *
2	Med. onions, chopped	4 t	coarse sea salt
3 T	olive oil or butter	16 C	vegetable stock
4-5 Lb	butternut squash, peeled, seeded, ½-in cubed	2 C	milk or half-and-half
		Taste	ground black pepper

* Can substitute 1 dried red bell pepper for the pepperoncini

In a heavy pan over low heat, cook celery, carrot and onion in oil or butter until tender but not brown (10-15 minutes). Add squash, potatoes, peppers and sea salt. Stir in stock, then cover and simmer until vegetables are tender (about 20 minutes). Remove pepperoncini and discard. Puree soup with an immersion blender. Add milk to desired consistency. Add pepper to taste. Serve in crocks, topped with toasted croutons of Stone House Asiago Bread.

Pond Hill Farm
Fresh Strawberry Soup

Serves 4

1 qt	fresh strawberries, hulled	1 C	red wine
1 T	cornstarch	½ C	sugar
1 C	orange juice	1C	sour cream

Reserve 4 slices of strawberry for garnish and puree in a blender all remaining ingredients except sour cream. Transfer to soup pot and heat just to boiling, stirring frequently. Remove from heat and whisk in the sour cream. Refrigerate, covered, until cold. Serve chilled with a dollop of sour cream and a strawberry slice in each bowl . *(The farm's Sharon Spencer says, "This is so pretty, it's a real treat as a first course at Easter. You can make it a day ahead.")*

Trillium

Corn and Crab Chowder

Serves 10

Stock

4	ears of corn in the husk	1	carrot, ½-inch dice
1	fresh thyme sprig	1	celery rib, ½-inch dice
1	bunch of parsley	½	white onion, ½-inch dice
1	bay leaf		

Soak corn in the husk in water for 3 hours and roast in the oven for 1 hour at 350 degrees. Once the corn is cool to the touch peel husk off and discard. With a sharp knife slice the corn off the cobs and reserve the kernels. Add the cobs to a 1-gallon soup pot with vegetables and herbs, submerge in 3 qt. cold water. Bring to a boil, reduce heat, and simmer 3 hours. Strain stock through cheesecloth and reserve. Discard solids. *(Hold refrigerated if not used immediately.)*

Chowder

2 qt	corn stock (above) or vegetable stock	8 T	crabmeat
1½ T	corn oil	1 C	heavy cream
1 C	chopped yellow onion	2 T	kosher salt
1¼ C	chopped carrots	1½ t	white pepper
1½ C	chopped celery	Pinch	cayenne pepper
1½ C	chopped green pepper	2 dash	bitters
2 T	minc ed garlic	2 T	chopped fresh tarragon
1 T	minced shallot	Garnish	chives and jumbo lump crabmeat
½ C	Dry Sack sherry		

In a 1-gallon pot, sweat onion, carrots, celery, green peppers, garlic, and shallots with corn oil. Add sherry and allow it to boil until liquid is reduced by half. Add crabmeat and salt. Pour 1-gallon of corn stock into pot, allow soup to boil, reduce heat, and simmer 1 hour. Stir in heavy cream, tarragon, cayenne, bitters, and white pepper. Taste and adjust seasonings. Garnish with lump crabmeat and chopped chives.

Andante
Smoky Butternut Squash Bisque
With Candied Pecans

Serves 10-12

Candied Pecans

3 C	pecan halves	2 T	rice vinegar	
¼ C	canola oil	Taste	sea salt, chipotle chili powder	
¾ C	brown sugar			

Toast pecan halves 20 minutes at 350°F. In a skillet, heat the oil, vinegar, and brown sugar enough to melt the sugar and get a little bubbling going on. Then add the roasted nuts and fold them in and stir for just a little bit, until they seem to have absorbed the liquid. Season, then pour onto a cookie sheet to cool, then try not to eat them all!

Bisque

8 C	butternut squash flesh	1 C	heavy cream
4 oz	unsalted butter	Taste	sea salt, chipotle chili powder, Liquid Smoke
4 C	chicken stock		Roux (optional
½ C	sweet Marsala	Garnish	Maytag blue cheese
1	sweet onion		

Peel squash, scrape out the seeds, and cut in 2-inch pieces. Peel and cut the onions likewise. Sauté onion first in the melted butter till translucent. Add squash and continue the sauté, stirring, until the mixture is really getting involved. Season with a little salt and chipotle. Add Marsala and stock, bring to a boil, then just simmer until the squash is very tender and fully cooked.

Strain the solids from the liquid, and puree in a food processor. Then join the puree back with the liquid, add the cream and reheat, stirring with a whip until almost back to a boil again. Check seasoning again, and add a drop of Liquid Smoke if you like. It really gives it an earthy, smoky flavor, combined with the flavor of the chipotle.

When the soup is almost at a boil again, thicken if necessary, with a little hot roux of equal parts flour and melted, unsalted butter, cooked a bit to eliminate the "raw" flavor. (*To cut a few calories, omit the roux and just let it be!*)

Check seasoning again to see if you want additional salt, chipotle or Marsala. then strain the soup through a wire mesh strainer and dish! Garnish with candied pecans and some Maytag blue cheese crumbles.

Wells Family Farm
Cracked Tomato Soup

Makes 1 quart

1 qt	**cracked tomatoes ***
1	**Med. onion, diced**

Taste salt

Core the tomatoes but leave the skins on. Combine with diced onion and process in batches in a blender to make a smooth mixture. Add salt to taste and simmer in a saucepan for two hours. When ready to serve you can, if you wish, add one or two dollops of sour cream for a creamy soup.

* Cracked and split tomatoes might not look pretty, but they're still good, so Phyllis and Mike Wells sell theirs at half price at their roadside stand in Williamsburg. Cracked tomatoes are good for canning of freezing if done right away. One year the Wellses had so many cracked tomatoes, they started using them to make this soup for themselves. Phyllis freezes it in 12-oz. containers. "With good bread," she said, "that makes a nice winter lunch for two. We're always surprised at the taste of summer in the middle of the winter!"

Authors
Cucumber Soup
With Tomato, Onion and Dill Garnish

Serves 6

1 T	**butter**	**2**	**garlic cloves, minced**
1	**Med. onion, diced**	**3 T**	**white wine vinegar**
4	**cucumbers, peeled, seeded and diced**	**Taste**	**salt, pepper**
1	**Sm. potato, peeled, diced**	**Garnish**	**seeded & chopped tomato;**
1½ C	**chicken broth**		**chopped green onion;**
1½ C	**sour cream or yogurt**		**chopped dill**

In a 2-qt. saucepan, sauté onion in butter until soft, add potato, cucumber and broth and cook over medium heat until potato is fork-tender. Let cool, then combine all ingredients in a blender and puree until smooth and creamy. Chill. Serve in bowls sprinkled with tomato pieces, dill and green onion.

Stone House Cafe
Farmhouse Cheddar Soup

Serves 8-10

½	stick butter	1	large russet potato, diced
6	scallions	1 C	milk or half-and-half
3	celery stalks, diced	½ Lb	grated Cheddar
2	carrots, diced	1 t	Tabasco
¼ C	all-purpose flour	1 t	Worcestershire
5 C	unsalted chicken or veg. stock	Taste	salt

Melt butter and sauté vegetables until soft. Add flour and cook 5 minutes. Add stock, 1 cup at a time. Add potato and cook 20 minutes. Puree or leave chunky (your option). Whisk in milk, cheese, and Tabasco and Worcestershire. Salt to taste. Serve with a sweet baguette from Stone House Bread.

North Peak
White Cheddar and Ale Soup

Serves 15-20

2 C	sliced yellow onions	¼ C	vegetable base
1 C	sliced carrots	2 T	chicken base
1 C	diced celery	1½ C	heavy cream
¼ C	fresh thyme, stems and leaves, chopped	2 C	milk
		1½ C	flour
2 T	minced garlic	1 stick	butter
1	bay leaf	8 C	white cheddar cheese
2 C	North Peak Golden Ale	Taste	salt and white pepper
3 qt	water		

Melt butter in stock pot. Add onions, carrots, and celery and sauté until translucent. Add flour and cook on low heat for 10 minutes, stirring constantly. Add thyme, garlic, bay leaf, and white pepper and cook five more minutes. Add ale, water, bases, heavy cream, and milk to the mixture and bring just to a boil. Puree and strain. Add cheese and puree until smooth.

Chef Nancy Allen
Creamy Carrot Soup
With Porcini Mushroom Garnish

Serves 8 to 10

¼ C	extra virgin olive oil	3½ C	boiling water
2	large onion, finely diced	Taste	salt and pepper
13 C	finely diced carrots		
2	garlic cloves, minced		

Heat the olive oil in a soup pot, and add the onion and soften over moderate heat. Add the carrots and cook. When they begin to soften, add the garlic and water. Bring the soup to a boil and then lower to a simmer and cook until the carrots are very soft. Remove the soup from the heat and either puree with an immersion blender, or strain the vegetables from the liquid and puree them in a blender, adding only as much liquid as you need to facilitate pureeing. Pour the puree back into the cooking liquid and stir. Reheat and season to taste with salt. Serve soup in bowls with a tablespoon of porcini garnish (below). Alternatively, garnish with a dollop of sour cream or a few tablespoons of cream and some chopped chives or parsley.

Porcini Garnish

1 oz	dried porcini mushrooms	2 T	unsalted butter
1 C	Marsala		

Rinse dried mushrooms briefly to remove any sand. Break up the porcini into smaller bits and simmer them in a small saucepan with the wine until wine is reduced by half and is syrupy. Remove from heat and while still hot, whisk in butter and season to taste. Ladle the soup into bowls and top with a spoonful of the mushrooms.

Monte Bianco
Panzanella

Serves 4-6 (but you won't use all the dressing)

Dressing

¼ C	red wine vinegar		½ t	fresh thyme, chopped
1 t	balsamic vinegar		¼ t	lemongrass, chopped
1 T	dry white wine (or red)		2/3 C	extra virgin olive oil
½ t	fresh marjoram, chopped			

Combine vinegars and wine and whisk in herbs, salt and pepper to taste. Slowly whisk in oil to emulsify.

Panzanella

Cut bread in small chunks. Thinly slice cucumber and scallion. Cut tomatoes in thin

1	day-old loaf of Italian bread		15	fresh basil leaves
1	small English cucumber		2	yellow tomatoes
1	small red pepper		2	red tomatoes
6	scallions, sliced			

wedges. Julienne the pepper and basil leaves. Combine all in a salad bowl, toss with dressing, and serve.

Sage Meadow Farm
Chinese Noodle Salad

Serves 8

6-8 C	lettuce and cabbage, finely chopped	**½ C**	slivered almonds, toasted
¼ Lb	snow peas or sugar snaps, cut in 2-3 pieces	**3**	green onions, thinly sliced
		1 pkg	ramen noodle soup mix
			Optional: cilantro

Oven-toast the almonds 5- to 10 minutes at 350°F. Coarsely crush the noodles from the soup mix and reserve the seasoning packet. Combine all in a bowl. Toss with dressing below.

Dressing

1/3 C	seasoned rice vinegar	**1/8 t**	black pepper
2 T	granulated sugar	**1 T**	toasted sesame oil

Mix vinegar, sugar, black pepper and soup seasonings, then vigorously whisk in the sesame oil. Pour on the salad, toss gently, and let stand 30 minutes before serving. Garnish with cilantro, if desired, just before serving.

Red Mesa Grill
Argentina Skirt Steak Salad
With Smoked-Tomato Ranch Dressing and Smoked Pinto Salsa

Serves 6

Dressing

1 C	prepared ranch dressing		1 t	mesquite seasoning
¼ C	mayonnaise		¼ C	finely diced tomato
2 T	western French dressing			

Blend ingredients thoroughly in a mixing bowl. (*Mesquite seasoning can be found in specialty food shops; use your own favorite ranch and western French dressing*).

Salsa

1 Lb	pinto beans		¼	green bell pepper, diced
1½ oz	Crisco or lard		¼	poblano pepper, diced
1½ C	chopped onion		1	jalapeño, minced
1½ T	salt		1½ t	Worcestershire
2 T	minced garlic		1 T	fresh lime juice
3	green onions, sliced thin		1 T	olive oil
¼	red bell pepper, diced		3 T	dried parsley flakes

Soak beans overnight, then put in a colander or perforated container and smoke for 30 minutes over hickory. Transfer to a stock pot and stir in lard, chopped onion, garlic, 1 T of salt and 3 cups of water. Simmer until tender. Drain, cool, and blend thoroughly with remaining ingredients

Steak

1	skirt or flank steak		½ C	dry red wine
1 C	olive oil		6	garlic cloves, crushed
½ C	soy sauce			

Mix marinade well; puncture steak with fork and marinate overnight, then char-grill to medium rare. Slice very thin. Keep warm.

Salad

½ C	chopped green bell pepper		½	onion, chopped
2	heads romaine			

Sauté onion and pepper. Wash, dry and chop lettuce, and toss with dressing. Arrange on large plates, and top with pepper and onion, smoked pinto salsa, and slices of steak. Finish with tortilla crisps.

Chef Nancy Allen
Maple City Shiitake Dressing

Makes 12 oz.

1 T	Dijon mustard	3 oz	stemmed shiitake mush-rooms, finely diced
4 T	rice vinegar		
3 T	shoyu or soy sauce	3 oz	toasted sesame oil
5 oz	canola oil		

Pour the mustard, vinegar and shoyu into a blender or processor and puree briefly. Heat a little canola oil in a small saucepan and cook the mushrooms over moderate heat until soft, then remove from heat and let cool slightly. Scrape the mushrooms into the blender and puree with the mustard mix for a few seconds. Then add the remaining canola and the sesame oil in a slow stream while the blender is running, to make an emulsion. Taste and adjust as needed.

The House
Thai Lime dressing

Makes 1½ cups

1	large garlic clove, smashed	1 T	tamari or soy sauce
1	scallion, chopped	½ T	granulated sugar
6	basil leaves, chiffonade	1 oz	lime juice
1 t	minced jalapeño	2 oz	canola oil
1 oz	rice wine vinegar	1 T	sesame oil

In a blender, macerate all ingredients except the oil to form a paste (add a few drops of water if necessary). Continue blending and slowly add oils to make an emulsion. Season to taste. (*The House uses this on a salad of seared tuna, soba noodles, vegetable Julienne, mango, and black sesame seeds.*)

Andante
Poppyseed Vinaigrette

Makes approx. 1 qt.

½ C	rice vinegar		½ C	mirin *
6	cloves garlic		¼ C	sugar
2	shallots		1 t	Chinese mustard powder
2 t	whole grain mustard		1 t	poppy seeds
2 t	Dijon mustard		1½ C	canola oil
2 t	sea salt		½ C	extra virgin olive oil
1 t	black pepper			

* *Mirin is available at Esperance in Charlevoix, or substitute dry vermouth*

Put all ingredients except oils and poppy seeds into a food processor, and pulse several times to mix thoroughly. Then, with machine running, slowly add the oils through the feed tube to make an emulsion. Finally, add the poppy seeds and pulse a few times to mix them in well. (*Andante's Bob Stark says this is an "excellent 'fusion' dressing for a salad of mixed organic field greens, candied pecans, plumped dried cherries, crumbled feta, and sliced Fuji apple.*)

H. O. Rose Room, Perry Hotel
Cherry Vinaigrette

Makes 1 Pint of Dressing

¾ C	oil		¼ C	sugar
½ C	heavy cream		¼ C	sweet, dark cherries, pitted
¼ C	raspberry vinegar			

Puree cherries. Whip sugar and vinegar until sugar dissolves. Add cream and whip until mixture starts to thicken. While continuing to whip, slowly drizzle in the oil until fully incorporated. (*The Perry's H. O. Rose Room serves this on a salad of greens topped with fruit, nuts and sliced green onion, and sprinkled with freshly ground black pepper.*)

Timmerin

Sarah's Sherry Vinaigrette

Makes 3 cups

1 C	sherry *	¾ C	Champagne vinegar
3½ T	Dijon mustard	¾ C	olive oil
1½ T	good quality honey	¾ C	safflower or other salad oil
1	shallot, peeled	Taste	kosher salt and black pepper

* Not cooking sherry, which contains additional sodium

In a small saucepan, reduce sherry by half. Transfer reduced sherry to a blender and add the mustard, honey, shallot, and vinegar. Season with Kosher salt and cracked black pepper and allow the mixture to steep for a few minutes while the sherry cools. Turn on the blender, open the top, and slowly drizzle in the salad oil, beginning drop by drop until emulsification begins, and continuing to add oil slowly. Taste on a piece of lettuce and adjust seasoning. Strain and refrigerate.

Chef Tim White: "Sous Chef Sarah Moseler created this simple vinaigrette. It goes well with a spinach salad with blue cheese and walnuts, maybe even some grilled onions. I've even had it at home as a sauce for wild king salmon and grilled chicken. It's really good and the recipe can easily be halved."

The House

Citrus Basil Dressing

Makes 1½ cups

½ C	chopped fresh basil (firmly packed)	1 oz	orange juice
		1 oz	lime juice
1 T	Dijon mustard	2 oz	water
1 oz	heavy duty mustard	6 oz	blended oil
1 oz	lemon juice	Taste	salt and white pepper

In a blender, combine all ingredients except oil and blend until everything is well mixed. Then continue blending while very slowly adding oil to make an emulsion. *(This goes well with goat cheese, blanched asparagus, roasted corn, grape tomatoes, and mixed greens.)*

Main Dishes

Andante
Braised Lamb Shanks
In Rioja Wine Sauce

Serves 4

4-6	lamb shanks	2	sprigs fresh rosemary
1	large sweet onion	2	bay leaves, crushed
1	large carrot	4½ C	red Rioja wine
2	ribs celery	3 C	chicken stock
1	fennel bulb	¾ C	red wine vinegar
8	cloves of garlic, crushed	Taste	sea salt and crushed black
2	sprigs fresh thyme		peppercorns

Rough-chop the vegetables as for a mirepoix, and divide in two equal parts. Mix 1½ cups of the wine and all the stock in a saucepan to make a braising liquid, and start bringing it to a boil. Season the shanks with sea salt and pepper and dredge in flour. In pan large enough to hold them and the braising liquid, brown them on all sides in olive oil. Remove the shanks from the pan and set aside. In the same pan, caramelize half the mirepoix, stirring in a little unsalted butter. At the same time, bring the braising liquid to a boil. When the mirepoix is browned and seasoned, put the shanks back in and pour in the boiling braising liquid. Cover tightly with aluminum foil and braise in oven 3 hours at 350°F.

When finished, remove the pan from the oven and let cool, then remove shanks from pan. Strain the liquid and reserve.

To make the Rioja sauce, caramelize the remaining mirepoix in a little unsalted butter, season it, then add ¾ cup of red wine vinegar and the remaining 3 cups of Rioja. Reduce this by half and strain it into the reserved braising liquid. Bring this mixture back to a boil and season it. If you wish, thicken it by adding a little butter-and-flour roux.

At this point, says chef Bob Stark, "The addition of some sautéed wild mushrooms of your choice is nice. I like to present the shank on some roasted garlic smashed potatoes, with the sauce over, and some salsa romesco and some crispy leeks." The salsa recipe is on P. 214.

Dining In, Dining Out

Bech's Mustard
Grilled Herbed Rack of Lamb

Serves 2

Dry Marinade

2 T	chopped fresh rosemary		1 t	fresh ground pepper
2	large garlic cloves, sliced		1	lemon, zest only, finely ground
1½ t	salt			

Mix all ingredients in a small bowl.

Lamb

1	lamb rack of about 2 Lbs (8 ribs)		1½ t	Bech's Great Lakes Dijon
1	clove garlic, slivered		2 T	dry marinade (above)
			3 T	olive oil

Make small slits between the rib bones and insert garlic slivers. Rub meat lightly with olive oil, then brush on mustard. Lightly press dry marinade into mustard. Cover exposed tips of bones with foil and let stand at room temperature for at least 30 minutes. Grill, turning several times, until meat thermometer registers 140°F (about 25-30 minutes). Cut into individual one-rib chops to serve.

La Bécasse
Roast Venison
With Red Wine Sauce

Serves 4

1 Lb	venison		2	stalks celery, chopped
1 C	red wine		1	bay leaf
3 oz	cider vinegar		1 T	thyme
1	carrot, chopped		1 T	whole juniper berries
1	onion, chopped		1 T	whole coriander

Combine ingredients and marinate meat in the refrigerator for 48 hours. Remove meat from marinade, reserving marinade. Dry meat and sauté until brown, then roast in oven at 350°F until done as desired. Bring marinade to boil, reduce by half, adding additional wine and seasoning to taste. Use as sauce.

Tapawingo
Smoked Bacon Wrapped Pork Loin
With Caramelized Apples and Onions

Serves 6

Apple Cider Brine

1 qt	apple cider		2	cloves
½ C	salt		2	bay leaves
½ C	brown sugar		3	garlic cloves, crushed
1 T	ground cinnamon		2 t	orange zest (no pith)
4	star anise			

Combine all ingredients for the brine.

Pork

1	pork loin, trimmed		1	Med. onion, coarse chop
	sliced smoked bacon as needed		Taste	butter, brown sugar, salt, pepper
1	apple, peeled, cored, sliced			

Submerge the pork loin in the brine and refrigerate 3 hours. Remove pork loin from the brine and pat dry with paper towel.

On parchment paper, overlap slices of bacon the width of the pork loin. Carefully roll the pork loin in the bacon and tie with string, using the parchment to hold the bacon in place until it's tied. Place the pork loin seam side down in the center of a roasting pan. Roast at 375°F for 30-35 minutes or until the internal temperature of the pork loin reaches 153°F. Remove pork loin from the roasting pan and rest for 15 to 20 minutes before slicing. Sautee the onions and apple slices in butter and sugar to caramelize. Season to taste and use as garnish on the plated roast.

Trillium
Veal Medallions Boursin
On Sautéed Spinach with Red Currant Jus

Serves 6

Sauce

4 T	butter	1½ Lb	boneless veal loin
5 T	minced shallots	3 T	olive oil
2 C	red wine	¾ Lb	fresh stemmed spinach
4 qt	beef or veal stock	¼ C	white wine
1 C	red currant jelly	6 oz	Boursin cheese

Sauté 3T shallots in 2T butter and, when translucent, add red wine and reduce by half. Add stock and reduce as desired. Add red currant jelly and simmer over low heat. *(If you substitute beef broth, thicken it with a cornstarch slurry instead of reducing it.)*

Veal and spinach
Cut veal into 2-oz medallions. Bring oil to high heat in a large sauté pan, add veal, brown both sides, and cook until done. Remove veal from pan and set aside. Add remaining shallots and butter to pan and, when hot, add spinach leaves and sauté lightly. Add white wine and stir to deglaze pan, and remove pan from heat.

Presentation
Divide Boursin in four equal pieces and pound each to a flat disk (it helps if cheese is between sheets of parchment paper). Pour 2-3 ounces of sauce in center of each plate. Arrange sautéed spinach on sauce. Place Boursin disks on spinach, and shingle the veal on top.

Douglas Lake Bar & Steakhouse
New Zealand Rack of Lamb

Serves 4

1	lamb rack, 2-3 Lb	2 T	oregano
8	garlic cloves	2 T	thyme
1	onion	2 T	basil
4 T	Dijon mustard	½ C	red wine vinegar
3 T	salt	½ C	balsamic vinegar

Make a marinade of last 9 ingredients. Marinate lamb 12 hours. Wrap bones in foil and grill to medium-rare or medium.

Leelanau Country Inn
Braised Beef Short Ribs

Serves 4

4 Lb	meaty beef short ribs	2 t	basil leaf
2 t	thyme	1	large onion, 1/8-inch sliced
2 t	whole oregano	4	Lg. tomatoes, poached and
2 t	black pepper, coarsely		skinned
	ground	1 C	water

Preheat oven to 350°F. Put ribs in a casserole. In a small mixing bowl, combine thyme, oregano, basil and pepper, and sprinkle mixture over the ribs. Cover the seasoned ribs with onion slices and bake, uncovered, for 20 minutes. Meanwhile, poach and skin the tomatoes. Remove ribs from oven and crush the tomatoes over them by hand. Reduce oven temperature to 250°F. Add water to casserole, cover, and return to oven for 4 hours. To serve, divide ribs evenly on four plates and top with tomato and onion. (*The Inn suggests serving this with half a cup of rice pilaf alongside.*)

The New York
Roast Pork or Veal Loin
With Dried Cherry and Wild Rice Stuffing

Serves 6

1	center-cut loin of veal or pork	2 T	minced shallots or onion
1 C	breakfast sausage	Taste	salt, pepper
1 C	cooked wild rice	Taste	chopped rosemary, thyme,
½ C	dried cherries		parsley

Butterfly the loin (or ask butcher to). Preheat oven to 400°F. Pound meat between layers of Saran wrap until evenly flat. Combine the remaining ingredients in a bowl and lay along the center of the butterflied loin. Fold the meat, tube-like, over the stuffing and tie with butcher's twine. Roast for 45 minutes at 400°F. Remove from oven and let rest on a platter or cutting board while you make a pan gravy with the fat and juices in the roasting pan.

Walloon Lake Inn
Rib Veal Chop
With Three-mushroom Stuffing

Serves 4

4	10-ounce veal rib chops	6 oz	portobellos, chopped
1 T	chopped fresh thyme	2 T	butter
2 T	chopped shallots	3 T	brandy
6 oz	shiitakes, chopped	Taste	olive oil, salt, pepper
6 oz	morels, chopped		

Preheat oven to 350°F. Sauté thyme and shallots in butter to soften. Add mushrooms and cook until mixture is almost dry. Stir in brandy and let cool. Slit the veal chop on one side to form a cavity about the diameter of a silver dollar, and stuff with mushroom mixture. Salt and pepper the outside of the chop and sear both sides in a pan with some olive oil. Bake about 20 minutes at 350°F. Remove and let rest for five minutes before serving. (*We make this at home with a flour-thickened, sherried sauce of sautéed mushrooms and chicken stock. – Eds.*)

Old Mission Tavern
Sautéed Beef Tenderloin
With Red Wine, Rosemary, Blue Cheese and Pine Nuts

Serves 2

12 oz	beef tenderloin	3 t	blue cheese
2	Med. shallots, minced	2 T	toasted pine nuts, coarsely chopped
1 C	red dry wine		
1 C	chicken stock	3 T	butter
¼ t	fresh rosemary, fine chop	Taste	salt, black pepper

Slice tenderloin into four equal medallions. Season medallions with salt and pepper and sauté in butter in a pan to desired doneness (about 3 minutes a side for medium-rare). Remove from pan and set aside. Add shallots to the pan and soften but do not brown (about 3 minutes). Add red wine and reduce by half. Add rosemary and chicken stock, and reduce again by half. Stir in 1t of blue cheese and season to taste. Plate medallions. Pour sauce over them and sprinkle with pine nuts and remaining blue cheese.

Villa Ristorante Italiano
Ossobuco alla Villa

Serves 6-8

1 C	finely chopped onion	1½ C	beef stock (or canned broth)
2/3 C	finely chopped carrot	1½ T	honey
2/3 C	finely chopped celery	1½ C	canned Italian tomatoes,
¼ C	butter		finely chopped
1 t	minced fresh garlic	½ t	dried thyme
1	lemon, zest only	4	leaves fresh basil (or ½ t dry)
½ C	vegetable oil	2	bay leaves
6-8	veal shanks	3	sprigs parsley (or ½ t dry)
¾ C	all-purpose flour	Taste	salt, freshly ground pepper
1 C	dry white wine		

Pre-heat the oven to 350°F. Choose a heavy, tightly-lidded casserole just large enough to contain the veal in one layer.

Cook the onion, carrot and celery in butter over medium heat for 8 to 10 minutes until the vegetables soften and wilt. Add the minced garlic and lemon zest at the end. Remove from heat. Place in casserole.

Truss the veal shanks with butcher's twine (*to keep thickness uniform so meat cooks evenly*) and lightly flour them. Heat the oil in a skillet over medium heat and brown the veal on all sides. Stand the pieces side by side on top of the vegetables in the casserole. Tip the skillet and draw off nearly all the fat, then deglaze the skillet with the wine, boiling it for 3 minutes while scraping up any brown residue in the pan. Pour this reduction over the veal in the casserole.

In the same skillet, bring the broth to a simmer and pour into the casserole and add the chopped tomatoes (with their juice), honey, thyme, basil, bay leaves, parsley, pepper and salt. The broth should come to the top of the veal. If it does not, add more stock or water. Bring the contents of the casserole to a simmer on top of stove. Cover tightly and put on the bottom shelf of the oven and cook about 2 hours or longer, basting the veal pieces every half hour. When done, the veal should be very tender, some of it falling away from the bones, and the sauce should be dense.

Trillium
Hickory Smoked Pork Tenderloin
With Creamy Aged White Cheddar Cheese Polenta

Serves 4

1½ Lb	**pork tenderloin**	**2 C**	**pure maple syrup**
8 C	**water**	**8 oz**	**hickory or cherry chips ***
4 C	**salt**		

* available at Meijer or other supermarkets

Brine-cure the pork tenderloin for 12 to 24 hours fully submerged in a mixture of the water, salt and maple syrup. Soak the wood chips in water for 30 minutes prior to smoking. If using a smoker, follow the directions on the smoker. If using a grill, put the soaked wood chips in a disposable aluminum pan over the fire with a grill or slotted cookie rack over the chips. When smoke begins rising, lay the pork on the top rack and cover it loosely with aluminum foil. Let pork smoke 30 minutes. (*Chef Christopher Mushall says brine-curing makes pork safe if cooked to an internal temperature of 140°F. "If you still can't get over the pink in your pork," he adds, "feel free to cook the tenderloin to 165."*)

Creamy Polenta

2 C	**yellow grits or fine cornmeal**	**½ Lb**	**butter**
2 C	**heavy cream**	**¼ C**	**aged Cheddar cheese ***
1 C	**water**	**Taste**	**salt and white pepper**

* The Trillium uses Black Diamond 4-year aged Canadian White Cheddar (see below).

Bring water, cream, and butter to boil. Shred the cheese while you wait for the water to boil. With a whisk, slowly add the cheese and cornmeal. Once the corn meal starts to thicken, remove the polenta from the heat and whisk in salt and pepper.

If the polenta stays on the heat, warns Mushall, "It will jump out of the pan, making a mess. It will severely burn you if it lands on your skin; you will only make this mistake once and will forever understand why we call it 'Italian napalm.' In the South, polenta is called 'grits.' This is an altered version of my Aunt Marie's recipe that she and I made in Calumet, Michigan. In the Trillium, we use Black Diamond 4-year aged Canadian White Cheddar. The aging process lends a slight, granular crunch, similar to Parmesan Reggiano. It is a little costly, but worth the money. You may substitute Muenster, Asiago, Parmesan. You can also add roasted garlic or Gorgonzola to the polenta.

Presentation

Place a scoop of polenta in the middle of the plate. Slice the smoked pork on the bias and lay slices over the polenta. Garnish with sautéed vegetables. *Mushall likes to add baby spinach lightly sautéed with olive oil, garlic, and shallots.*

Grey Gables Inn
Braised Colorado Lamb Shanks
Hunter Style

Serves 4

4	16-18-oz. Colorado lamb shanks (hind shank)	1 C	red wine
	flour as needed	2 C	chopped tomatoes
		1 Lb	sliced mushrooms
3 C	oil, for browning	2	bay leaves
3	garlic cloves, chopped	2	fresh thyme sprigs
2	carrots, rough chop	4	carrots, cut into sticks
3	celery stalks, rough chop	4	celery stalks, cut into sticks
1	Med. onion, rough chop	2	Med. red onion, sliced
3 C	veal stock		

Preheat oven to 350°F. Lightly flour the lamb shanks. Place heavy-bottomed pot on stove over medium heat, add the oil to pot and when hot, add the floured lamb shanks. Brown all sides of meat and remove from pot. Drain most oil, and place all rough-chopped vegetables and garlic in the pot until well browned. Add the red wine, veal stock, tomatoes, mushrooms, bay leaf, thyme, and shanks. Bring to a boil and place the pot in oven uncovered. Cook shanks 2½ hours. If sauce reduces too much, add 1 C of water.

While shanks are cooking, roast the carrot, celery and onion in a separate pot for 30 minutes, with olive oil, fresh herbs of your choice, salt, and pepper. Cool and set aside.

When lamb is done, remove pot from oven and take out shanks. Remove excess fat from sauce and puree the remainder and season with salt and pepper. Arrange lamb on platter with whipped potatoes, pour sauce over lamb and garnish with reheated roasted vegetables.

Grand Hotel
Buffalo Tenderloin
With Wild Mushroom Salad

Serves 4

Wild Mushroom Salad

1 T	butter	1 t	curry powder
1	shallot, diced	2 T	chopped tarragon, parsley
1	clove garlic, minced	Taste	salt and pepper
1/3 C	sliced shiitake mushrooms	1/3 C	hazelnut oil
1/3 C	crimini mushrooms	1/3 C	rice vinegar
1/3 C	morels	½ C	olive oil

In skillet, over medium heat, melt butter and sauté shallots and garlic to soften. Add mushrooms, curry, herbs, and season to taste. Add oils and rice vinegar, combine thoroughly, remove from heat, and pour mixture into a bowl to infuse and set aside.

Blackberry Sauce

1 T	olive oil	2 T	soy sauce
2	shallots, diced	1 C	meat stock
2 T	pickled ginger	2 T	thyme
1 T	tomato paste	½ C	fresh blackberries
3 T	blackberry jam		

Heat oil in a saucepan, add shallots and ginger, and sauté for one minute. Add tomato paste, blackberry jam, soy sauce, meat stock, and thyme, and reduce by half. Remove from heat and strain. Adjust seasonings, add fresh blackberries, and set sauce aside.

Wild Rice

1 T	butter	2 T	pecans
1	shallot, diced	1 T	chopped basil
1 C	cooked wild rice	Taste	salt, pepper

Melt butter in a sauté pan over low heat and add shallots, wild rice, pecans, basil, and seasonings. Combine thoroughly and heat.

Buffalo

8	2-oz. buffalo tenderloin medallions	Taste	salt and pepper

Season medallions with salt and pepper, coat lightly with oil, and sear in a skillet over medium-high heat until medium rare. Lay medallions alongside plated rice and mushroom salad, spoon sauce over medallions and serve.

Chef Charles
Pizza Rustica

Makes a 9-inch pie

Pastry

2 1/8 C	all-purpose flour	2	large eggs, beaten
2 t	baking powder	1	beaten egg yolk to brush on
4 oz	cold salted butter		pastry

Combine the flour and baking powder. Cut in the butter until a fine crumb consistency is obtained. Add the beaten whole eggs to bind the crumb into a dough. Divide the dough in half, shape rounds and refrigerate for one hour.

Filling

4	large eggs, beaten		finely chopped
1 Lb	ricotta cheese	4 oz	ham, thinly sliced and finely
¼ C	grated Parmesan		chopped
½ Lb	grated provolone (or a blend of provolone and mozzarella)	8 oz	Italian sausage, cooked
		1 t	freshly chopped basil
		2 t	freshly chopped parsley
4 oz	prosciutto, thinly sliced and	Taste	ground black pepper

Preheat oven to 400°F. Finely chop the cooked sausage. Combine all ingredients well in a work bowl. Roll the dough rounds on a lightly floured surface. Place one half in the bottom of a 9- or 10-inch pie pan. Pour in the filling. Top with the second piece of rolled dough. Crimp dough edges together, pierce top with a fork to release steam and brush the top of the pie with the beaten egg yolk. Bake 15 minutes at 400°F, then lower heat to 325°F and bake another 35 to 40 minutes, until golden brown. Let stand at room temperature at least 30 to 45 minutes before serving.

This pie can be prepared several hours ahead and refrigerated before baking.

Chef Charles Egeler doesn't make this pizza at the restaurant. "I simply can't with our style of oven," he says. He makes it at home, he says, "for a luncheon or brunch entree accompanied by antipasto." The name is exactly what it implies: "Rustic Pizza." Egeler says he has used many variations for the filling, using different cheeses, and salami as one of the meats. Herbs can range from basil to oregano or marjoram. The parsley and ricotta with egg base for the filling is pretty standard. Some recipes use a yeast dough for the crust, and usually refer to the dish as "Torta Rustica."

T. J. Charlie's
John's Italian Chicken

Serves 4

4	8-oz chicken breasts		1 C	dry white wine
4	links sweet Italian sausage		4 T	cornstarch
4	cloves garlic		4 T	water
2 T	olive oil		1 C	fresh mushrooms
1 C	chicken broth			

In a heavy skillet, sauté garlic in olive oil. Remove garlic. Sauté chicken until light brown on both sides. Place chicken in casserole dish. Sauté Italian sausage until brown on all sides and arrange with chicken. Discard all but 4 T of pan juice and de-glaze with wine. Add chicken stock and bring to a boil. Turn heat down and thicken with a slurry of cornstarch and water. Simmer until sauce coats the back of a spoon. Season with salt and pepper to taste. Add fresh mushrooms and pour over the chicken and sausage. Bake 1 hour at 350°F. (*John Heeke suggests serving with rice pilaf and roasted red peppers.*)

Pond Hill Farm
Melon and Bacon Pasta

Serves 2

¼ C	olive oil		Taste	salt and pepper
1½ C	diced cantaloupe		½ C	crisp bacon, crumbled
¼ t	crushed red pepper flakes		½ C	fresh basil leaves, snipped
2 T	lemon juice and grated zest		8 oz	medium pasta shells, cooked and drained
3 T	grated parmesan cheese			

In a serving bowl, combine oil, melon, lemon and zest, cheese and spices. Let come to room temperature. Toss with hot pasta, then top with bacon and basil before serving.

Chef Nancy Allen
Flat but Flavorful Chicken
On Greens

Serves 4

4	boneless, skinless chicken breasts	2	Lg. ripe tomatoes, cored and diced
2 T	chopped fresh herbs	7 oz	mesclun greens
3 T	extra virgin olive oil	7 T	Italian dressing
Taste	salt and freshly ground black pepper		

Trim gristle and fat from chicken. Brine them if you wish. Butterfly chicken and then place one between two large pieces of saran wrap. With a wooden rolling pin, gently and evenly pound the breast until it is about ¼-inch thick. Repeat with remaining breasts. Toss them with the herbs and oil. Preheat a grill or grill pan. Salt and pepper breasts to taste and place them on the heated grill or pan. Cook the first side until you can see the edges of the breasts begin to turn opaque and the breasts develop grill marks. Flip the breasts and cook the second side until they're done (5 to 7 minutes total time). Toss the tomatoes and greens with dressing. Divide the salad among four plates and lay a grilled chicken breast on top of each. (*Allen designed this dish for the web-site* minutemeals.com, *and it became their most popular recipe.*)

The New York
Chicken Breast with Crab Stuffing

With Roasted Red Pepper Aioli and Corn and Potato Risotto

Serves 6

Roasted Red Pepper Aioli

¼ C	mayonnaise	½ C	minced garlic
¼ C	puree of roasted red peppers		

Combine ingredients and refrigerate until ready to use.

Crab Stuffing

1 Lb	jumbo lump crabmeat, drained and picked for shells	3	Lg. eggs
		1 C	breadcrumbs
½ each	red, yellow, green bell pepper, finely diced	1 t	chopped garlic
		½ t	Tabasco
8	green onions, thinly sliced	1 t	chopped oregano
½ C	Dijon mustard	1 T	chopped parsley
1 T	Worcestershire sauce	Taste	salt, pepper

Combine ingredients until wet.

Chicken

6	boneless breast halves, skin on	1 C	demi-glaze or sauce espagnole *(from specialty stores)*
2 T	olive oil or butter		

Cut a pocket in each breast, starting at the thick end. Be sure to cut evenly and go the full length of the breast. Stuff breasts with crab stuffing, using a spoon or a large pastry bag with no tip. Rub outside of breasts with oil or butter and bake at 400°F until done (20-30 minutes). While the chicken is cooking, prepare the risotto.

Corn and Potato Risotto

1 C	diced onion	1 C	fresh or frozen corn
1 T	butter	1 C	heavy cream
3 C	peeled, cubed russet potatoes	Taste	salt and pepper
½ C	dry white wine		

Soften onion in butter over medium heat, but do <u>not</u> brown; add diced potato and white wine, and reduce by half. Add the corn and cream and simmer until potatoes are cooked and the cream thickens (about 20 minutes). Season to taste.

Presentation

Spoon risotto in center of plate. Ring it with demi-glaze. "Shingle" chicken slices on top and drizzle with aioli.

Monte Bianco
Chicken Piccata

Serves 2

4	boneless, skinless chicken breast halves	3 T	capers
2 T	extra virgin olive oil	1	small lemon (juice only)
1 C	chicken broth	2 T	unsalted butter
1/3 C	dry white wine	¼ C	flour
		Taste	salt and pepper

Season flour with salt and pepper. Dust chicken breasts with flour mixture. In a large skillet, heat olive oil over medium heat. Add chicken and sauté about 3 to 4 minutes a side. Transfer chicken to a plate. Drain oil from skillet and deglaze with wine, then add broth, lemon juice, and capers. Add chicken to the skillet and cook about 3 minutes more a side or until thoroughly cooked. Remove chicken to a warm plate for serving. Whisk butter into skillet until sauce is slightly thickened, and pour sauce over

Bech's Mustard
Vi's Chicken

Serves 6

3 T	unsalted butter, melted	1 T	curry powder
1 C	honey	2½ Lb	boneless, skinless chicken thighs
4 T	Bech's Great Lakes Dijon mustard		

Place chicken thighs in a large baking dish. Whisk other ingredients together and pour over chicken. Bake 1 hour at 350°F. Serve with rice.

Rowe Inn

Pistachio Crusted Chicken

Serves 4

Mustard Cream Sauce

½ C	dry white wine		3 T	Dijon mustard
1	chopped shallot		1 T	chopped fresh basil
1 C	whipping cream			

Boil white wine and shallots in heavy saucepan over high heat until liquid is reduced by half. Add Dijon mustard and whipping cream and simmer until reduced to one cup and slightly thickened. Add the basil and season with salt and ground pepper to taste.

Chicken

1 C	shelled raw pistachios		1 T	chopped fresh rosemary
¾ C	dry bread crumbs, fine grind		4	chicken breast halves,
¼ C	Dijon mustard			skinless & boneless
2 T	chopped fresh basil		¼ C	clarified butter
1 T	chopped fresh dill			

Finely grind the pistachios in a food processor. Mix in the bread crumbs and place the mixture in a shallow dish. In a small bowl, combine the mustard and herbs. Spread the mustard mixture over the chicken breasts and then dip them into the pistachio mixture, coating completely.

Heat clarified butter in a skillet over medium heat and brown two of the chicken breasts until golden brown — about 2 minutes a side. Transfer chicken to baking sheet and remove any leftover nuts from skillet, then repeat browning with remaining two chicken breasts, adding more butter to skillet as necessary. Bake chicken at 350°F until cooked through, about 7 minutes. Serve with mustard cream sauce.

Chef Nancy Allen
Macadamia Nut Chicken Breasts
With Banana Chutney

Serves 6

Banana Chutney

2 T	butter (chop into small bits)	4	large, firm bananas
3 T	chopped, crystallized ginger-root	2 T	maple syrup or brown sugar
		½	lime, juice only
¼ t	cinnamon	Pinch	salt
1/8 t	cardamom	Taste	chopped cilantro (up to 4 T)

Peel banana and cut into ½-inch cubes. Heat a small saucepan over medium heat and add the butter. When it has melted, add the ginger and spices and cook 30 seconds, then add the banana, maple syrup, and 2 to 3 tablespoons of water. Lower the heat, cover the pot, and cook until the banana is tender, stirring frequently (about 3 to 4 minutes). Add the lime juice, salt, cilantro, and additional syrup to taste.

Chicken

6	boneless, skinless chicken breast halves	3	eggs
		Taste	salt and pepper
¾ C	macadamia nuts		oil and unsalted butter (for sautéing)
¾ C	fine dry breadcrumbs		
½ C	all-purpose flour		

Place the chicken breasts between two pieces of saran wrap and pound lightly with a rolling pin until they are somewhat evened out and flattened. Place the macadamia nuts with half the breadcrumbs in food processor or blender and pulse until finely ground. Mix the nuts with the remaining breadcrumbs in a shallow bowl.

Place the flour in a second shallow bowl. Lightly beat the eggs in a third shallow bowl with salt and pepper. Heat a heavy 12-inch skillet over medium heat. Meanwhile, one by one dip chicken into the flour, then the eggs, then into the nut-crumb mixture, and set on a plate.

When the pan is hot, add butter and oil and, when they're hot, <u>lower</u> the heat and add the chicken breasts. (If the heat is too high they will burn before cooking through.) Cook until golden and done, about 3 to 4 minutes per side. (You may also preheat the oven to 400°F and finish cooking the breasts in the oven after they are sautéed a perfect golden brown.) Plate the cooked chicken breasts garnished with a spoonful or two of the chutney.

Monte Bianco
Rollatini di Pollo

Serves 4

White Cream Sauce

1½ t	chopped garlic	Dash	nutmeg
1 T	olive oil	Pinch	white pepper
1½ pt	heavy cream	Taste	salt

Cover bottom of heavy pot with olive oil and sweat garlic over medium heat. Add cream, nutmeg and pepper, whisk, and reduce to desired consistency (it should remain fairly free flowing). Season with salt to taste, strain and reserve.

Rollatini

4	chicken breast halves (boneless, skinless)	4	thin slices mozzarella
1 t	olive oil	4	figs, sliced thin
4	very thin slices prosciutto	2 T	Gorgonzola, crumbled

Wash and dry chicken breasts and trim excess fat. Butterfly breasts and pound to about ¼-inch thickness. Layer prosciutto, mozzarella and fig slices on breasts, tuck in sides of breast and roll. Wrap securely in plastic wrap and chill until firm (at least one hour).

Pre-heat oven to 350°F. Unwrap breast rolls and bake in a lightly oiled baking dish until firm to touch, about 20 or 30 minutes. *(If necessary, tie breast rolls or pin them with toothpicks, then remove after they're cooked.)*

Heat white cream sauce in heavy skillet, stir in Gorgonzola , and cook over medium flame until cheese melts and sauce flows fairly freely. *(You can also add a little meat glaze to the sauce.)* Slice chicken breasts on diagonal and fan on warm plates. Pour sauce around edges of chicken.

Monte Blanco often serves this with roasted redskin potatoes and a steamed, fresh, seasonal vegetable. At home, we sometimes substitute very thinly sliced pepperoni for the prosciutto, and dried cherries for the figs. — Eds.

Chef Nancy Allen
Thai Red Chicken Coconut Curry

Serves 6

1 Lb	boneless, skinless chicken breasts		to taste
½ C	coconut fat skimmed from cold coconut milk	½ C	tiny cherry tomatoes
		6	Kaffir lime leaves
1 T	Thai red- curry paste, to taste	1½ C	cups mixed vegetables (e.g., snow peas, broccoli, bamboo shoots, carrots) cut in small, thin bite-sized pieces
3 C	coconut milk		
2 T	fish sauce (nam pla)	½ C	Thai basil or basil leaves, finely sliced
1 T	palm sugar or maple syrup,		

To get coconut fat, chill a can of sweetened coconut milk and skim the fat off the top. Trim all gristle and fat from chicken and cut the meat into bite-sized chunks and set aside. Heat the coconut fat in the bottom of a saucepan until the water evaporates and it thickens. Add the curry paste and cook for a minute or two in the coconut fat. Add the chicken pieces and stir-fry for 2 minutes to infuse the chicken with flavor. Add the coconut milk, fish sauce, palm sugar, tomatoes and the lime leaves. Add any non-green vegetables like carrots. Simmer until chicken is done, about 8 minutes. Add the remaining green or delicate vegetables and cook until just done. Scatter the basil on top. Taste and adjust the seasonings.

Garrett's on Water Street
Pan Roasted Pheasant Breast
With Black Currants, Sweet Potato, Root Vegetable Puree, Herbed Parisienne Potato

Serves 2

	thigh meat from pheasant carcass		with shallots and dry sherry, drained
3 oz	pancetta or belly pork, minced	3 oz	fresh, white breadcrumbs to bind
2 oz	stale baguette panada (soaked in 1½ oz cream)	Pinch	fresh chopped parsley
1 C	heavy cream	Pinch	rosemary
½ C	lobster mushrooms, cooked	Pinch	thyme
		Pinch	salt and pepper

Mousse

Separate thighs from carcass, and remove and discard thigh skin and bones. Mix meat with minced pork and sauté the mixture lightly until just cooked (*approx. 5 minutes*). Remove from heat and place in a food processor with mushrooms, herbs and bread panada. Process with 1C heavy cream for 5 minutes. Slowly add breadcrumbs to get firm consistency. Salt and pepper to taste. Set aside in refrigerator.

1	pheasant (4½ -5 lb.), dressed	½ oz	Cassis
6	strips lightly smoked bacon	1 T	Champagne vinegar
2 oz	clarified butter	2 T	honey
2 T	olive oil	1 T	sugar
3 C	reduced pheasant demi-glace	6 C	veal demi-glaze
1 t	chopped fresh thyme	2 C	mirepoix of onion, carrot, and celery
1 t	chopped fresh rosemary		
½ oz	Cognac		

Pheasant

Remove breasts from carcass and butterfly them. Spoon 2-3 ounces of mousse onto each and fold over to cover. Wrap each breast, mummy-like, in bacon slices (3 per breast should do). Brush with clarified butter and roast in oven for 10-12 minutes. Remove and crisp bacon under salamander.

Brown pheasant legs and all bones with mirepoix in olive oil in   oven. Remove and place bones and vegetables in heavy saucepan. Add veal demi glace and reduce by half. Strain and set aside.

In a saucepan, mix vinegar and sugar and reduce to caramel. Add pheasant glace and washed black currants. Cook 5 minutes. Add brandy and cassis. Cook 5 minutes more, then add fresh herbs and place sauce in processor to puree. Strain sauce, add honey and salt and pepper to taste.

Cont. at bottom of next page →

Old Mission Tavern
Chicken Breast Artichoke

Serves 2

2	6 ounce chicken breasts	4 oz	white wine
2 T	butter	1 t	chicken base
½ C	flour	1 C	heavy cream
8 oz	artichoke hearts	¾ t	ground fresh garlic
3	chopped green onions, white and green part	Taste	salt and pepper
3 oz	sliced shiitake mushrooms		

Dredge chicken in flour seasoned with salt and pepper, then sauté in butter until done but not dry (about 4 minutes a side). Set aside and keep warm. Add artichoke hearts, onions and mushrooms, to skillet, and sauté 2 minutes (add butter if necessary). Add white wine, chicken base and cream. Reduce until thickened. Plate breasts, spoon sauce over them, and serve with rice or linguine.

– Continued from previous page

Shred peeled sweet potatoes into long shards (use grater attachment on a food processor). Mold into bird-nest shape using a potato-basket mold. Fry at 325°F until golden. Set aside. Boil peeled, washed sweet potatoes (approximately 2 Lbs.) along with half an acorn squash and 3 parsnips until tender. Strain and season with 2T sweet butter, pinch fresh nutmeg, salt and white pepper. Place in pastry bag and set aside. Using a melon baller, take 12 perfect balls from two large peeled baking potatoes. Blanch in boiling water 8 minutes. Cool and then sauté potato balls in clarified butter until golden. Sprinkle with a mixture of fresh chopped parsley, rosemary, chervil and thyme. Drain. Salt and pepper.

Assembly

Place pheasant breast on cutting board. Cut into 5 equal-sized rondelles. Heap approximately 3 oz. of green cabbage confit in center of plate. Carefully lay pheasant slices across cabbage, using pastry bag to place a rosette of mousse between slices. Decorate by placing a turned mushroom cap on each rosette. Spoon strained sauce around pheasant. Place sweet potato nest on plate. Fill with root puree. Place seasoned potato bails on top. Garnish plate with cluster of fresh black currants, sprig of fresh rosemary, fried sweet potato frills and fresh watercress. Finish with glazed miniature baby vegetables.

Trattoria Funistrada
Duck and Mushroom Risotto

Serves 4

5 C	chicken broth	1½ C	Arborio rice
1/3 C	extra virgin olive oil	¾ C	Chianti or other dry red wine
1	medium onion, diced	½	cooked duck (or chicken)
8 oz	mushrooms, chopped fine	Taste	salt and pepper
2	cloves garlic, minced		

Bring broth to a simmer. Skin and de-bone the bird, add the bones to the stock. Finely dice the skin and meat separately. Heat the oil in a large heavy saucepan over medium high heat, add the skin and sauté to crisp (2-3 minutes). Add mushrooms and onions and sauté until soft (5 minutes). Add garlic and rice, stirring with wooden spoon for 2 minutes. Add wine and continue stirring until liquid is absorbed. Add a ladle or two of stock and keep stirring and adding stock as it is absorbed. After 10 minutes add the duck to the pot and continue stirring and ladling until the broth is exhausted (approximately 10 more minutes). Remove from heat and cover for 5 minutes before serving.

NOTE: Near the end of cooking start checking the rice for doneness; grains should remain intact with a small central "pearl" and a tender exterior. You can use a little water to finish if the stock runs out before the rice is finished. This dish should be too runny to hold a molded shape but firm enough to serve on a plate. Try using 2 cups diced turkey in place of the duck (or chicken).

Timmerin

Crispy Duck Leg Confit

Serves 12 as appetizer

The Cure

2 C	kosher salt	3	fresh rosemary sprigs
1½ C	granulated sugar	½	bunch fresh thyme
1 T	juniper berries	2 T	whole black peppercorns
1 T	whole cumin seeds, toasted	5	bay leaves
½ head	garlic	12	duck legs
2	shallots, peeled		

Pulse the juniper berries, cumin, peppercorns and bay leaves in a spice grinder, then place in the bowl of a food processor and add garlic and shallot. By hand, roughly chop the herbs and add them to the bowl. Pulse until the garlic and shallots are finely chopped. Transfer to a mixing bowl and mix thoroughly with the salt and sugar. This should be enough cure to do 12 duck legs. *(The cure will keep indefinitely in an air-tight container in the fridge.)* Layer the cure and the duck legs in a large colander or perforated pan, starting with cure at the bottom, and more cure between layers of duck legs, and cure on top. Put the colander in a bowl large enough to hold it and catch the fluid the cure will draw out. Refrigerate, covered, 24-48 hours.

Confit

2 Lb   rendered duck fat (check at specialty meat shops)

Preheat oven to 300°F. Remove the legs from the colander and discard the bowl of liquid. In a heavy pot or casserole, layer the duck legs and fat and put over a burner to melt the fat and bring it to a quick boil. Transfer the pan to oven and bake at least two hours, until the meat is fork tender and nearly falling off the bone. Remove from oven and let legs cool a bit before placing in a storage container. When the fat is cool, strain and pour it over the legs to cover them. This seals the duck from air to prevent spoilage. Covered in fat, the legs will last up to three months in the refrigerator. To serve, bring to room temperature to soften fat, remove legs and scrape off excess fat. Put legs skin side up on a sheet pan or sauté pan and roast at 450°F until heated through. You can use broiler for a few minutes to brown up and crisp the skin at the end.

Chef Tim White says, "We continually get compliments about this dish, which can be used with every season's accompaniments. It pairs perfectly with fruit sauces and gastriques; it can be shredded and added to white beans or mixed with wild rice. It's a lengthy process, but like all things comforting and soulful, worth the effort. While it is definitely not for the calorie conscious, the legs absorb less fat than you'd get by deep frying your favorite fish. The recipe works equally well with other poultry, such as chicken or goose. The cure smells wonderful. I sometimes omit the sugar and use the excess to season steaks for the charcoal grill at home."

Coho Café
Wok-seared Sesame Shrimp

Serves 8

Sauce

1½ C	sugar		1 C	pineapple juice
¾ C	cold water		1 T	cornstarch
1½ C	chicken stock		2 T	water to make a slurry
1 C	soy sauce			

Boil sugar and water in a saucepan to 250°F to create caramel. Avoid stirring. Slowly add chicken stock (be careful in adding liquid to hot caramel!) Let reduce by half (about 6-7 minutes), then add soy sauce and pineapple juice. Return to a boil and add cornstarch slurry to thicken.

Shrimp

1 T	sesame oil		2 Lb	shrimp, peeled & de-veined
1 t	chopped garlic		1 Lb	fresh spinach
1 t	chopped jalapeños		2 T	black sesame seeds
1 t	chopped fresh ginger			

Heat oil in a wok. Add the garlic, ginger and jalapenos to hot oil and sweat. Add the shrimp and cook until done. Add sauce and let reduce in pan for 3 or 4 minutes. Remove from heat and toss with the fresh spinach. Serve immediately, garnished with sesame seeds.

The Boathouse
Seared Sea Scallops in Prosciutto

With Asparagus Coulis, Balsamic Reduction, Sun-dried Tomato Ratatouille

Serves 4-6

Ratatouille

1	small white onion, minced	1 C	canned, diced tomato
2 T	garlic, minced	1 C	sun-dried tomato re-hydrated
1	red bell pepper, seeded and		in hot water
	¼-inch diced	½ C	tomato or V-8 juice
1	large eggplant, peeled and	8-10	large basil leaves, chiffonade
	diced	1 T	granulated sugar
1	large zucchini, diced		

Dice eggplant first, then sprinkle liberally with kosher salt and place in a strainer. (This removes bitterness, helps break down cell walls, and draws out the water which prevents it from soaking up excess oil.) Sweat the onion in 2 oz. of oil over medium heat, until translucent. Add garlic and sweat. Add bell pepper and cook for 2-3 minutes to soften. Add the zucchini and eggplant and cook 5-7 minutes. Add both the canned and the re-hydrated tomatoes and the juice, and simmer for 10-15 minutes until all vegetables are tender but not mushy. Remove from heat and stir in basil. Season with salt, pepper and sugar. (*This ratatouille works well as a pasta sauce and to accompany salmon, whitefish or scallops. It can also serve as a side dish on its own. Leftovers can be used in soup—a classic Italian minestrone, for instance.*)

Scallops

12-24	large sea scallops	6	very thin slices prosciutto

Thoroughly drain and dry scallops, so internal moisture won't cook them through before they brown. Wrap prosciutto around the sides of scallops and pin in place with toothpicks, leaving the flat tops and bottoms exposed. Pan-sear them on high heat, turning once, until opaque and lightly browned on both sides.

Sauce

To make the coulis, Chef Jim Morse purées extra asparagus stalks with chicken stock, cream, spinach and basil. He reduces the balsamic vinegar very slowly on low heat to avoid boiling. (*"This takes time," he says, but he adds: "The reduction has long shelf-life and is very versatile"*).

Terry's Place
Shrimp Scampi

Serves 4

6 T	unsalted butter, softened	½ C	dry white wine
2 T	chopped shallots	20	Lg. shrimp (21-25/lb)
2 T	chopped fresh garlic	1 lb	fettuccine or cappellini
2 T	chopped fresh parsley	Taste	salt, pepper

Cook pasta, drain and set aside. In a medium sauté pan combine 1 T butter, shallots, garlic, parsley and shrimp, and sauté over high heat for about 1 minute. Turn shrimp, add wine and remaining butter, and reduce slightly. Add cooked pasta and toss, making certain all butter has melted and blended thoroughly. Salt and pepper to taste. *(This is a generous dish, and you might find it serves more than four.)*

Poppycock's
Grilled Salmon
With Mushroom-Leek Ragout

Serves 4

Ragout

3	julienned leek whites	2 oz	sweet vermouth
2 C	cream	2 C	sliced mushrooms
1 t	minced garlic	Taste	salt, pepper

Heat leeks and mushrooms in a pot until they steam. Add garlic, vermouth, cream and simmer until cream thickens and vegetables are cooked (about 12 minutes). Season with salt and pepper. Keep warm, and spoon over grilled salmon.

Salmon

4	6-oz salmon filets	Taste	salt, pepper
1 T	vegetable oil		

Lightly oil filets, season with salt and pepper, and char-grill.

Whitney's Oyster Bar
Whitney's Shrimp
With Mustard-Chive Chantilly

Serves 4

Mustard-Chive Chantilly

1 C	heavy whipping cream	1 T	chives
2 oz	Dijon mustard	Taste	salt and pepper
2	egg yolks		

Whip cream until it starts to thicken. Add mustard, chive and egg yolks. Whip until very thick, and add salt and pepper. (*Chuck and Gina Whitney warn us that to get this right, you have to "whip forever, or until it is really thick."*)

Shrimp

20	Med. Shrimp	¼ t	black pepper
3 C	bread crumbs	4	eggs
4 oz	Old Bay seasoning	1 oz	heavy cream
½ t	thyme		

Peel and de-vein shrimp. Make a wash of eggs and cream and thoroughly dip shrimp in wash, then dredge in a mixture of bread crumbs, Old Bay, thyme and pepper. Sauté in hot oil over medium-high flame. Remove, drain on a towel, and serve with the mustard-chive sauce.

Funistrada
Steamed Mussels

Serves 2

2 Lb	live fresh mussels		½ t	dried basil
2 T	butter		12 oz	American-style lager beer,
2 T	extra virgin olive oil			divided
1	clove garlic, minced			

Clean and de-beard the mussels, discarding any that are hollow or don't close when tapped. Heat butter and oil in a heavy, 6- or 8-quart, lidded pot. Add the garlic and allow to perfume without browning. Add basil, mussels, and 2–3 ounces of the beer to the pot and cover. Enjoy sipping the remaining beer while you stand by and shake the pot every five or six minutes until the mussels are open. Discard any that refuse to open, as they are <u>nasty</u>. Serve with crusty bread to soak up the mussels' liquor.

Chef Tom Reay says the restaurant uses garlic-infused olive oil and skips the minced garlic part. "It takes about 45 minutes to infuse 3 liters of oil," he says, "and we don't have to worry about burning the minced garlic during the service rush."

Walloon Lake Inn
Rainbow Trout Hemingway
With Lemon-Brandy Butter Sauce

Serves 4

4	9-oz trout, boned		3 T	fresh lemon juice
6 T	butter		¼ C	brandy
2 T	chopped shallots		Taste	salt and pepper to taste
1 C	sliced mushrooms			

Preheat a heavy sauté pan. Add 1 T butter, and when it starts to brown, place trout in pan, flesh side down, and brown briefly (2-3 minutes). Repeat for all trout. Place all trout on an oiled cookie sheet and bake at 400°F until flesh is firm, about 15 minutes. Meanwhile, sauté shallots and mushrooms in butter, add lemon juice and brandy (use care in case the brandy flames). Season with salt and pepper and pour over plated trout. *(The Inn's David Beier says, "It is essential that the trout be fresh. By the time an Idaho trout makes it to Northern Michigan, it's too late.")*

Amical
Salmon in Phyllo

Serves 1

6 oz	salmon, skinless fillet	2 T	fresh basil
2	sheets) phyllo dough	¼ C	fresh spinach
2 T	bread crumbs	1 t	parsley, fresh chopped
1 T	Parmesan, grated	1 t	red pepper, diced, as garnish
2 T	butter, melted	Sprig	fresh herb, as garnish
1 t	basil pesto		

Slice salmon into two thin 3-oz. portions. Lay out 1 sheet of phyllo dough, brush with butter and sprinkle evenly with Parmesan and bread crumbs. Lay the other sheet on top and repeat the process. Pat the fish dry with a towel and place in the center of the sheets, one next to the other. Top with pesto, then chopped spinach & basil. Fold one end back over the fish and herbs, then brush with butter. Fold in the edges and wrap the other part of the phyllo around the salmon to form a package. Brush with butter and sprinkle with breadcrumb-Parmesan mixture. Bake 10-13 minutes at 350°F, preferably in a convection oven with the fan on. When finished, cut on the bias, plate and serve with a suitable sauce. *(See below.)* Garnish with parsley, pepper and herb.

Authors
Lemon Beurre Blanc

Serves 4

1 C	dry white wine	5	white peppercorns
1 T	chopped shallot	¼ Lb	cold, unsalted butter, cut into small pieces
½	lemon (juice only)		

In a saucepan combine wine, shallot, lemon juice and peppercorns. Bring to boil and reduce liquid to about 2 T. Remove the pan from heat. Strain out solids and discard. Over <u>low</u> heat, whisk in butter a few pieces at a time to form a smooth emulsion.

Stubb's Sweetwater Grill

Broiled Walleye

With Basil and Pistachio Pesto

Serves 4

Pesto

¼ lb	fresh basil	1 oz	Parmesan cheese
2 oz	pistachio nuts	2 oz	extra virgin olive oil
1 oz	roasted garlic	1/8 t	cayenne pepper
1 t	fresh garlic	Taste	salt and freshly cracked black
1 T	balsamic vinegar		pepper

Place all pesto ingredients except oil in a processor and pulse until mixture is a coarse puree. Slowly drizzle in the oil while continuing to process until mixture is emulsified.

Walleye

4	6-oz walleye filets	4 oz	white wine
½ C	fresh bread crumbs	6 oz	chicken stock
¼ C	Parmesan cheese		

Preheat oven to 400°F. Combine wine and stock for use as broiling liquid. Scale walleye filets and remove all pin bones. Place filets, skin side down, in a large, lightly buttered, broiling pan. Avoid any overlap. Spread pesto liberally and evenly over filets, then sprinkle with bread crumbs and Parmesan. Carefully add wine-stock mixture to pan, using just enough to cover the bottom of the pan and the sides of the fish, but not the tops. Place pan in oven at 400F for about 8 minutes, then place under low-broil flame until coating is golden and fish is fully cooked.

Rowe Inn
Roasted Sea Bass Provençal

Serves 4

¼ C	oil-packed sun-dried toma-toes, chopped and drained (reserve 2 T of the oil)	1 T	minced fresh thyme (or 1½ t dried)
		½ C	dry white wine
2 T	drained capers	½ C	bottled clam juice
I T	chopped garlic	4	7 oz sea bass fillets

Preheat oven to 450°F. Heat 2 T reserved tomato-packing oil in a large, heavy, oven-proof skillet over medium-high heat. Add tomatoes, capers, garlic and thyme and cook, stirring, for 1 minute. Add wine and clam juice and boil until liquid is reduced almost to a glaze, about 3 minutes. Sprinkle fish with salt and pepper. Add to skillet; turn to coat with sauce. Place skillet in oven. Roast until fish is just opaque in center (about 15 minutes). Transfer fish and sauce to platter.

Andante
Grilled Chilean Sea Bass
With Miso-Citrus Marinade

Serves 4

4 pcs	Chilean sea bass or other fish for grilling	2 T	sugar
		½ C	white miso
¼ C	sake	1 T	minced ginger root
¼ C	ponzu*		

*Ponzu is a combination of lemon juice, soy sauce and sake

All ingredients into food processor bowl except oil and fish Oil drizzled in through the feed tube with the machine running. Marinate fish in the mixture, refrigerated, over-night. Grill fish.

Chef Bob Stark says this "makes for a lacquered-type, crispy crust, that is killer on the grill." At the restaurant he serves it with sushi rice (P. 210) and mango salsa (P. 211).

The Fish
Stuffed Whitefish
With Shrimp Mousse and Lemon-herb Beurre Blanc

Serves 4

Shrimp Mousse

6 oz	shrimp	1	egg
1 T	parsley, stems removed	¾ C	heavy cream
3 oz	walleye, skinned and boned	¾ t	minced shallot
1 t	salt		

Divide the shrimp in two equal measures. In a food processor, pulse half the shrimp and half the parsley until coarsely ground. Remove to a bowl and reserve. Put the remaining shrimp in the processor with the walleye and salt, and puree. Add egg and blend, scraping down sides of container occasionally. Continue processing while adding the cream in a slow stream. Scrape down container sides occasionally. Remove mousse from processor, fold in the shallot and the reserved shrimp and parsley. Refrigerate at least one hour before use.

Lemon-herb Beurre Blanc

1 t	chopped chives	1	shallot, chopped
1 t	chopped parsley (reserve stem)	5	whole black peppercorns
¼ t	chopped rosemary (reserve stem)	½ C	lemon juice
¼ t	chopped thyme (reserve stem)	½ C	white wine
1	bay leaf	½ Lb	unsalted butter, half-inch diced

Combined chopped herb leaves and set aside. In a small saucepan, combine herb stems, bay leaf, peppercorns, chopped shallot, lemon juice, and white wine. Slowly cook over low heat until reduced to about two tablespoons. Add diced butter, one or two pieces at a time, whisking steadily until all butter is incorporated in a creamy sauce. Strain out all the solids. Add chopped herb leaves and season with salt to taste. Sauce will hold up to 15 minutes at room temperature, a bit longer in a thermos. (Do *not* refrigerate).

Whitefish

2 Lb	whitefish, skinned and boned	¼ Lb	unsalted butter, half-inch diced
1 T	minced garlic		
2 Lb	fresh spinach, stems removed		Non-stick vegetable spray

Preheat oven to 500°F. Divide whitefish into eight equal portions. Lay four pieces of fish flat on a baking sheet coated with non-stick spray (fish pieces can be placed close together for the bottom layer). Divide the shrimp mousse among the four portions of whitefish, and place the remaining fish pieces atop each portion of mousse. Season

Continued at bottom of next page →

Leelanau Country Inn
Barbecued Bluefish
With Lemon Cajun Butter

Serves 4

Lemon Cajun Butter

6 T	butter, softened	1 t	chopped fresh parsley
1	Med. shallot, finely chopped	2 t	lemon juice
½ t	garlic puree		

Combine thoroughly in a small mixing bowl and work by hand until all liquids are absorbed by the butter. Place in refrigerator to set up.

Bluefish

4	8-oz filets of cape bluefish	1 t	garlic puree
2 T	olive oil	1 t	finely chopped onion
½ t	salt	¼ t	paprika
½ t	ground black pepper	½ t	cayenne pepper
¼ t	sugar		

Make barbecue spice by mixing onion and dry ingredients in a small bowl. Brush both sides of each filet with oil, then sprinkle barbecue spice on fish to cover both sides. Allow to set in refrigerator for 30 minutes.

Grill filets on an open-flame grill that has been preheated so the rack is very hot. This will sear the filets so the flesh won't stick to the grill. Place coated filets on the grill skin side down and cook until the skin is crisp (about 7 minutes). Turn the filets and cook an additional 7 minutes. Remove from grill, plate immediately, and top each filet with 2 T of lemon Cajun butter. Serve immediately.

– Continued from previous page

with salt and bake 15 until meat thermometer shows internal temperature of 160°F (about 15 minutes). While fish is baking, sauté garlic in half the butter in a large pan for about one minute over moderate heat. Add the spinach and cook until half wilted. Add the remaining butter and continue cooking until spinach has almost completely wilted. Season to taste with salt and pepper. Divide the spinach among four plates. Top each with one whitefish portion, and drizzle with lemon-herb beurre blanc. Serve

The Authors
Poached Halibut
In Tomato-Fennel Broth with Leek and Roasted Redskins

Serves 4

Vegetable Broth

3 C	clam or fish stock	1 t	orange zest
6 oz	tomato sauce (or V-8)	1 oz	olive oil
2 oz	dry white wine	4	garlic cloves, minced
1 T	fresh lemon juice	2	leeks, ribbon sliced
1 t	fresh tarragon, chopped	½	fennel bulb, med. dice
Pinch	saffron threads, crushed (opt)	2 T	tomato paste
1	bay leaf		

Prepare broth by bringing stock to a simmer and adding tomato sauce, wine, lemon juice, tarragon, saffron, bay leaf, and orange zest. Simmer slowly for several minutes.

In a large skillet or sauce pan, sauté garlic briefly in oil to release fragrance, then add leeks and fennel, cover, and sweat until translucent. Stir in tomato paste and sauté 2-3 minutes until the entire mixture has color. Add broth, bring to boil, lower heat and simmer until the vegetables are tender (20-30 min). Season to taste with salt and pepper. Remove from heat and set aside. (*Broth can be made a little ahead and held.*)

Fish and Presentation

4 pcs	fresh halibut, 4-6 oz. each *	4 T	chopped fresh parsley
8	Sm. redskin potatoes, halved		(garnish)

* Fish pieces should be uniform for even poaching. We also use sea bass or mahimahi done this way.

Separately boil or roast redskin quarters until fork tender. Drain and reserve.

Add fish to the broth and poach gently until done (about 8 min for ½-inch filets, 10-12 minutes if 1-inch thick). Transfer fish and potato quarters to warm soup plates, ladle vegetable and broth over them, garnish with parsley, and serve immediately with garlic bread or crusty baguette.

Chef Nancy Allen
Egg Pasta
With City Kitchen's Chengdu Peanut Sauce

Serves 8

Peanut Sauce

¼ C	canola oil	½ C	sesame butter
½ C	chopped pickled ginger or	2/3 C	soy sauce
	¼ C minced ginger root	5 T	maple syrup
¼ C	minced garlic	5 T	black rice vinegar
½ C	peanut butter		

To make the peanut sauce, heat the oil, ginger and garlic in a large pot over medium low heat. Let the mixture simmer for 3 to 5 minutes. Whisk in the remaining sauce ingredients. Taste the sauce and adjust it to your liking. Set it aside. It will improve in flavor as it sits.

Vegetables and Pasta

1 head	broccoli, washed and cut into long stemmed florets	1 Lb	egg noodles
4	carrots, scrubbed and sliced	2	scallions, finely chopped, for garnish
1	red bell pepper, seeded and julienned	½ C	roasted peanuts, chopped, for garnish

To prepare the dish, steam the vegetables till tender. Cook pasta till al dente. Drain the pasta and toss with the peanut sauce and vegetables. Pile the pasta and vegetables high on a plate and garnish with the peanuts and scallions.

This was the most requested recipe at Allen's City Kitchen in Traverse City. – Eds.

Grey Hare Inn Vineyard B&B
Crêpes du Nord
With Herbes de Provençe Cream Sauce

Makes 12 crepes

Crêpes

1¼ C	all-purpose flour, sifted	1 C	milk
½ t	salt	3 T	unsalted butter, melted
4	eggs	1¼ C	cold water

In a blender or food processor blend all ingredients at high speed for 30 seconds, scrape down sides and blend 30 more seconds. Pour batter into mixing bowl and refrigerate 1 hour. To make six-inch crêpes pour a scant 1/3 cup of batter into a hot, buttered crepe pan. Cook over medium-high heat until surface is firm enough, then flip over into a second pan, and cook about 30 seconds, or until golden. *(The crêpes may be made ahead and frozen, then thawed for use.)*

Sauce

2 T	butter	1 C	half and half
3 T	flour	¾ t	herbes de Provençe

Melt butter in a sauce pan and whisk in the flour to make a roux. Continue whisking over low heat until mixture just begins to brown (about 3 minutes) to be sure flour is saturated and has no "raw flour" taste. Add the cream and herbes de Provençe and continue whisking over low heat until the sauce thickens and reduces slightly, or about 10 minutes. Add small amounts of additional cream if necessary to retain desired sauce consistency. Turn heat to very low simmer and hold, covered, for up to 30 minutes until ready to use. Re-whisk prior to saucing the crêpes.

Filling

6	2-inch dried morels	1 C	cooked 7-grain wild rice mix
12	Med. button mushrooms		(from Oryana)
6	Med. scallions	12	jumbo eggs, beaten lightly

Reconstitute dried morels in simmering water for 15 minutes. Slice button mushrooms and green onions (whites and 2" of green) into ¼-inch pieces. Dice morels more finely. Sauté onions and mushrooms over medium heat about seven minutes or until just starting to brown. *(Filling can be held at this point while you make the sauce.)* Stir in the rice and eggs and cook over medium-low heat until the eggs are done but still slightly runny.

To assemble, place 2 crêpes on each plate and spoon enough filling left-to-right across the middle of each to form a 1-inch tube of filling when you fold the crêpe. Start by folding the near third of the near crêpe over the filling, then fold the other

Continued at bottom of next page →

Sage Meadow Farm
Quick Greens and Pasta

Serves 2

½	onion, fine-chopped	1	bunch kale or Swiss chard
1	garlic clove, minced	1-2 oz	balsamic to drizzle (or red
1 T	olive oil		wine)
¼ C	sun-dried tomatoes, fine-chopped	1 C	feta, crumbled
			thin spaghetti for two

While pasta is cooking, sauté onion and garlic in olive oil until soft. Add sun-dried tomatoes, cut in small pieces. Tear greens into bite-sized pieces and add to pan, and drizzle with a little balsamic. Cover and let cook until greens are wilted. Drain cooked pasta well, return to a bowl and cover with the greens. Sprinkle feta on top and serve.

– Continued from preceding page

edge over to enclose filling in a roll. Repeat with the second crêpe, rolling as you go so the crepe rolls end up side by side. The idea is to minimizes handling of the delicate crêpes. Spoon cream sauce on crêpes and garnish. (*The B&B serves these with asparagus spears and Canadian bacon*). Just before serving, reheat the plate for 45 seconds on high microwave, then add garnish of edible flowers—violets or nasturtium—and a twist of orange slice.

(*This fusion of French and Up North cuisine is served regularly at the B&B, often accompanied by wine-poached pears, page 227.*)

Trillium
Wild Mushrooms
with Angel-Hair Pasta

Serves 4

Pasta

4 oz	dried angel hair (or 8 oz fresh)	1 t	chopped fresh oregano
3 qt	boiling salted water	1 t	chopped fresh tarragon
1 t	chopped fresh basil	¼ t	chopped fresh thyme
		3 T	butter

Bring water to boiling, add pasta and cook until tender, stirring occasionally. Drain, add butter and chopped herbs, toss, and hold covered.

Sauce and Mushroom Mix

1 C	dried morels	2 C	fresh shiitakes
2 T	minced shallots	2 C	fresh oyster mushrooms
2 T	butter	2 T	minced shallots
1 C	dry white wine	1 T	minced garlic
2 C	morel juice	3 T	butter
3 C	heavy whipping cream		

Reconstitute dried morels by soaking in 3 C water. Remove morels and set aside on paper towel to drain. Reserve soaking liquid. In a 3-quart sauce pot, sauté the shallots in butter until translucent. Add wine and reserved morel juice. Reduce by half. Add whipping cream and reduce to desired thickness (simmer on low heat). De-stem shiitake and oyster mushrooms and cut larger mushrooms to bite size. Sauté shallots and garlic with butter until translucent. Add all mushrooms and cook until tender. Add cream sauce and cook to desired thickness.

Presentation

Arrange mushrooms around perimeter of plate, pour remaining sauce over them, arrange pasta in center. Garnish with a fresh herb sprig.

Folgarelli's
Eggplant Lasagna

Serves 8-10

4	large eggplants	¼ Lb	Imported Parmesan Reggiano
1 jar	Folgarelli's house-brand red marinara sauce	1 C	Folgarelli's imported olive oil
		1	red bell pepper
1½ Lb	skim-milk mozzarella (shredded)	1	yellow bell pepper

Preheat oven to 350°F. Trim ends of eggplant and cut lengthwise in ¼ to ½ inch slices, leaving the skin on. Heat a large frying pan with half of the olive oil in it (you'll probably brown the eggplant in two batches, so save the rest of the oil for the next batch). Lightly brown eggplant slices on both sides, and drain on paper towel. Set aside. Core tops of both peppers and slice in ¼-inch rounds. Set aside.

Place browned eggplant in 9-x-10-inch glass baking dish so it covers the bottom. Place pepper rounds on top so that peppers touch but do not overlie each other. Top with ¾ pound mozzarella, and then spread a thin layer of half a jar of Folgarelli's sauce. Repeat the eggplant-pepper-mozzarella-sauce layers, and then spread Parmesan on top of the second layer of sauce. Bake for 45 to 55 minutes. Let set on stove for 10 minutes. Cut and serve.

Old Mission Tavern
Blue Cheese Spinach Pasta
With Bacon

Serves 2

3	strips bacon	3 C	cooked linguine
3 T	olive oil	2 T	blue cheese (crumbled)
1	clove garlic, chopped	¼ C	Parmesan
Dash	black pepper	½ C	mozzarella (shredded)
2 C	spinach (fresh)		

Cook and crumble the bacon and reserve. Sauté garlic in oil until lightly brown. Add pepper and spinach, and stir until well wilted. Add linguine, Parmesan and mozzarella. Toss until cheese is melted. Place in serving dish and top with blue cheese. Run under broiler about one minute. Add crumbled bacon and serve with garlic bread or plain sour dough roll.

Black Star Farms
Asparagus-Shallot Frittata
With Mushroom Ragout, Tarragon Infused Raclette Sauce and Scallion Curls

Serves 4

Scallion curls

4	scallions	Ice and water	

In advance, make the curls as follows: Cut 3-4 inches from the center of each scallion where it turns from white to green, then slice into very thin strips, lengthwise. Submerge in ice water about 2 hours to curl. Remove, drain and set aside.

Sauce

1½ C	heavy cream	1½ C	grated Leelanau raclette
¼ C	fresh tarragon, chopped	Taste	salt and pepper

Over low heat, reduce heavy cream by half. Add tarragon, simmer for 5 minutes, then strain solids out and discard. With cream over a low flame, slowly add cheese, stirring constantly, until the two have combined to make a sauce (add more cheese if thicker sauce is desired). Season with salt and pepper to taste.

Ragouts

1-2	shallots, chopped	3-5	Roma tomatoes, seeded,
2-4 T	unsalted butter		cored & chopped
5-10	button mushrooms (depends on size), finely chopped	1	clove garlic, minced

Sauté shallots in butter 2-3 minutes, remove with slotted spoon and set aside. Sauté mushrooms in butter over medium heat 7-10 minutes, stirring occasionally. Add garlic and sauté another minute then add tomatoes, sauté 1 more minute, remove from heat and set aside.

Frittata

12	asparagus spears	Taste	salt and pepper
4	eggs, beaten	2-3 t	clarified butter
Taste	Tabasco		

Cut woody stems off asparagus (peel remaining stems if very thick). Blanch asparagus in boiling water 1-2 minutes, and immerse in ice water 5 minutes. Drain and dry. Toss the asparagus with the shallots and butter ragout mixture to coat. Season eggs with Tabasco and the pepper. Heat a sauté pan over medium flame and, using ½t clarified butter for each frittata, pour about ¼ of the beaten eggs into the pan. Lay 3 coated asparagus spears on the egg with some extra shallots in center, as soon as bottom side of egg is cooked, but still slightly liquid in center, fold one side over, then the other to enfold the spears, and remove to a non-stick sheet pan. Repeat for remaining frittatas.

Continued at bottom of next page→

Latitude

Morel Scrambled Eggs

With Fontina Cheese

Serves 4

1 Lb	morels	2	garlic cloves, chopped
9	eggs	1¾ C	Fontina cheese
1 C	heavy cream	3 T	parsley
4 T	butter	Taste	salt and pepper
2 T	shallots, fine dice	4 slices	country bread, toasted

Wash morels by immersing briefly in salted water. Do *not* soak. Agitate and drain. Cut off the stems and chop them. Check insides of morel caps for insects and debris. Melt 2 T butter over medium heat in a large skillet and add the mushrooms and shallots, and stir and sauté for about 5 minutes. Add the garlic and cook an additional minute. Season with salt and pepper, remove from the pan and reserve. Heat the remaining butter in another pan until just hot. Whisk together the eggs and cream, and half the parsley. Season with salt and pepper and cook, stirring constantly until the mixture is the texture of thick cream. Do not over cook. Stir in half the mushrooms and half the cheese and remove from the heat. Serve each helping of eggs atop a piece of toast, and top the eggs with the remaining cheese, mushrooms and parsley.

– Continued from bottom of preceding page

Put sheet pan and the pot of mushroom-tomato ragout in the oven and bake all for 5-7 minutes a 350°F, until the frittatas are slightly brown and puffed up. Remove from oven. Put a bed of mushroom ragout on each plate, lay on a frittata, and ladle raclette sauce over it, and top with scallion curls.

This is a favorite at Black Star, where it's made with fresh tarragon from the garden and Leelanau Cheese Raclette from the creamery that's 5-7 months aged. The frittatas are accompanied by roasted Yukon Gold potatoes, also from the garden, and locally cured and smoked cherry bacon from Pleva's Meats in Cedar.

Sides, Sauces & Stuff

Leelanau Cheese
Swiss-Style Potato Gratin

Serves 4

I t	butter	8 oz	raclette cheese, grated or thinly sliced
1 Lb	potatoes, peeled and thinly sliced in rounds	2/3 C	dry white wine
Taste	salt and black pepper	4 T	milk
2	cloves garlic, minced		

Preheat oven to 375°F. Grease generously small casserole dish with butter. In medium bowl, gently toss potato slices with salt, pepper, and garlic. Place layer of potatoes in prepared dish. Sprinkle with generous amount of cheese. Repeat with another layer of potatoes and more cheese. Top with remaining potatoes. Pour wine and milk over layered potatoes. Sprinkle top with remaining cheese. Cover dish with foil and bake for 40 minutes. Remove foil and bake additional 15 to 20 minutes or until top is golden brown.

Tapawingo
Roasted Potato Salad

Serves 8

Potatoes

10	small, new, red potatoes, halved *	8 T	unsalted butter
8	cloves garlic, peeled, and smashed	1 t	teaspoon freshly cracked pepper
7	rosemary sprigs	Taste	salt

* Can substitute equivalent amount of peeled white potatoes cut in larger chunks

Combine all ingredients in a pan, cover with foil, and bake 15 minutes at 400°F. Uncover and continue baking, stirring occasionally, until potatoes are light and golden—about 15 minutes.

Dressing

4 t	Dijon mustard	Taste	cayenne pepper
2	egg yolks	2/3 C	olive oil
1 t	coarse salt	4 T	balsamic vinegar
½ t	cracked pepper		

In a bowl, whisk together the mustard, egg yolks, salt, and peppers. Add oil slowly, alternating with the vinegar. Set aside.

Assembly

	roasted potatoes (above)	½ C	finely diced yellow pepper
2/3 C	cooked, crumbled bacon	¼ C	thinly sliced scallions
½ C	finely diced red onion	Taste	salt and pepper
½ C	finely diced red pepper		

While potatoes are still warm, combine with bacon, red onions, bell peppers, scallions, salt and pepper. Toss with dressing, and garnish with chopped parsley, if desired. Serve warm, or at room temperature for best flavor.

Andante

Coconut Sushi Rice

Serves 4

Awase-zu

1 C	rice vinegar	3 T	mirin *
¾ C	sugar	1 T	salt

Mirin is available at Esperance in Charlevoix, or substitute dry vermouth

Heat ingredients in a saucepan until the sugar is dissolved.

Sushi Rice

1 C	sushi rice	Taste	shredded fresh coconut

Soak 1 C sushi rice 1 hour in enough water to cover. Drain and rinse in a strainer. Put into a small pot with a tight fitting lid with 1¼ C water and bring to a boil. Turn down to medium low, cover and cook for 8 minutes, then turn down to low, and cook for additional 12 minutes. Remove the rice from the heat and let it rest for 20 minutes. Then turn it out into a bowl, and season and moisten with Awase-zu. Then add shredded coconut to taste. Serve at room temperature, or reheat in the microwave. (*The restaurant serves this with grilled Chilean sea bass in a miso-citrus marinade – P. 197*).

Authors

Tangy Green Beans

Serves 6

1 Lb	green beans, stemmed, trimmed, de-strung	3	garlic cloves, minced
1 T	olive oil	¼ C	chicken stock or broth
1 T	orange zest	1-2 T	butter
1 T	lemon zest	Taste	salt, pepper

Boil beans in a large pot in salted water for 4-5 minutes. Drain in a colander. Heat oil in a skillet over medium heat and, when hot, add garlic and citrus zest. Cook, stirring, 1-2 minutes. Add broth, bring to boil, turn down heat and simmer about a minute. Add blanched beans and butter and toss until beans are fully re-warmed and coated with sauce. Season and serve.

Wells Family Farm
Oven Broiled Eggplant

Serves 4

1	eggplant	freshly grated Parmesan
	olive oil	

Slice an eggplant thinly and spread each slice sparingly with olive oil. Then dip each slice in grated Parmesan, covering both sides. Arrange the slices on a non-stick or slightly oiled cookie sheet and broil them on each side just until they are golden brown and crunchy outside and soft and tender inside.

Andante
Spicy Mango Salsa

Serves 4

1	mango	2 T	lime juice
1	red pepper	Taste	sea salt
½	jalapeño	2 T	minced cilantro
1 t	minced ginger root	2 T	thinly sliced scallion (mostly
1½ t	sambal oelek*		the green part)

* Sambal oelek is a South Asian condiment paste of chiles and salt mixed with a combination of oil, vinegar and/or brown sugar. Available at Esperance in Charlevoix.

Control the "spicy" by adjusting the amount of sambal. Peel and dice mango small, please. Toast red pepper over open gas flame, cool, rub off the skin, eliminate the seeds and thicker ribs. Dice. Thinly slice the green onion. Also dice the seeded jalapeno. Add the ginger root and the lime juice and season with some sea salt, sambal oelek, and cilantro. (*Says Chef Bob Stark; "Use this stuff on your fish!" Following his own advice, he uses it in the restaurant on grilled, miso-citrus marinated, Chilean sea bass.*)

Boathouse
Potato Gnocchi

Serves 4-6

2 Lbs	russet potatoes		2 T	kosher salt
1½ C	flour		1 t	ground black pepper
5	Lg. egg yolks			

Bake the potatoes until fully cooked (about 1 hour). Break them open and scoop out the flesh, and press it through a potato ricer. Place the riced potato on a board and make a well in the center. Place half the flour in the well and add the egg yolks, salt and pepper. Add a small amount of the remaining flour and chop with a dough cutter or dull knife to incorporate. Continue adding flour a small amount at a time until the dough is firm and uniform but not overly sticky.

Cut off a chunk of the dough and roll it out into a thin log, ½-inch in diameter. From the log, cut pieces ¾-inch long and, with a fork, run each piece down the back of the tines to form grooves. Placed the shaped pieces on a floured sheet pan, taking care not to let them stick together. When all gnocchi are formed, chill for an hour then cook in boiling salted water until they rise to the surface. Remove with a slotted spoon, let drain on paper towel, and use immediately.

Chef Jim Morse says you can hold uncooked gnocchi several hours on the sheet pan in a refrigerator. You can also freeze uncooked gnocchi up to two months. Put the sheet pan in the freezer, and, once the gnocchi are solid, transfer them to a plastic bag. You can cook them straight from the freezer, although it may take a minute or two longer. Gnocchi, like any pasta or dumpling, can be served in cream or tomato sauces, tossed with pesto, or in soups, casseroles or gratins. The Boathouse serves them in several ways, one of which is with pulled chicken, Serrano ham, spinach, peas, and a yellow-pepper cream sauce with horseradish crust.

Grey Hare Inn Vineyard B&B
Potato Strada
With Rosemary, Garlic, Fontina Cheese

Serves 8

½ loaf	sliced Italian bread (enough for 2 layers in a 2 qt. casserole dish)	1	large garlic clove, minced
		3	medium red potatoes, ¼-inch dice
8 oz	Fontina cheese, grated	1	stick softened butter
1	medium shallot, finely chopped	6	jumbo or large eggs
		1¾ C	half and half
1 T	chopped fresh rosemary	1 T	chopped parsley

Bake bread 20 minutes a side on a baking sheet at 200°F. Meanwhile, boil potatoes in water until just tender but still firm. Drain, then fry in 4 T melted butter over medium heat until they begin to brown. Add shallots and continue to sauté until shallots are translucent. Push mixture to one side of pan and put a sliver of butter in other side and press garlic into it to cook briefly, then toss garlic with potato mixture. Remove from heat, add rosemary, toss, and let cool.

Remove bread from oven and cool. Liberally butter a square, 2-quart casserole and lightly butter one side of dried bread slices. Place a layer of bread, buttered side up, in casserole. Sprinkle half the potato mixture on top, then half the cheese. Repeat for a second layer of bread, potato, and cheese. Thoroughly whisk eggs and parsley in a bowl, whisk in half-and-half, and pour mixture evenly over surface of casserole. Cover dish with plastic wrap so it rests on surface of top layer with enough weight on top to keep bread immersed. Rest in refrigerator at least 4 hours (overnight is fine).

Bring to room temperature and bake 60-70 minutes in preheated 325°F oven. Let rest at room temperature 10-20 minutes so layers set firmly. Slice into squares. Serve warm, garnished with fresh rosemary or thyme sprigs.

Mary's Kitchen Port
Mexican Sweet Potato

Serves 8

5 Lbs	sweet potatoes	2 T	cayenne
2 oz	olive oil	1 C	fresh cilantro, chopped
2 T	cumin	4 oz	lime juice
1 T	sea salt		

Wash, peel, and chop potato into 2-inch pieces. Place in a bowl. Add olive oil, cumin, sea salt, and cayenne. Toss. Line a cookie sheet with parchment paper and place potatoes loosely on parchment. Roast at 400°F for 20 minutes. Cool for 5 minutes. Add fresh cilantro and lime juice.

Andante
Miso-Sesame Vinaigrette
For Grilled Fish

Serves 4

¼ C	rice vinegar	1 t	minced garlic
2 T	chicken stock	½	seeded jalapeño
2 T	white miso	1 t	Dijon mustard
1 T	sugar	½ C	canola oil
1	egg yolk	1 T	toasted sesame oil
1 T	tahini	1 T	toasted sesame seeds
1 t	minced ginger root		

First, toast the sesame seeds. Then, everything except the sesame seeds and oil into the bowl of a food processor. With machine running, drizzle in the oil. Then stop and pulse in the sesame seeds. (*Chef Bob Stark: "Great sauce, cold or at room temperature, for grilled fish, or any darn fish, I think!"*)

Authors
Carrot Soufflé

Serves 8

2 C	cooked carrots, pureed	1 T	flour
2 t	lemon juice	1 t	salt
2 T	minced white or yellow onion	¼ t	cinnamon powder
2 T	sugar	1 C	milk
4 T	butter, softened	3	eggs

Preheat oven to 350°F. Beat all ingredients together until mixture is smooth, and pour into a lightly buttered 2-quart casserole. Bake, uncovered, 45-60 minutes, until center is firm to the touch. (*Carrots can be pureed a few hours ahead and, with lemon juice , kept in a lidded container.*)

Wells Family Farm
Pesto

Makes 3 to 4 cups

1½ C	olive oil	1½ C	grated Parmesan
5	cloves garlic	3 C	fresh basil
½ C	pine nuts		

Blend these ingredients in your blender adding basil a bit at a time until creamy.

Says Phyllis Wells: "We serve it over linguini. The extra we put into plastic freezer bags and enjoy all winter. I usually put about ½ cup into each freezer bag. Some people freeze it in ice cube trays, then put the cubes in freezer bags. It's so easy to work with. Thaw it in a microwave serving dish before it defrosts." Wells usually has German red garlic starting the second week of August. They have daily fresh basil in packages of about 1 C each from July 1 until September 30, or first frost.

Andante
Salsa Romesco

4	Roma tomatoes	1 t	roasted garlic
2	ancho chiles (dried poblano)	1 t	sherry vinegar
2	slices country bread	¼ C	olive oil
1	jalapeño	Taste	sea salt
½ C	almonds	Taste	crushed black peppercorns

Toast the chiles in a hot skillet on all sides until they are pliable, then cut in half. Scrape out and discard the seeds. Soak the flesh in hot water for 20 minutes, then drain. Cut tomatoes in half, brush with olive oil and season to taste, and grill on both sides. Let cool. Toast the sliced bread in olive oil, then cool and drain. Toast the nuts in a little olive oil, then cool. Combine <u>all</u> ingredients in a food processor and pulse. Not too much, however! A little chunky is good.

Authors
Cheese Grits Soufflé

Serves 8

1 qt	milk	1/8 t	cayenne pepper
1 C	quick-cook grits	3 C	shredded Jarlsberg cheese
½ C	butter	6	eggs, beaten well
1½ t	salt		

Preheat oven to 350°F. In a large, heavy saucepan, bring milk just to a boil and stir in grits with a whisk. Reduce heat and continue stirring until mixture becomes thick and mushy (3-4 minutes). Remove from heat. Add butter in pieces, then add salt, cayenne pepper, and cheese. beat all together well, using a wooden spoon. Finally, thoroughly stir in the eggs.

Pour mixture into a deep, well-buttered, 2-quart casserole or soufflé dish. Bake, uncovered, for 1 hour and 10 minutes, or until well-puffed and golden. (*We often serve this with roasted pork tenderloin sauced with a pear-port reduction. To halve the recipe, use a 1-quart casserole and bake 45-50 minutes.*)

Authors
Salmon Chanted Evening
Two Spooning Sauces for Char-grilled Salmon

Makes Sauce for 8-10 servings

Dilled Curry-mustard Sauce

3 T	mayonnaise		½ t	curry powder
1 T	sour cream		½ t	Dijon mustard
1 t	chopped fresh dill		¼ t	horseradish
	(or ½ t dried)			

Whisk all ingredients together. Store covered in refrigerator.

Honeyed Ginger-lime Sauce

4 T	mayonnaise		½ t	minced fresh ginger
½ t	lime juice			or ginger paste
½ t	honey		½ t	soy sauce

Whisk all ingredients together. Store covered in refrigerator.

A few years ago, we and our friends Louis and Nancy Sanford returned from a Lake Michigan fishing expedition with serious surplus, so we whittled it down one evening by grilling salmon steaks for 60-odd friends. We invented these sauces to accompany them. The flavors are not shy, so it's best to serve the sauces on the side and let diners help themselves. Please experiment with the relative amounts of ingredients. We're constantly adjusting these to taste. We steaked the fish since we had so many to feed, but first we fileted, skinned and boned the them, and trimmed away every shred of fat and dark flesh. Then we cut our 2-inch steaks, rubbed each piece lightly with olive oil, salt and pepper, and grilled them over a very hot fire. We tried to make it 4-5 minutes a side, but with that many, the times varied, and we found the salmon stood up very well when grilled considerably longer. Some of it was crisp about the edges, and more than a few guests commented how much they liked that. – Eds.

Desserts & Sweet Things

Altonen's Farm Market
Grandma Julia Altonen's Apple Pie

Serves 8

Crust (single-crust – double to add a top crust)

¼ C	all-purpose flour		½ C	vegetable shortening
1 t	sugar		3 T	ice water (approximately)
1 t	salt			

Combine flour, sugar, salt and shortening until mixture looks crumbly. Slowly add water. Mixture will gather in a ball. Roll out dough on floured board to fit the bottom of a 9-inch pie pan and to make top crust (if needed).

Apple Filling

¾ C	sugar		1 t	cinnamon
3 T	flour		2 T	butter
½ t	salt		6-8	tart apples (e.g., Northern Spy)

Mix first 4 ingredients thoroughly. Cut in 1 to 2 T butter. Set aside. Wash, quarter, core and thinly slice the apples. Arrange one half of the apple slices atop the bottom crust in pie pan. Sprinkle with half the filling mixture. Repeat with a second layer of apple topped with filling mixture. Add a top crust or lattice crust, if desired. Bake 10 minutes at 400°F. Reduce heat to 325°F and bake 30 to 40 minutes more, until apples are tender and crust is browned.

Timmerin

Bittersweet Chocolate Crème Brûlée

Serves 12

1 qt	heavy cream (not ultra pasteurized)	½ lb	bittersweet chocolate chips (or finely chopped bulk chocolate)
11	egg yolks *		
1 C	sugar	Pinch	kosher salt
1 oz	unsweetened cocoa powder		Sugar for topping

* In separating the eggs, save the whites and freeze individually like ice cubes for use in angel food cake or omelets.

In a saucepan, heat the cream until a few bubbles rise to the surface. Let cool 5 minutes. Meanwhile, beat the egg yolks and sugar together and stir in the chocolate and cocoa powder. Stir about 1 cup of the cream into the mixture to temper the eggs, then pour the sugar and egg mixture back into the warm cream in the saucepan and stir over low heat until chocolate is melted.

Strain before pouring into shallow ramekins. Put ramekins in a large baking pan containing enough hot water to come half way up the sides of the dishes. Bake in a still oven at 300°F for 30 to 45 minutes, or until the custard sets. When all are set, remove the pan and let the water cool slightly. Remove the ramekins and refrigerate. *(Note: Baking time can vary, and it may be as much as an hour and a quarter; that's just the way the custard cooks. The deeper the dishes, the longer the cooking takes. The centers should be just set, so that when you carefully wiggle the ramekins, the center just barely wiggles.)*

For the crunchy sugar topping, sprinkle the tops of the custards with sugar to lightly coat the entire surface of each. Then use a kitchen torch to carefully brown and caramelize the sugar.

American Spoon Foods
Independence Cake

2½ C	all-purpose flour		1 t	vanilla extract
½ t	cinnamon		1 t	baking soda
1 t	freshly grated nutmeg		1 C	buttermilk
½ t	double-acting baking powder		1 jar	Blueberry Spoon Fruit ®
1 C	sweet butter		1 jar	Sour Cherry Spoon Fruit ®
1½ C	granulated sugar		1 T	confectioners' sugar
4	Lg. eggs (room temperature)			

* *Blueberry Spoon Fruit and Sour Cherry Spoon Fruit are
American Spoon Foods products and trademarks.*

Preheat oven to 350°F. Grease three, round, 9-inch cake pans and line them with parchment paper. Sift flour, cinnamon, nutmeg and baking powder together in one bowl. In a large mixing bowl, cream the butter and gradually add granulated sugar, blending well. Beat in the eggs, one at a time, until mixture is light and fluffy. Add vanilla and blend well. Dissolve baking soda in buttermilk in a small bowl. Beginning and ending with the flour mixture, alternately add flour mixture and buttermilk mixture to the butter mixture. Divide batter into prepared pans and bake in preheated oven for 20-25 minutes or until edges begin to pull away from sides of pans and center springs back with pressed lightly. Cool in pans for 10 minutes, then turn out onto wire racks and cool completely. Spread bottom layer with Blueberry Spoon Fruit, set middle layer on top and spread with Sour Cherry Spoon Fruit. Put on top layer and sift confectioners' sugar onto it.

Tapawingo
Souffléed Lemon "Pudding"

Serves 8

1 t	unsalted butter, at room temperature	¾ C	freshly squeezed lemon juice
½ C	all-purpose flour	1 T	freshly grated lemon zest
1¾ C	sugar	3	large eggs, separated
4 T	unsalted butter, melted	2 C	buttermilk

Preheat oven to 350°F. Beat the separated egg yolks. Lightly butter eight 6-ounce soufflé dishes. In a large bowl combine the flour and 1½ C of the sugar, and mix well. Add the melted butter, lemon juice, lemon zest, and the beaten yolks. Stir in the buttermilk. Beat the egg white with the remaining ¼ C of sugar until stiff, and gently fold into the first mixture. Pour into the dishes, and place the dishes in a hot water bath (a larger baking dish with about an inch of hot water in it). Bake until brown on top and puffed above the rim of the dishes — about 25 to 30 minutes. (*Tapawingo's Pete Peterson says, "This is wonderful served warm, or chilled."*)

Monte Bianco
Zabaglione con Frutti

Serves 4

4	egg yolks	4 C	sliced fresh fruit (raspberries, strawberries, blueberries)
½ C	sugar		
1 C	dry Marsala wine	4	mint sprigs, for garnish

In a double boiler, over simmering water, combine all ingredients except the fruit, and whisk briskly until mixture is thick and creamy. Place berries in wine glasses and pour zabaglione over them. Garnish with fresh mint.

Chateau Chantal
Cherry Cheese Strata

Serves 6

16	slices French bread	2/3 C	sugar
4 oz	cream cheese, softened	1½ t	orange zest
½ C	Chateau Chantal Cherry Merlot Jam	1 t	vanilla extract
		¼ C	almond slices
1 C	frozen cherries	¼ C	turbinado (raw) sugar
4	eggs, slightly beaten	Garnish	vanilla yogurt
2 C	half-and-half		

Preheat oven to 350°F. Coat a 2-qt. baking dish with non-stick spray. Spread cream cheese on enough bread slices to form one layer in the baking dash, packed tightly. Spread jam on top of the bread slices, scatter frozen cherries over that, and lay on another layer of bread slices. Use any extra bread in bit-size pieces to fill in between slices. Combine eggs in a bowl with half-and-half, sugar, zest and vanilla, and pour over the bread in the baking dish. Sprinkle with turbinado sugar and almond slices. Bake, uncovered, until a knife inserted in center of dish comes out clean (about 45 minutes). Remove from oven and let stand 15 minutes before serving, garnished with a spoon of vanilla yogurt.

Grey Gables Inn
Chocolate Bread Pudding

Serves 6

8 oz	Valrhona pistoles or other melting chocolate, chips	6	Lg. all-butter croissants, diced
1 pt	heavy whipping cream	½ t	vanilla extract
4	egg yolks	Pinch	kosher salt

Pre-heat oven to 325°F. Heat whipping cream until wisps of steam are visible, but do not allow to boil. Pour hot cream over chopped chocolate and stir until chocolate is completely melted. Cool, and then add whipped egg yolks, vanilla, and salt. When well combined, add diced croissants and fold them into the chocolate batter until all the pieces are well coated. Lightly butter ovenproof ramekins and fill with pudding mixture, lightly pressing down with a spoon. Place puddings in a water bath and bake 20 to 25 minutes. Serve with whipped cream or your favorite ice cream.

Authors
Clarine's Apple Tart

Serves 6-8

3	Granny Smith apples	1	egg
½ C	sugar	1	pie crust (use your favorite;
½ C	heavy cream		Pillsbury works fine)
1 t	vanilla		Powdered sugar for dusting

Heat oven to 375°F. Roll pie crust thinly to fit a 9-10 inch tart pan. Peel and core apples and cut in very thin "half-moon" slices. Lay slices on the crust in concentric rings, starting at outside of pie. Lay slices so the straight edges pointed at center of pie and each slice half overlapping two-thirds of the last one. Lay a second layer the same way, atop the first. (Three medium apples generally yield enough slices to make two complete layers on a 9-inch pie.) Bake the crust and apples for 15 minutes. Mix the remaining ingredients and pour over the apples. Return to the oven and bake another 25 minutes. Dust powder sugar over warm pie. (*This is from our friend Clarine Olson, and is one of our favorites at home. A simple recipe, it makes a beautiful presentation.*)

Windows
Chocolate Pâte

Serves 6-8

1 Lb	semi-sweet chocolate	12 oz	butter
1 C	coffee	8	eggs
1 C	sugar	Garnish	whipped cream

Boil coffee and sugar together until sugar has completely dissolved. Melt chocolate in double boiler and slowly add coffee. Mix well. Beat in butter a little at a time, alternating with eggs until everything is smooth and well blended. Pour into a greased loaf pan, bake in a water bath at 300°F for 2 to 2½ hours. Serve warm with freshly whipped cream.

Chateau Chantal
Ice-wine Truffles

Makes 36 small truffles

1/3 C	whipping cream	2 T	butter, softened
½ Lb	semi-sweet chocolate, finely chopped	¼ C	cocoa powder
		1 t	powdered sugar
1/3 C	Chateau Chantal ice wine		

Bring cream just to a boil in a bowl and add chocolate. Blend. Then stir in ice wine. Remove from heat and let cool, then beat in the butter and set aside until it mixture is firm enough to handle. Meanwhile, sweeten coca powder with powdered sugar and spread on a shallow plate. Drop chocolate-butter mixture, one spoonful at a time, into powder mixture to coat, and roll each truffle into a ball between palms of your hands (coat hands with coca mixture to prevent sticking). You may have to adjust temperature of truffle mixture; if truffles are too firm to shape without breaking, warm them to soften; if too soft, chill until they firm up. Truffles look most "authentic" when they are a little irregular in shape. When all are coated, agitate gently in a dry strainer to shake off excess power. Store in an airtight container for up to 10 days in refrigerator, and up to 3 months frozen. Bring to room temperature before serving them, in a candy dish or individual fluted paper cup.

Mary's Kitchen Port
Chocolate Chew Cookies

This makes a <u>lot</u> of big cookies—enough for a church bake sale. Adjust quantities accordingly.

1¼ Lb	sweet butter, softened	1½ C	cocoa
3½ C	granulated sugar	1¼ Lb	flour (5 cups)
4	eggs	1 t	salt
4 t	vanilla	2 t	baking soda

Beat ingredients until fluffy. Fold in flour; Use a scoop to transfer to cookie sheet and bake 14 minutes at 325°F.

Carriage House at the Iroquois
Peanut Butter Pie

Makes 2 pies

Crust

1 C	graham cracker crumbs		¼ C	sugar
¾ C	ground pecans		¼ C	melted butter

Mix until well blended. Press evenly into two 9-inch pie pans. Bake at 350°F for 5 to 8 minutes, or until golden brown.

Filling

12 oz	cream cheese, room temperature		8 oz	creamy peanut butter
			2 C	whipping cream, whipped to stiff peaks
8 oz	powdered sugar			

Cream together cream cheese and peanut butter until very smooth. Scrape bowl often. Add powdered sugar and beat until well combined. Gently fold in whipped cream until thoroughly incorporated. Divide between the two cooled pie crusts. Smooth top and make small peak design on top.

La Bécasse
Hazelnut Pudding

Serves 10

½ lb	butter		5 oz	dry breadcrumbs
2/3 C	confectioners sugar		Dash	salt
6	eggs, separated		Garnish	confectioner's sugar, crème Anglaise, fresh strawberries, lingonberry jam
1 oz	brandy			
½ C	granulated sugar			
6 oz	toasted, ground hazelnuts			

Butter ten 6-ounce ramekins. Cream butter with confectioners sugar. Beat in egg yolks one at a time. Beat in brandy. In a separate bowl, beat egg whites until foamy. Gradually beat in granulated sugar. Fold toasted nuts, bread crumbs and salt into the creamed butter mixture. Add 1/3 of the egg white. Continue folding. Fold in remaining egg whites. Turn mixture into ramekins and cover each with foil. Place in water bath and bake at 350°F until puddings are firm, about 35 minutes. To serve, turn warm puddings out of ramekins onto plates, sprinkle with confectioners sugar and garnish with crème Anglaise, fresh strawberries and lingonberry jam.

Authors
Walnut Cake
With Chocolate Cream

Serves 10 to 12

Cake

9-10 oz	**English walnuts**		**1 C**	**sugar**
6	**eggs, separated**			

Butter and flour two 9-inch cake pans. In a food processor or blender, pulverize the walnut meats into fine powder. You'll need 2 C, so add walnuts if necessary. In a large bowl, beat the egg whites until stiff. In a separate bowl, beat the egg yolks until lemon-colored and fluffy. Gradually beat the sugar into the egg yolks, and then fold that mixture into the egg whites. Finally, fold in the powdered walnuts. Pre-heat oven to 350°F. Pour the batter into prepared cake pans and bake 25-30 minutes, or until the cake pulls away from the sides and is lightly browned. *Immediately* invert the pans on racks. Cool slightly then remove cakes from pans and let stand 2 to 4 hours.

Chocolate Cream

3 oz	**unsweetened chocolate**		**1½ C**	**heavy cream**
5 T	**sugar**			

Melt the chocolate in a medium-sized saucepan over medium heat. Whisk in the sugar, and then the cream. Stir constantly until the mixture *almost* comes to a boil, and then immediately remove from heat. Chill up to (but not more than) 2 hours.

Just before frosting the cake, beat the chocolate mixture until it has the consistency of whipped cream. Spread between cake layers and then on the top and sides of the assembled cake. Sprinkle shavings of chocolate or raspberries on top if you want, as garnish. Refrigerate overnight.

This cake is elegant and light-textured. We sometimes serve it with a raspberry coulis.—Eds.

Grey Hare Inn Vineyard B&B
Grapes in Grappa
with Mascarpone Sauce

Makes 6 desserts

Sauce

1½ C	green grapes	8 oz	mascarpone cheese
½ T	grappa	Taste	confectioner's sugar

Chop grapes in a food processor, and strain to get half a cup of juice. Discard solids. Place mascarpone and confectioner's sugar in the mixer with standard paddle or whisk attachment, and blend on low speed while gradually adding grape juice in a steady stream. Scrape sides of bowl, then whip on medium high speed for a minute or so until sauce appears well blended and is slightly thickened. Stop blending if it begins to separate. Stir in the grappa.

Grapes

1	bunch red seedless grapes	1	lemon, zest only
1	bunch green seedless grapes	6	mint sprigs, for garnish
1/3 C	grappa		

Quarter three cups worth of red and green grapes and marinate in the grappa in a bowl for 2 hours before serving (longer is okay, although alcohol taste will increase with time). Refrigerate, tossing periodically. Apportion sauce into parfaits or martini glasses and top with the marinated grapes, then garnish with lemon zest and a sprig of mint.

Grey Hare's Cindy Ruzak: "Grappa, a liquor distilled from grape skins, is expensive, but no substitute works as well. Seedless concord grapes, or blueberries, will add color when available." This dish is often served at the Grey Hare Inn as a first course before a strada, but can also be used as a dessert by doubling the amount of confectioner's sugar and adding a full tablespoon of grappa to the sauce at the end.

Folgarelli's
Dolce Pears in Moscato

Serves 6

6	Bosc pears	1 Lb	dolce Gorgonzola
1 C	Moscato wine	Garnish	chocolate, for melting

Warm oven to 250 degrees. Wash pears in cold water, slice lengthwise and core (no need to remove stem). Place face down in baking dish and add Moscato. Bake in glass dish for 1½ hours *(Donna Folgarelli says she starts them baking as she starts preparing the meal, and lets the pears cook slowly until it's time to make dessert.)* When pears are done, place them face-up on warm plates. Place a nice dollop of dolce Gorgonzola in center of each and drizzle with melted chocolate in a Z design. For a nicer presentation, the dish can also be drizzled with the chocolate before the pear is in place. Serve immediately.

Trillium
Huckleberry Ice Cream

Serves 8-10

6	egg yolks	2 C	huckleberries
1 C	half-and-Half	4 t	lemon juice
1¼ C	sugar	2 t	Black Star Farms cherry eau
2 C	heavy cream		de vie

In mixing bowl, whisk yolks slowly and gently. Heat the half-and-half, and ¾ C sugar in a non-reactive saucepan. Stir continuously over low heat until the mixture is steaming and the sugar has dissolved. Very slowly begin to add the hot cream to the egg yolks, constantly stirring, scrape the bottom of the pan with a rubber spatula. Cook the ice cream base custard mixture until it is thick enough to coat the back of a spoon. Remove from the heat and strain through a fine mesh sieve. In a saucepan, stir the berries and the sugar until the sugar has dissolved and the berries have released their juices. Puree the berries and add them to the ice cream base custard. Freeze as stated on the ice cream maker. Serve. *(Trillium Chef Christopher Mushall says, "We get our freshest huckleberries in late summer and early fall. This recipe can be used with raspberries, blackberries, strawberries, or just about any other fresh fruit you might want. Be sure to wear an apron! These babies get messy.)*

Old Mission Tavern
Coffee Ice Cream

Serves 4

2 C	whole milk	6	egg yolks
¼ C	coarsely ground coffee bean *	¼ C	sugar
1	vanilla bean	¼ C	heavy cream
2 oz	Godiva chocolate liqueur		

* Chef Ken Stoppa specifies a coarse grind so coffee is easy to strain out. Use whole milk, not 2%.

Put milk, coffee beans, vanilla, and liqueur in saucepan and bring to a boil, then remove from heat and let steep for an hour. Strain. Discard solids. Set liquid aside. Beat egg yolks and sugar until fluffy. Add the heavy cream and a little of the milk mixture, stir together, and return to the remaining milk mixture. Stir over medium heat and bring to about the custard stage (170°F, or until it begins to thicken). Remove from heat and let cool, then freeze in an ice cream machine. *Old Mission Tavern uses this in their chocolate mocha ice cream pie, one of their most popular desserts.*

Authors
Indian Pudding

Serves 6

3 C	whole milk	½ t	ground cinnamon
¼ C	cornmeal	1/8 t	baking soda
¼ C	sugar	¼ C	dark molasses
½ t	salt	Garnish	whipped cream, ground
½ t	ground ginger		nutmeg

In a medium saucepan over low heat, heat 2 C of the milk just until bubbles form around the edge. With a whisk, gradually stir in cornmeal. Cook over low heat, stirring constantly, for 15 minutes or until slightly thickened. Remove from heat. Heat oven to 275°F. In a small bowl, combine sugar, salt, ginger, cinnamon, and soda; stir this into cornmeal mixture. Stir in molasses and remaining 1 C of milk. Pour into a buttered 1-quart casserole. Bake 2 hours or until softly set. Cool to room temperature. Serve warm with whipped cream and sprinkling of nutmeg. *(This Colonial pudding recipe was served at Fraunces Tavern in New York City, which was built in 1719 and is still a restaurant. The seeds of The Revolution were planted there in 1768, and it is where General Washington bid his official farewell to his troops in 1796. – Eds.)*

Julienne Tomato
Pâte à Choux

Makes approx. 6 éclairs or puffs, or 20 miniatures

8 oz	water	6 oz	bread flour
4 oz	margarine	4	Lg. eggs

Preheat oven to 350°F. In a heavy-bottomed sauce pot, heat water and margarine to boiling. Reduce heat and add flour. Cook 5 minutes, stirring periodically with a wooden spoon. Beat in a stand-mixer on low speed until steam is no longer present. Slowly add eggs one at a time and mix until incorporated.

Now comes the fun part

Says pastry chef Julie Adams: "Choux is wonderfully versatile and can be used for many things. Pipe out of a pastry bag into 2-inch circle for cream puffs; pipe out of a pastry bag into 2-inch rings for turbans; pipe out of a pastry bag into 1-inch tubes for éclairs. Increase the sizes for larger items.

Bake on heavy, parchment-lined cookie sheet until golden brown and no butter bubbles remain.

Fill with custard, whip cream, mousses etc. Dip in caramel or chocolate or sprinkle with powdered sugar. Try a savory alternative: In the final mixing process add cheese for savory puffs (e.g., pecorino Romano, grated Gruyère, pick your favorite). Serve alone or stuffed with chicken or tuna salad.

Carriage House at the Iroquois Hotel
Blueberry Lemon Muffins

Makes 12

1¾ C	sifted all-purpose flour	1/3 C	cooking oil
¼ C	sugar	1 C	fresh blueberries or 1 cup
2½ t	baking powder		frozen whole blueberries,
¾ t	salt		thawed
¾ C	milk	2 T	sugar
1	well beaten egg	1 t	grated lemon peel

Sift together flour, sugar, baking powder and salt in to mixing bowl. Make well in the center of flour mixture. Combine milk, egg and oil. Add all at once to dry ingredients. Stir quickly, just until dry ingredients are moistened.

Toss together blueberries and the 2 T sugar; gently stir into batter along with lemon peel. Fill greased 2½-inch muffin pans 2/3 full. Bake at 400°F for about 25 minutes. While muffins are still warm, dip tops in melted butter, then in a little granulated sugar.

Pond Hill Farm
Seven Minute Chocolate Mousse

Serves 8

6 oz	semi sweet chocolate chips	4	eggs, separated
1/3 C	very hot, strong coffee	2 T	cream de cacao liqueur

Stir chocolate chips into coffee. Add egg yolk and liqueur and blend 30 seconds more. Set aside. In a 4-quart bowl beat the 4 egg whites to stiff peaks. Fold in chocolate mixture. Put in individual ramekins, glasses or a bowl. Refrigerate until cold. Garnish with whipped cream if desired. (*This is easy and can be made ahead. You can put it in a graham cracker crust and make a pie or a Charlotte with lady fingers.*)

Authors
Hot Chocolate Cake
With Raspberry Sauce

Serves 4

8 oz	butter	4	egg yolks
8 oz	semi-sweet chocolate	9 oz	all-purpose flour
1 oz	amaretto	8 oz	sugar
3	eggs		

Melt butter and chocolate over a double boiler. Fold in amaretto, eggs and yolks. Sift flour and sugar and fold into mixture until combined (do not over-mix). Place into buttered 4-oz ramekins. Bake at 375°F for 17 minutes. Should be firm on outside but still soft and not set up in the center. Remove from ramekins and serve on dessert plates with raspberry sauce and ice cream. (*The batter can be prepared up to 4 hours ahead and refrigerated.*)

Raspberry Sauce

10 oz	frozen raspberries (with sugar), thawed	1 t	lemon juice
			Ice cream
3 T	raspberry jam		

Strain raspberries, reserving ¼ C raspberry juices. Puree berries, ¼ C juices, jam and lemon juice in processor. Strain, pressing on solids to extract as much fruit and juice as possible. (*Can be made 2 days ahead and kept, covered, in refrigerator. This rich and chocolatey cake recipe came from a chef at the Woodstock Inn in Vermont.*)

As We Go to Press . . .

The restaurant scene is in constant flux, and when places open or close soon after publication, we sometimes feel left behind. We try to avoid profiling any restaurants we think likely to close soon, but we don't have a crystal ball (two places that burned down soon after our first guide appeared remained in the book for a year, like ghosts). We aren't about to start recommending unborn restaurants, either. But when principals in a new venture have good track records, we're quite comfortable telling you of their plans:

Jim Milliman of Hattie's in Suttons Bay is adding a second restaurant, a new bistro named "Hanna," at 118 Cass St. in downtown Traverse City. The emphasis: fresh seafood and dishes that are "less detailed" than on Hattie's up-scale menu. Ovens left from a pizzeria formerly on the premises provide gourmet pizzas as well.

"Trattoria Stella" is to be the name of an Italian restaurant in Building 50 at Grand Traverse Commons. Owners are Amanda and Paul Danielson (she formerly managed Grand Traverse Resort's Trillium and he managed for Schelde restaurants and at Windows). They describe it as "very traditional," with butcher paper over white tablecloths, a 20-seat table-bar, a classic Italian menu and wine list, and "strong representation" of regional Northern Michigan wines and food products. The restaurant retains the original brick walls and structural arches of the historic building and incorporates several intimate dining areas, including one entire wing of semi-private alcoves.

On our website, **bayshorebooks.com**, we provide frequent updates on the Northern Michigan restaurant scene, along with our current newspaper columns and reviews.

Cooking Schools and Classes

In recent years, as more and more food lovers have settled down Up North, cooking schools and classes have proliferated like morels in May. Restaurants hereabouts are always on the lookout for ways to stay up and running all winter, and many do so by transforming themselves into classrooms for a few days each month in the off-season and inviting us to learn how to work magic in the kitchen.

A few years ago, Sherri gave Graydon a two-day class at Tapawingo, and still considers it the best gift she ever gave herself. After he came home, armed with new recipes and ideas, she told a friend, "It's as if I had a personal chef. I could hardly get him out of the kitchen."

We both still enjoy the benefits of that little gift, and since have attended other classes, both individually and together. We find it adds romance to our life when we set out to please each other with good food. We also think it helps us dance more lightly and expertly together in the kitchen.

Ladies needn't worry about sending their guys, either. The kitchen is very much a man's place, too. At a course we once took with Chef Nancy Allen, six of the ten students were men.

The classes we're familiar with are no-nonsense, hands-on instruction, and in the more extensive ones, the students prepare their own sumptuous "graduation" meals, in some cases inviting friends and relatives to their tables. Some classes are just a few hours, others run days. At least one restaurant offers full-time, four-day sessions that include optional room and board at the restaurant.

Instruction tends to be friendly and expert, and often includes the basics of kitchen equipment as well as prep, *mise en place*, and cooking techniques.

Most send the students home with yummy recipes, too. Graydon still keeps our kitchen stocked with savory, herbed, oven-dried tomatoes he learned to make at Tapawingo. When we find fresh fennel at our grocery, he delights in fixing it as Chef Nancy Allen taught him in a class on Tuscan cookery — sliced, brushed with olive oil, sprinkled with sea salt and grilled.

For serious professional training, check out the Great Lakes Culinary Institute at Traverse City's Northwestern Michigan College. It has kept the region's restaurants staffed with pros for years, and just recently moved into stunning new quarters, complete with lavishly equipped kitchens and class-rooms and a full-scale restaurant of its own with a view of the bay any commercial establishment would die for.

While the institute is geared mainly to professional training, there are also occasional one-time courses and evening classes for serious amateurs as well.

The restaurant is called the "Lobdell," for a Michigan restaurant-management family that made a generous gift to the college to help build it. It is gorgeous — airy, spare, elegant, and contemporary, with solid glass walls that take maximum advantage of the view.

The kitchens are as visible as the bay, in plain sight behind a wall of glass as you enter.

As part of their very practical training, NMC's culinary students plan, prepare, and serve periodic luncheons and dinners for the paying public, often with an ethnic or other theme. The meals we've enjoyed there have been interesting, well-balanced for color, texture, and flavor, and not at all textbookish, boring, or dull. Students, maybe, but this is a real-world restaurant with a faculty that knows the ropes.

For details schedules and classes (or to look into training for a professional career) see data in the box below.

Classes and Schools — the Data

We list here some courses offered in the past, to give you an idea of what's available Up North. Such courses are generally in the off-season, and schedules are seldom determined before mid-September. We suggest checking with restaurants in early autumn, or keeping an eye on their websites and watching for newspaper announcements. Tuition varies widely, depending on length of course and amenities (such as meals, room and board); fees have ranged in the past from $35 for a three-hour class to $400+ for multi-day, residential programs. For schedules and details, contact these sources directly.

Chateau Chantal, Old Mission (classes by Chef Nancy Allen for B&B guests); 231-223-4110; www.chateauchantal.com

Creative Expressions, Onekama; 231-889-4236; www.culinaryplayground.com

Douglas Lake Bar & Steakhouse, Pellston; 231-539-8588; www.douglaslakebar.com

Folgarelli's, Traverse City; 941-7651; www.folgarellis.com

Great Lakes Culinary Institute, Traverse City; 231-995-1197; www.nmc.edu/glci

Latitude, Bay Harbor; 231-439-2750; www.latituderestaurant.com

Nancy Allen, instruction in your home. E-mail to nallenchef@aol.com

Tapawingo, Ellsworth; 231-588-7971; tapawingo.net

Walloon Lake Inn, Walloon Lake; 800-956-4665 ; www.walloonlakeinn.com

---

Index

The illustrations in this book are photographs,
digitally converted into line drawings by Adobe Photoshop.

About the Authors

SHERRI DECAMP provides inside perspective on the hospitality industry as co-founder of The Professional Guest, a consulting firm that provides detailed evaluations of restaurants, lounges and guest services for a nationwide clientele of four– and five-star luxury hotels and resorts. She and her partner sold the company in 2002 to an Atlanta firm. Prior to founding her own company in 1997, she was director of sales at Grand Traverse Resort. That followed a 20-year career in education, first as an elementary teacher and later in the design and marketing of corporate experiential training programs. She holds a BA from Western Michigan and a Masters in education from Michigan State University.

GRAYDON DECAMP wrote entertaining, authoritative, pull-no-punches restaurant reviews as senior editor of *Traverse* magazine in the early 1990s following retirement from a long career as a politics columnist and city editor for Cincinnati's two daily newspapers. He has written books about the U. S. Naval Academy and his former newspaper, the Cincinnati Enquirer (*Old Lady of Vine Street)* and was editor of the official history of Michigan's Mackinac Island State Parks. He also writes for *Food Arts* and other magazines. He holds a BA in psychology from Williams College.

THIS IS THE DECAMPS' second food and restaurant guide to Northern Michigan. Their first, *The Connoisseur Up North,* became a regional best-seller from the day it was published in 1996 and remained in print eight years through five printings and four revisions. In *Dining In, Dining Out, in Northern Michigan* the DeCamps expand their scope beyond restaurants and recipes, to include farms and farm markets, wine and wineries, delis and shops and other resources for readers who, like them, enjoy good meals at home as well as in restaurants.

The DeCamps live in Elk Rapids and, like so many who choose to live Up North, they enjoy spending much of their time outdoors, on or in skis, snowshoes, bicycles, boots and boats. ("How else," they ask, "could we manage to eat the way we do?") They are active in the region's arts community and in environmental and conservancy organizations dedicated to protecting the natural beauty of Northern Michigan. They also write the "Connoisseur Up North" column of restaurant and food reviews for the Traverse City *Record-Eagle.*